Using Debate in the (

Debate holds enormous potential to build 21st-century skills such as critical thinking, communication, collaboration, and conflict resolution in the K–12 classroom, but teachers often struggle to implement and contextualize it effectively. *Using Debate in the Classroom* draws on research from a variety of academic disciplines to explain the benefits of debate across subject areas, and describes how teachers can use debate to enliven their curriculum and support the aims of the Common Core. Topics include:

- Introducing debate as a pedagogical practice to engage students, improve school culture, and disrupt the school-to-prison pipeline.
- Using debate to teach critical literacy and improve students' reading, writing, and speaking skills.
- Implementing role-playing techniques to strengthen information literacy and reasoning skills.
- Building students' empathy, perspective taking skills, and cultural humility as they confront difficult social issues through debate.

Appendices provide a variety of tools to assist K–12 teachers in implementing debate in the classroom, including ready-made debate activities, student hand-outs, and a step-by-step guide to introducing students to debate in just one week.

Karyl A. Davis directs communications for the Glenn Pelham Foundation for Debate Education and is the owner and principal creative of the consulting firm kd Alice Communications.

M. Leslie Wade Zorwick is Associate Professor of Psychology at Hendrix College.

James Roland is Senior Director of Community Programs and Engaged Scholarship at the Barkley Forum Center for Debate Education at Emory University.

Melissa Maxcy Wade is President of the Glenn Pelham Foundation for Debate Education.

Using Debate in the Classroom

Encouraging Critical Thinking,
Communication, and Collaboration

Edited by Karyl A. Davis, M. Leslie
Wade Zorwick, James Roland, and
Melissa Maxcy Wade

Routledge
Taylor & Francis Group

NEW YORK AND LONDON

First published 2016
by Routledge
711 Third Avenue, New York, NY 10017

and by Routledge
2 Park Square, Milton Park, Abingdon, Oxon, OX14 4RN

Routledge is an imprint of the Taylor & Francis Group, an informa business

© 2016 Taylor & Francis

Library of Congress Cataloging in Publication Data
Names: Davis, Karyl A., editor.
Title: Using debate in the classroom : encouraging critical thinking, communication, and collaboration / edited by Karyl A. Davis, M. Leslie Wade Zorwick, James Roland, and Melissa Maxcy Wade.
Description: New York : Routledge is an imprint of the Taylor & Francis Group, an Informa business, [2016] | Includes bibliographical references and index.
Identifiers: LCCN 2015050456 | ISBN 9781138899537 (hardback) | ISBN 9781138899544 (pbk.) | ISBN 9781315707808 (e-book)
Subjects: LCSH: Debates and debating—Study and teaching. | Critical thinking. | Communication in education. | Group work in education.
Classification: LCC PN4181 .U75 2016 | DDC 808.53071—dc23
LC record available at http://lccn.loc.gov/2015050456

ISBN: 978-1-138-89953-7 (hbk)
ISBN: 978-1-138-89954-4 (pbk)
ISBN: 978-1-315-70780-8 (ebk)

Typeset in Goudy
by Swales & Willis Ltd, Exeter, Devon, UK

Printed and bound in Great Britain by
TJ International Ltd, Padstow, Cornwall

For Debate Educators – Past, Present, and Future

Contents

Foreword

John Sexton

Debate formed my mind, shaped the way I look at the world, and prepared me for a vocation in the world of thought. In short, debate changed my life.

Debate entered my life when a great high-school teacher (called simply "Charlie" by all of us) suggested that I was too narrowly focused on classroom studies and that I would be a better person – and a smarter one – if I joined the debate team. That led to my own four years of debating, followed by 15 years of coaching debate. Not surprisingly, I have given to hundreds (maybe thousands) of others the advice that Charlie gave to me.

If you care about cultivating your mind, there simply is no better use of your time than serious debate. Here's why.

1   Debaters learn to listen and to engage meaningfully in conversation with those with whom they disagree.

    We debaters are committed to a contest of ideas. We understand that, in order to communicate and persuade, it is critical to understand in a nuanced way what our opponent is saying, and to understand our opponent's argument in its strongest form. This builds our capacity to listen.

    To listen is to be open, to hear what our conversation partner is saying. Think about it: in debate you can't refute an argument if you don't understand it. If you don't listen carefully, and you respond to the version with which you are familiar as opposed to what is actually being said, you lose the debate.

2   Debaters learn to spot and confront illogicalities, while simultaneously extending the same critical examination to their own personal beliefs and preconceptions. Debaters learn to defend stances not out of a personal attachment to a conclusion but based on logic and evidence. Debate proves that controversial topics traditionally exempt from critical analysis *can* be discussed in a civil, useful manner. Debaters learn to value the rationality of positions and to oppose demagoguery.

3   Debaters appreciate depth and nuance and are willing to grapple with complex ideas. Debaters must be creative thinkers. They must be adept at both analytical and synthetic thinking. What good debaters and good lawyers

combine is an analysis of intellectual problems, synthesis and organization of material, identification of possibilities and totalities that other people don't see. Debaters also see holes in the sense of gaps that other people don't see and then they fill in those gaps.

This skill is all the more important in this age when the attention span of people is shrinking. The deficiency in public policy discussion can be traced to the fact that we are becoming more and more a culture of immediate gratification and short attention span, and we're moving away from being a society that values depth and is willing to delay gratification. Debate is a good antidote to that because it is based upon the premise that serious discussions of ideas should not stop at a first level. In debate, extending the argument is extremely important. Debaters understand that conversations about ideas have to go into several levels of extension.

4 Debaters understand the importance of effective communication, animated by a consciousness of their audience and the malleability of their words. Debaters understand the malleability of language. One of the maturing processes experienced by a competitive debater is maturing out of the sophomoric explanation of a defeat in a round because the judge made a mistake, and maturing into an understanding that a judge comes into a round as a tabula rasa upon which the speakers write. In order to write, the speakers have to communicate their ideas into that judge's mind. In that process of communication, the sophisticated communicator has to understand that words can be heard in different ways and that a combination of words in a sentence or a combination of sentences in a paragraph have a kaleidoscopic quality to them. You must be aware of your listener – in the context of competitive debate, the judge; in the context of life, any partner in conversation – and how your listener is likely to perceive certain words and the order or the frame in which they appear. You must be conscious not only of the way you mean the words, but of the way the words can be perceived by those who enter conversation with you.

5 Debaters identify their goals and then formulate the steps necessary to achieve them. Debaters start with an ability to motivate themselves, to set and see a goal, to set and see the intermediate steps that will get them to that goal, neatly summarized in the Confucian metaphor about knowing that you can move a mountain one spoonful at a time.

Debaters incorporate almost subconsciously this maxim. If a debater wants to get to point x, and point x is a particular debate tournament, and by the date of that tournament you've got to have yourself ready on your case and you may want a variation case for particular teams, and you've got to be prepared for affirmative cases you're going to meet, without even thinking about it, debaters at the highest level begin moving toward that goal of being ready for a tournament. They instinctively incorporate the need to plan steps as a way to get to that goal. This quality prepares them to embrace enormous tasks and to plan intermediate steps. It becomes second nature to them. That knack is extraordinarily rare at all levels.

Debate creates citizens with these capacities. This book provides an extraordinary guide to the world of debate and how, exactly, it manages this feat.

Preface

Melissa Maxcy Wade

In 1964 I found debate in a Texas classroom and about the same time, around the country, my future husband and many lifelong friends were also discovering this activity that would change all of our lives. For more than 50 years debate has animated my passion as a competitive participant, coach, educator, social justice activist, non-profit director, U.S. presidential debate commentator, and business consultant. Decades of friends and family, including our children, attended the annual Emory National Debate Institute to learn the skills of communication, collaboration, critical thinking, and conflict resolution. Respectful communication understands critical thinking as a process, which moves from critical listening to question formation to data collection, not to get to the right answer, but to get to the next round of questions. Respectful communication understands conflict as necessary to advancing the nuances of ideas and subjecting them to robust criticism, so that they grow into solutions and facilitate deeper interpersonal relationships. Respectful communication understands collaboration as something humans do as social beings drawn to various social, work, education, religious, and ceremonial communities for purpose.

At no time in our history has the need for constructive national debate been more important. We face profound global problems: climate change, social unrest, ethnic cleansing, burgeoning refugee populations, terrorism, and ever-present nuclear weapons. Ubiquitous social media can both educate us, as in the Black Lives Matter movement, and divide us, as in the self-reinforcing insularity of online groups that helped inspire Dylan Roof to kill nine members of the Emanuel AME Church in Charleston. Debate education is a pivotal component of productive civic action.

Using Debate in the Classroom: Encouraging Critical Thinking, Communication, and Collaboration makes the case that debate, argumentation, and advocacy training offers an optimal delivery system for many skills that people seek to cultivate in the 21st century. Debate is special, in that it offers a flexible tool that can be used to efficiently teach practices related to communication, critical thinking, collaboration, conflict resolution, and even civic awareness. Academic debate encourages respectful civil discourse that is thoughtful, evidenced, and well reasoned. This discourse includes the kinds of communication that are used in classrooms, business meetings, group discussions, and governmental proceedings. Debate has value in diverse educational settings, including K–12, higher education, continuing professional education, and workforce training.

This book draws on research from multiple academic disciplines to explain why debate is associated with so many positive outcomes. The authors examine effects ranging from improvement in grades and school retention to broader positive effects like the development of scientific literacy, prejudice reduction, cultural humility formation, information management, digital literacy, and improvement of critical thinking skills. Both competitive and classroom debate engage students in active learning, which promotes problem-based collaboration in the safe space of mediated conflict through assigned advocacy. Academic experts from debate, psychology, communications, law, education, African and gender studies, English, and science make a powerful case for debate education's impact on developing empathy and perspective taking, engaging students in collaborative game-based play, promoting cultural humility, managing and curating digital information, improving critical thinking and listening, reducing the school-to-prison pipeline, launching social justice movements, building scientific literacy, and increasing school attendance while reducing drop-out rates. All of these results are associated with a variety of positive academic, personal, and social outcomes.

Education strategies designed to build critical thinking such as Common Core State Standards and scientific literacy such as Next Generation Science Standards are first steps toward re-thinking education in the 21st century. It is my hope that debate will find students in the classroom, teach them respectful communication, and inspire their passion to make a difference in the world, as it did for me over 50 years ago.

Acknowledgments

The time and energy of a great many people went into the making of this volume and we want to take a moment to thank them. Thanks to our authors – Catherine Beane, Freddi-Jo Bruschke, Jon Bruschke, Brittney Cooper, Susan Cridland-Hughes, Ed Lee, Ajay Nair, Gordon Stables, Patrick Wade, Carol Winkler – for all being such a pleasure to work with and for making time for this project in their already busy lives. Thanks to Joe Bellon, Isaac Wolf, Kamal Ghali, Sanjay Ghandi, Ouida Jo Vincent, Holly Raider, Hank Tomlinson, and Greg Huber for having early conversations with us about the direction of this book and for their openness and willingness to help us make it as good as it could possibly be. And we are incredibly grateful to John Sexton for taking the time to write the foreword for this book.

We want to thank Cully Clark for shepherding the book proposal to find a home at Routledge. We want to thank Jim Wade and Steve Stein with their help on our Appendix materials. And we want to thank Bruce Albrecht for helping to secure funding to support this work through the Glenn Pelham Foundation for Debate Education. Leslie Zorwick had the time to work on this project through a sabbatical grant funded by Hendrix College, so thank you to the people at Hendrix who made that possible. And special thanks go to Quinn Menhart for his tireless work to make sure that we were following APA citation guidelines.

We also want to thank our contacts at Routledge, including Catherine Bernard, Marlena Sullivan, and Catherine Hanley. Our team at Routledge made this process smooth and they were supportive and helpful throughout.

Finally, we want to thank our families and loved ones, who were kind as we had even more work to do than usual and were patient with our many long Skype calls. We couldn't have done this without our respective home support networks of Ed Lee, Tom and Mellie Zorwick, Ranyatta Casey Roland, and Jim Wade.

An Introduction to Classroom Debate

A Tool for Educating Minds and Hearts

Karyl A. Davis, M. Leslie Wade Zorwick, James Roland, and Melissa Maxcy Wade

"My students are sometimes unaware that argumentation is not the same as plain old arguing. This subject [debate] really enlightens them to the discourse going on around them."

"Most average students are lacking in confidence when it comes to their opinions and beliefs and have not been asked to justify their answers very often . . . using argumentation and advocacy in the regular speech classroom teaches those students to justify their opinions, to use text clues and quotes, and to become better writers overall."

"It is so vital that we get students to think deeper about social and political issues. It is odd to me that [in] this 'information age' we are still a society that believes gossip through spam and [F]acebook. Our young people need to know how to consider sources for accuracy and make decisions based on the best information they can get. It is a personal mission for me to share with them how to share their knowledge and opinion in ways that are informed and ways that encourage discussion with those of other opinions."

These quotations come from a survey of middle-school, high-school, and college teachers in the 2013–2014 academic year who use debate in their classrooms. These teachers point to three critical arguments that provide the foundation for this book. First, the average student does not necessarily understand that arguing is not argumentation. Making a claim does not mean that claim has been explained, justified, or evidenced. Many people's frustration with national politics and news points to our desire for more explanation, justification, and evidence, as opposed to platitudes that fail to communicate very much. Second, many students do not feel confident in their own abilities to assert their claims because they are rarely asked to explain, justify, and provide evidence to support their positions. Helping students find the confidence to explain, justify, and provide evidence translates into improved oral and written communication skills, as well as a stronger belief in their ability to command the attention of others. Third, we are living in an era in which unfettered access to information makes the ability to evaluate the explanations, justifications, and evidence associated with claims incredibly important. Students must be taught the tools both to share their knowledge effectively and to evaluate the knowledge presented by others because both are precursors to effective communication and interaction.

In our society, we frequently reduce issues of importance, whether they be social, political, environmental, or legal issues, to polarizing soundbites instead of having nuanced discussions on the evidence. We often fail to listen critically to one another and to engage respectfully with one another. We ensconce ourselves in actual and virtual communities with people who think like us, but this insular way of approaching the world will not serve students or our communities in the 21st century. The 21st century requires a re-thinking in education that prepares students with the skills needed to thrive in a diverse, global, digital environment; we believe students can learn these skills effectively and efficiently through debate. The Black Lives Matter movement and tragedies like the Emanuel African Methodist Episcopal Church shooting bring home the importance of dialogue. We need to create communities where all voices engage around important topics such as racism, poverty, and access to justice. We need debate.

As editors of this book, we have varying degrees of experience with classroom and extracurricular debate, and we all feel strongly in the transformative power of debate for students and teachers. As educators, we have all had experiences in which we have seen students blossom through the use of debate as they realize people will listen to them and that their words have power. We also believe that there are few educational strategies and approaches that come with as many varied benefits as debate, where students take ownership over their learning and where they work collaboratively with other students to develop literacy, writing, and speaking skills. Additionally, we remember what it was like to be a student in the classroom, engaging with public speaking, advocacy, and debate for the first time. For all of us, learning the power of our own voices transformed us profoundly. With our backgrounds and work experiences in educational, legal, business, non-profit, and social justice settings, we agree that the skills we developed in speech and debate continue in a myriad of ways to impact our professional lives.

In order to understand the power of debate education and the timeliness of its application, we begin this book with a discussion of what we mean by debate education and an exploration of how the benefits of debate align with educational policies that strive to prepare students for success in the 21st century, with a particular focus on using debate to meet the goals established in the Common Core State Standards. Debate is a flexible teaching method that encourages critical thinking, communication, and collaboration. Teachers of all subjects and experience levels can use debate to meet curriculum objectives. Through debate, students acquire skills that will carry over to college, careers, and life. The chapters of this volume will make the case that debate promotes respectful dialogue (see Cooper, Chapter 1), conflict resolution (see Beane, Chapter 2), evidence evaluation (see J. Bruschke, Chapter 3), literacy skills (see Cridland-Hughes, Chapter 4), information processing (see Stables, Chapter 5), academic success (see Winkler, Chapter 6), scientific reasoning (see F. J. Bruschke, Chapter 7), critical thinking (see Wade, Chapter 8), empathy (see Zorwick, Chapter 9), and cultural humility (see Lee and Nair,

Chapter 10). Not only do students acquire these varied and important skills through debate, but they also learn to apply these skills to real-world problems in a way that empowers them to envision a better world.

Because of the power of debate education to transform classrooms into engaged learning centers, this book argues that all teachers should use debate in their classrooms, and each chapter provides reasons and evidence in support of this claim. In making the case for debate, we are presenting a volume that advocates a strong position based on clearly identified and well-evidenced reasons why debate works. In fact, it is the skill set we learned as debaters that prepared us to argue strongly in favor of debate as an optimal learning strategy for teachers. This book is not just about debate, it is an embodiment of the value of discourse.

What Is Debate Education?

As editors of this book, we believe that debate is a fundamental part of human nature and at the core of human interaction. Children debate with their parents whether or not they should get dessert, students internally debate the pros and cons of the colleges they are considering, and co-workers debate one another in order to come up with ideal solutions for challenges in the workplace. Regardless of whether or not people publicly share their opinions, everybody is opinionated and disagreement among people requires the use of critical thinking, effective communication, and elements of persuasion. Yet, for something that is such an innate part of human existence, many people do not have a good understanding of what debate entails. Many people incorrectly assume that debate means arguing and yelling or that debate only refers to specifically structured events, such as a presidential debate. In this book, we want to argue that debate is a very broad approach to engaging with topics; it is a flexible and adaptive pedagogical tool that allows students to engage in content, while simultaneously developing their critical thinking, communication, and collaboration skills. Debate is not about winning. Debate is about inquiry and analysis. It is about asking questions. It is about knowing how to sift through information to acquire the best data possible and making choices based upon the information gathered. It is about finding the confidence to clearly communicate ideas even when they are unpopular. It is about listening to and respecting others even when you disagree with them, and, while debate does not always resolve differences of opinion, it can help participants have productive communication across those differences.

One critical distinction when introducing the idea of classroom debate is that *having* an argument is different from *making* an argument. When we talk about making an argument in debate, we mean generating a claim (the position), a warrant (the reasons why), and evidence to support the claim and warrant (Toulmin, 1958). One benefit of debate is that it teaches students that claims always need warrants and that evidence makes these "reasons why" more powerful. Given that humans seem predisposed to debate, we suspect the readers of this book will have had the uniquely frustrating experience of interacting with someone who makes unsubstantiated claims. From children who say they do not like things before they have even tried them to bosses demanding their workers follow new procedures without explaining why, we know that it is frustrating when claims come without warrants. Part of the goal of debate is to make the search for warrants automatic and the need for warrants obvious.

There are many possible formats for types of debate. In particular, there are many types of extracurricular debate, including: Lincoln–Douglas debate, public forum debate, student congress/congressional debate, model U.N., mock trial, and policy debate. Though different in form, all types of extracurricular debate have the same core ideas. While extracurricular options have specific sets of roles, time limits, topics, and expectations for participants, in every instance, debate is a process of practicing and developing the skills that make students better at communicating and thinking. It is not the type of debate, but rather the act of engaging these skills that is transformative.

Debate allows students to cultivate their voice, intellect, and capacity to see things from a variety of perspectives. We strongly believe that both extracurricular debate activities and in-class debate activities have the power to develop these skills and that teachers have a range of ways to offer their students debate experiences. One benefit to assigned advocacy and debate in the classroom is that teachers can assign students to defend positions different from the students' own position. Research suggests that students are more likely to change their minds and develop more nuanced understandings of topics when they are forced to see both sides of an issue (see Zorwick, Chapter 9). Part of our goal in the Appendices is to offer a series of models that can be used to structure classroom debates, or assignments that involve advocacy and argumentation, and to make them accessible to as many teachers and classrooms as possible.

There are two definitions that we all agree point to our broad conceptualization of debate. First, Freely and Steinberg (2008) describe debate as "The process of inquiry and advocacy; the seeking of a reasoned judgment on a proposition" (p. 2). This conceptualization points to debate as an approach that supports students as they ask questions and learn to advocate for positions, while contextualizing students' work with the expectation of critical thinking. Second, Branham (1991) defines debate as "the process by which opinions are advanced, supported, disputed, and defended" (p. 1). This definition builds on the first by adding clash between conflicting ideas and creating an environment where students learn the skills to defend positions. Both definitions fit nicely with the quotations from teachers that began this introduction. Teachers are eager to find pedagogical approaches that will allow their students to think more deeply about information before developing their opinions and to learn to confidently defend their positions, once developed.

Even in our current age of educational reform, it is uncommon to find any one instructional tool that (a) helps students to acquire new skills, (b) helps them to apply these skills, and (c) teaches students to use those skills responsibly. We argue that the ways in which debate facilitates *skill acquisition*, *skill application*, and *accountability* make debate a unique educational tool. As a technique, debate gets more done in the classroom in less time than many other instructional methods. In addition, debate develops an exciting range of skills, from literacy to critical thinking to social skills, all of which will be examined in more detail in the chapters that follow this introduction.

When we speak about *skill acquisition*, we refer to the process of gathering and collecting the critical thinking, social, and literacy skills that improve learning *and* communication. Though we all have opinions, we do not express them in the same ways. The inherent variability in communication approaches is one reason debate is important for students – and teachers – to have in their mental toolboxes; debate is a tool which shapes, fixes, and molds communication across differences and helps people communicate with a wide variety of audiences.

When we speak about *skill application*, we refer to the use and practice of these newly acquired skills. We believe that educational methods have little benefit to students unless there is an application component, and debate exercises *necessarily* require the application of skills into an active, engaging debate. In fact, the best way to get better at debate is to do it frequently. We think of debate not as a static technique or idea, but rather as something we do, which involves the repetition of several skills essential to academic (e.g. critical thinking, reading, research, etc.) and social (e.g. empathy, critical listening, etc.) success. The practice and application of debate is more than speaking; it is processing information, preparing arguments, writing up the arguments, and learning to present claims and warrants effectively and persuasively. If we judge the effectiveness of a lesson by how many objectives and learning outcomes it can successfully and efficiently teach students, debate is the most effective educational technique that we, as well as countless other educators, have found.

In identifying *accountability*, we argue that learning is not a responsibility-free zone. The most impactful learning comes from understanding the connections between people and the world at large. In many ways, the current educational environment is one plagued with students who only complete tasks "because the teacher said so" and with a focus on learning and teaching only the material that will be on the standardized test. One challenge faced by educators is how to make learning engaging for apathetic students, who are currently not engaged in the learning process or in preparing for high-stakes testing. The nature of debate requires and encourages students to be accountable to the learning process itself. When debating, students have to consider argument development, construction, presentation, and defense. Accountability in debate education teaches students that effective communication involves consideration, concern, and respect for opposing views. We believe that the cornerstone of good relationships is effective communication and that students need to practice writing, speaking, and listening in order to become better communicators. Debate is an empirically proven vehicle for delivering the skills needed for effective communication, and we believe these skills are an important step in teaching students to engage carefully and thoughtfully with social issues and to interact respectfully with others.

Benefits of Debate Education

Debate, as defined above, is a powerful educational tool, and the heart of this book focuses on the reasons why. In this complex and global world, the skills students must learn have changed. Students require levels of information and technology literacy unfathomable even a decade ago (National Education Association [NEA], n.d.). Students need skills that will enable them to compete on a global scale and will enable them to work respectfully with others across difference (NEA, n.d.). Routine-based jobs, like manufacturing, are disappearing, and the critical thinking and communication skills required of analytic and interactive jobs, such as teaching, are becoming more important (NEA, n.d.). As the NEA (n.d.) articulates, "What was considered a good education 50 years ago . . . is no longer enough for success in college, career, and citizenship in the 21st century" (p. 3).

The Common Core State Standards (CCSS) are the most recent iteration of education policy meant to address the needs of students in the 21st century. In contrast to No Child Left Behind, CCSS focus more on measuring skill development than on content acquisition (Wallace, 2013). While opinion varies as to the effectiveness of CCSS, more than 40 states have adopted them (Common Core State Standards Initiative, "About the Standards," n.d.), and teachers in those states must work to meet them. Even in non-adoption states, teachers still strive to instruct students in skill sets that are highly prized in the CCSS, including critical thinking, communication, creativity, and collaboration, because teachers see the impact such skills have on their students' success (NEA, n.d.).

CCSS emphasize a number of skills strongly associated with debate. Debate gets students to read and analyze material, and debate forces students to make connections between ideas and the world around them. According the Common Core State Standards for English Language Arts (CCSS-ELA):

> Students who meet the standards . . . habitually perform the critical reading necessary to pick carefully through the staggering amount of information available today in print and digitally. They actively seek the wide, deep, and thoughtful engagement with high-quality literary and informational texts that builds knowledge, enlarges experience, and broadens worldviews.
> (National Governors Association Center for Best Practices &
> Council of Chief State School Officers, 2010a, p. 3)

Specific skills identified in the Common Core State Standards and developed by debate include argument construction, close critical reading, and evidence evaluation (Riffer & Jacobi, 2013). In addition, there are many standards that, upon close examination, reveal the depth of connection between CCSS and debate. One standard in the Speaking and Listening subsection of CCSS-ELA requires students to "Present claims and findings, emphasizing salient points in a focused, coherent manner with relevant evidence, sound valid reasoning, and well-chosen details; use appropriate eye contact, adequate volume, and clear pronunciation" (National Governors Association Center for Best Practices & Council of Chief State School Officers, 2010a, standard SL.8.4). Students meet each aspect of this standard in a debate; as students share their ideas with their classmates, they make strategic decisions about what they are going to say and how they are going to say it, and they learn from the choices that they make in the debate how to communicate their thoughts clearly and effectively.

The connections between the Common Core State Standards and debate extend beyond the language arts, where people may assume a natural affinity exists, to math and science, where people may find the relationship less obvious. Because math and science instruction in middle school and high school often focuses on well-established principles or findings of fact, it is understandable that teachers might underestimate debate's utility. However, "[o]ne hallmark of mathematical understanding is the ability to justify, in a way appropriate to the student's mathematical maturity, *why* a particular mathematical statement is true or where a mathematical rule comes from" (National Governors Association Center for Best Practices & Council of Chief State School Officers, 2010b, p. 4). We believe that when students reason through math problems or hypothesize an explanation for a scientific phenomenon, they are engaging the same skill set required for debate. Teachers can use debate in math and science classrooms, just as in English and history classrooms, as a tool for students to think critically, reason, construct arguments, and communicate ideas. By teaching students in math and science courses to identify their positions with reasons and evidence in the context of debate, teachers work to ensure that future mathematicians and scientists possess not just the analytical skills to develop solutions, but also the communication skills to convey their ideas.

While students need to acquire 21st-century skills, such as argument construction and evidence evaluation, they also need to know how to apply those skills to real-world problems. A focus on success in life beyond the classroom permeates the CCSS for English Language Arts and Math, as well as related standards (Common Core State Standards Initiative, "English Language Arts Standards," n.d.; National Governor's Association Center for Best Practices & Council of Chief State School Officers, 2010b; National Council of the Social Studies [NCSS], 2013). By applying the skills they are learning to real-world issues, students are not merely learning for a test; they are learning so that they can make decisions and communicate those decisions in a way that is respectful and responsible, a way that is accountable to themselves and others. In the future, when students decide a course of action in the workplace, disagree with the ideas held by peers and supervisors, or engage in issues confronting their community, they can draw upon the academic and social skills they learned in debate. Debate pushes students to learn more than the facts in their textbooks, more than basic writing and study skills (Wallace, 2013). This focus on real-world application in debate brings learning to life for students. In fact, survey results of debaters in the Atlanta Urban Debate League suggest that students crave instruction that lets them make connections to real-world problems. When questioned about what they liked most about debate, student responses included: "We get to debate with others and learn about the USA's social issues"; "How the topics are of real global issues"; and "Learning something new about the world in each round" (AUDL, 2015).

While it is important that students are able and willing to engage real-world problems, acquiring the requisite skills and applying those skills is not enough; students need to learn accountability in order to use those skills responsibly. We believe that when students start using debate to learn about the world, they simultaneously learn how to advocate in order to make the world a better place. By providing a space where students' opinions are sought and valued, debate teaches students to become advocates for their positions. Students, in the process, develop an understanding that they can influence and impact others through their speech. They learn that accountability involves considering how their ideas, and the way they articulate their ideas, will affect others. They begin to consider how their choices might benefit the community and not simply their individual success (Kuhn, 2005, p. 12; Wade, in press). When students research and discuss both sides of an issue, they look at the world through another person's eyes. When they listen carefully to the other side and provide reasons and evidence for their position, they engage in respectful dialogue.

We need students to care about their education and how they use their education; in particular, we need them to care about participating in civic life. If students do not care, they are not likely to apply the skills they have learned for the benefit of our larger community (Kuhn, 2005, p. 14). A democracy requires robust dialogue and debate. Voters, jurors, legislators, judges, politicians, and those affected by the decisions that each group makes need to engage in discussions about problems and policies that affect our communities.

Empowering students to engage in real-world problems through debate is valuable not only because of the positive impact it has on students, but also because of the positive impact it has on teachers. The education profession loses approximately 500,000 teachers each year, which has the potential to undermine efforts to prepare students for the 21st century and to meet the Common Core State Standards (Zorwick & Wade, 2015). School systems invest time and resources in on-the-job training and continuing education programs that help teachers implement educational policies, such as the Common Core State Standards, but as teachers leave the profession, students and colleagues no longer benefit from the knowledge those teachers gained during their careers. Fortunately, an additional benefit of debate is the positive effect it has on job satisfaction for teachers (see Zorwick & Wade, 2015). Debate has the power to re-energize teachers by helping them remember what they love about teaching: seeing understanding dawn in a student's eyes, seeing a student's confidence blossom, seeing a student express empathy and compassion for others. In the Zorwick and Wade (2015a) survey of teachers, "More than 70% of . . . teachers indicated they were more likely to continue teaching because of their experience using argumentation and debate activities in their classrooms" (p. 52). Specifically, the researchers found that as a result of classroom debate, over 80% of respondents enjoyed teaching more and expressed increased confidence in the classroom (Zorwick & Wade, 2015).

Because debate improves the way that students learn and communicate, teachers feel more successful in their work. A teacher of debate and one of the authors in this book, Susan Cridland-Hughes, summarized debate's impact on teachers best when she said:

> [Debate] gives you hope. When you are talking to a student who is energized by an idea, it is so much more powerful when they find it on their own instead of you handing it to them. And you realize that in training them to have opinions . . . they have every tool they need to really make a difference.
> (Atlanta Urban Debate League [AUDL], 2011)

Based upon our experience as educators, and supported by the research presented in this book, we believe that debate presents the best opportunity for teachers to teach the skills needed in the 21st century – and we are not alone in that belief. At the National Association for Urban Debate Leagues 2012 Annual Dinner, U.S. Secretary of Education Arne Duncan argued, "Competitive urban debate is almost uniquely suited to building what's been called the 'Four C's' of 21st century skills – critical thinking, communication, collaboration, and creativity. And to that list I might add a fifth 'C' – for civic awareness and engagement" (U.S. Department of Education, 2012). By educating students using debate, we supply them with the skills and fortitude they will need to address the challenging issues that confront our society.

Conclusion

Martin Luther King (1947) said, "Intelligence plus character – that is the goal of true education" (p. 5). Debate education offers us a way to realize King's vision, a way to teach skills of the mind and character of the heart through skill acquisition, skill application, and accountability. Alumni of extracurricular speech and debate include presidents, congressional representatives, and supreme court justices, including Franklin D. Roosevelt, John F. Kennedy, Lyndon Johnson, Richard Nixon, Jimmy Carter, Bill Clinton, Russ Feingold, Richard Luger, Barbara Jordan, Phil Graham, John Kerry, George McGovern, Hillary Clinton, Antonin Scalia, Steven Breyer, Samuel Alito, and Sonia Sotomayor (Zorwick & Wade, in press). Despite a long history of debate in American education, however, debate remains an extracurricular activity in most schools. It is time for this to change. It is time for debate in every classroom. It is time for the widespread use of debate as a pedagogical tool that teaches the critical thinking and communication skills that lead to academic achievement, conflict resolution, and leadership. It is time to teach minds and hearts through skill acquisition, skill application, and accountability.

Engaging students in debate education will have ripple effects in our communities, as problem-solving, civic-minded students become leaders who are willing to speak up and take action on important issues. By establishing what we mean by debate education and discussing the benefits of its use in the classroom, we have started a discussion that will continue in the pages to follow – about the value of debate education, why it works, and what effect it can have on students, as well as teachers. We hope this brings readers one step closer to deciding that all teachers should incorporate debate in their classrooms. We hope that it brings teachers closer to the reason they first started teaching, to their own teaching goals, and to a goal we hope we share: to change the world through debate.

References

Atlanta Urban Debate League. (2015). [Student End-of-Year Survey 2014–2015]. Unpublished raw data.

Atlanta Urban Debate League. (Producer). (2011, August 17). *Life With Debate* [Video file]. Retrieved from https://www.youtube.com/watch?v=2qinOMPShKk.

Branham, R. (1991). *Debate and Critical Analysis: The Harmony of Conflict.* Hilldale, NJ: Lawrence Erlbaum Associates.

Common Core State Standards Initiative. (n.d.). *About the Standards.* Retrieved from http://www.corestandards.org/about-the-standards/.

Common Core State Standards Initiative. (n.d.). *English Language Arts Standards.* Retrieved November 28, 2015, from http://www.corestandards.org/ELA-Literacy/.

Freely, A., & Steinberg, D. (2008). *Argumentation and Debate* (12th ed.). Boston, MA: Wadsworth Publishing.

King, M. L. (1947). The Purpose of Education. *The Maroon Tiger.* Retrieved from http://www.drmartinlutherkingjr.com/thepurposeofeducation.htm.

Kuhn, D. (2005). *Education for Thinkers.* Cambridge, MA: Harvard University Press.

National Council for the Social Studies [NCSS]. (2013). *The College, Career, and Civic Life (C3) Framework for Social Studies State Standards: Guidance for Enhancing the Rigor of Civics, Economics, Geography, and History.* Silver Spring, MD: NCSS.

National Education Association [NEA]. (n.d.). *Preparing 21st Century Students for a Global Society.* Retrieved from http://www.nea.org/assets/docs/A-Guide-to-Four-Cs.pdf.

National Governors Association Center for Best Practices & Council of Chief State School Officers. (2010a). *Common Core State Standards for English Language Arts & Literacy in History/Social Studies, Science, and Technical Subjects.* Washington, DC: Authors.

National Governors Association Center for Best Practices & Council of Chief State School Officers. (2010b). *Common Core State Standards for Mathematics.* Washington, DC: Authors.

Riffer, C., & Jacobi, A. (2013). Answering the call for classroom and career readiness. *The Rostrum, 87*(5), 16–26

Toulmin, S. (1958). *The Uses of Argument.* New York: Cambridge University Press.

U.S. Department of Education. (2012). *The Power of Debate: Building the Five "C's" for the 21st Century.* Retrieved from http://www.ed.gov/news/speeches/power-debate%E2%80%94building-five-cs-21st-century.

Wade, M. (in press). Pathways to civic education: Urban Debate Leagues as communities of practice. In J. M. Hogan, J. A. Kurr, M. J. Bergmaier, & J. D. Johnson (Eds.), *Speech and Debate as Education for Citizenship.* University Park, PA: Penn State University Press.

Wallace, E. (2013). Speech and debate: Making the case for the Common Core. *The Rostrum, 87*(5), 13–14.

Zorwick, L., & Wade, J. (2015). Using forensic activity to develop the skills identified in Common Core State Standards. *The Rostrum, 90*(1), 46–52.

Zorwick, L., & Wade, J. (in press). Debate as a vehicle for civic education. *Communication Education.*

1   Take No Prisoners

The Role of Debate in a Liberatory Education

Brittney Cooper

In October 2015, the Black Lives Matter (BLM) movement petitioned the Democratic National Committee (DNC) to sponsor a presidential debate with candidates for the 2016 election, focused solely on the concerns of the BLM. The DNC declined the request for debate but did offer to help the BLM host a presidential candidate forum or townhall. This led to a series of conversations about the structure and format of public debates and townhalls, and about which form of activity would allow Black publics to interact substantively with those politicians seeking to lead the country. The BLM's request for a presidential debate came just weeks after news of a group of prison inmates in a maximum-security prison in upstate New York defeated a group of Harvard University debaters. The incarcerated debaters were students in the Bard Prison Initiative, a program housed at Bard College, that offers college coursework to inmates.

More than 60 years ago, Malcolm X honed his oratorical talents on a prison debate team. Today communities of color have been ravaged by the far-reaching effects of the prison industrial complex, and its role in the enforcement of tough-on-crime policies that have led to the mass incarceration of Black and Latino/a men and women. Far too many of our youth have a better chance of encountering debate training in prison than in the classroom. This is unacceptable. Bringing debate into prisons offers us a clear picture of the kind of intellectual talents that continue to languish behind bars. And the issue of mass incarceration and over-policing of Black communities is one of the critical issues that the BLM has placed on the agenda as a critical topic for public debate and liberation.

Together these examples demonstrate that participating in and understanding how debates work are a critical part of active participation in a democracy. Moreover, having access to good debating skills is a critical literacy to which all students should have access. The ability to understand and evaluate the relative merits of competing positions is not merely an intellectual exercise. These skills materially impact the quality of life of American citizens and all people. Moreover, when matters of rights and freedoms are involved, these skills become increasingly important. If students do not know how to both ascertain and evaluate the key premises and ideas behind the range of arguments that emerge in American politics, arguments that inevitably shape their own quality of life, then our students have not been well educated and they have not been adequately prepared to be engaged and thoughtful citizens.

In the first few decades immediately following the end of slavery, Black communities placed an extremely high value not only on access to a good-quality public education, but also on access to a robust public sphere in which Black communities, including women, men and children, could come and debate issues that mattered. They wanted access to spaces in which they could litigate qualities of leadership, strategies and plans for racial advancement, and general ideas about what it meant to be Black in the slowly receding shadow of enslavement. For communities deeply invested in the quest for freedom, the right to have opinions and to publicly share and deliberate about those opinions served as a mark of freedom. Similarly, in the contemporary moment, the burgeoning Black Lives Matter movement acknowledges that our movements are made clearer and sharper through robust and vigorous debate, disagreement, and consensus-building. But in order for leaders to use those skills as adults, they must first learn them in the classroom.

This chapter offers a brief history of debate within Black communities in the period between Emancipation and the Civil Rights Movement, with a particular focus on debate activities from the 1920s through the 1960s. Community debate programs and the emergence of collegiate debate in this period fit on the one hand with the importance of debate in the creation and cementation of a Black public sphere, but it also sets the stage for the cultures of debate that emerge during the Civil Rights Movement. The range of questions and issues with which these earlier communities concerned themselves are instructive for how educators might use debate in classrooms today. Therefore, I interrogate the manner in which local communities in the first half of the 20th century thought about the importance of debate as a form of political education for citizens. Then I turn briefly to a few of the iconic debates that took place during the Civil Rights Movement. These stories offer a vital and necessary reminder that the expansion of American democracy always requires a commitment to vigorous and sustained debate. In light of that history, we should consider debate a vital part of a good education.

In May of 1892, Ida B. Wells, a journalist and newspaper owner in Memphis, Tennessee, launched a career as a public intellectual and advocate after three of her friends were lynched. After she wrote a blistering editorial in her paper, the *Memphis Free Speech & Headlight*, townspeople burned down the newspaper's office and banished Wells from town. She fled to Brooklyn, New York, where she stayed with the famous African American poet and writer Frances Ellen Watkins Harper. In New York, Wells ensconced herself in a vibrant social scene that included the weekly meetings of many African American literary societies, where participants would perform musical selections, give talks about prepared papers and engage in formal debates.

One popular outlet for such debates was the Bethel Literary Association in New York. There debates which pitted pairs of debaters against each other covered a wide range of topics including "Resolved, that we need wealth more than we do education"; "Resolved, that we should encourage western emigration"; "Labor is a greater power than capital"; "That we owe no party a debt of gratitude"; and "That we need industrial more than academical education" (Peterson, 2011, pp. 346–347). Carla Peterson (2011) notes that the Bethel Literary Association was remarkable for its inclusion of female debaters: "Not only did women now share a public venue with men, but they argued with them over policy on equal terms" (pp. 347–348).

The leading Black lyceum in the city, the Brooklyn Literary Union, known for its debates, was less welcoming to women. The Union had strict debating guidelines. Four debaters gave ten-minute presentations. Then there was a 45-minute discussion, followed by a vote from the audience (Giddings, 2008, p. 234). Women were rarely among those featured as lecturers or debaters. However, during the late summer or early fall of 1892, Wells participated in a debate at the Brooklyn Literary Union, against, among others, Maritcha Lyons, a well-respected school principal from an old New York family. Though Wells had been gaining a local reputation as a compelling speaker, Lyons bested her in the debate. Wells took defeat in her stride, adopting Lyons as her mentor.

Lyons, together with Victoria Earle Matthews, another active member of the Brooklyn Black literati, put together the event that launched Wells's formal career as a public lecturer. In their mentor–mentee relationships, Lyons imparted to Wells two main lessons. "'Be so familiar with your discussion that you are literally saturated with it; think, meditate, and reflect, to develop all the points in a logical sequence.' Lyons also told Wells to learn how to 'manage the voice; if thought is prolific, expression of ideas will become automatic'" (Giddings, 2008, p. 235). In the ensuing months and years after her encounter with Lyons, Wells went on to become the most visible and vocal anti-lynching advocate of her generation, helping for the next 30 years to bring visibility to the epidemic of lynchings of African American men, women and children. By the early 1910s, the National Association for the Advancement of Colored People (NAACP) made anti-lynching one of its key political issues, largely because of the public foundation laid by Ida B. Wells.

In the mid 1920s, Pauli Murray, a famous Civil Rights attorney, writer, professor, and the first Black woman to be ordained an Episcopal priest, joined the debate team of the Hillside High School, the newly built "colored" high school for students in Durham, North Carolina. "We had a debating team, a glee club, organized baseball, boys' and girls' basketball teams, a school newspaper, and a yearbook," she wrote (Murray, 1987, pp. 59–60). All of these were "innovations utterly new to colored high school students in our town" (Murray, 1987, pp. 59–60). Moreover, she wrote, "our sports teams and debating team competed with those of other high schools in the state, and it was the first time that colored students in Durham had an opportunity to travel to other cities and expand our horizons. These modest advances were important milestones for us. They sustained our hope and gave us a sense of achievement at a time when the prevailing view that Negroes were inherently inferior remained unchallenged"

(Murray, 1987, pp. 59–60). Murray suggests that access to a debate team and other modern forms of extracurricular activity increased the rigor of her educational experience and chipped away at the sense of inferiority that a separate and unequal system of public education had produced in Black children, an argument that would be critical to the overturning of the Plessy decision in 1954. Moreover, debate and other activities marked the modernization of the American high school. Among many firsts, Pauli Murray graduated at the top of her class at Howard University Law School in 1944, producing a senior thesis that formed the basis for the legal strategy in the Brown desegregation decision. In addition to her work on the inclusion of the word "sex" in the 1964 Civil Rights Act, Murray also played a role in the dismantling of the all-white, all-male jury system. The first seeds of her voluminous career as a writer, thinker, academic, and poet undoubtedly had some of their genesis in the years she spent "preparing for inter-high school debates on the debating team."

This abbreviated history of Black debaters is a critical part of the intellectual and political history of African American people. To trace that history offers us a picture of the intellectual environs in which African American people honed and refined the arguments and strategies that shaped Black political discourse in the period between the end of Reconstruction and the Civil Rights Movement. This history of Blacks in debate also gives us a picture of the kind of training that it took to shape an African American leadership class in the post-slavery period. The robust cultures of debating that Black people created in the antebellum North and then throughout the country after Emancipation were critical in building a Black public or counterpublic sphere, a place where Black people could debate together about the collective fate of African Americans. In these nascent iterations of a Black public sphere, gender politics, and more specifically the participation of women, constituted a site of battle; thus, I began with the women because it is important to make visible the variety of ways that women participated in and helped to fundamentally shape the inter-workings of these spaces.

Several years ago, while I was conducting research for a project on the African American Club Women's Movement in Shreveport, Louisiana, in the pages of the *Shreveport Sun*, the state's oldest Black weekly, I unexpectedly began to see prominent front-page headlines advertising the debates of Black colleges near and far. For instance, the front page of the May 28, 1927 issue of the *Sun* proudly proclaims "Wiley College Debating Team Defeats Howard Univ, 3 Points." The famed Wiley College debate team was frequently the focus of the *Sun*'s coverage, in part because Marshall, Texas, home of Wiley College, is located only 30 miles from Shreveport, just across the Texas state line.

Debate and forensic activities were so popular in Shreveport that Black women who participated in the club movement also staged debates about particular issues. In one such debate, the town's Mary Church Terrell Club debated the topic "Resolved: That the South offers greater inducements and better advantages to our people than any other part of the country" ("Negative win in Debate", 1927). Mrs. Z. E. Baker and Mrs. R. E. Brown argued the affirmative;

the club's president Cora M. Allen and Mrs. Alice Davis argued the negative. In 1927, African Americans were exiting the South in droves as part of the Great Migration to the North in search of better jobs and more reasonable racial conditions. As fairly well-to-do club women with stable middle-class existences, women like Cora Allen, wife of the Rev. Luke Allen who pastored the largest Black church in town, were part of cadre of Black people who opted not to migrate. But the team of Allen and Davis prevailed in the debate, effectively defending the advantages of leaving the South. The debate is important, however, because it makes clear that the choice of whether to migrate or not, was in fact a debate, rather than a foregone conclusion.

The *Sun* covered a range of forensic activities, including those of Black colleges and universities throughout the country, and also debates at local churches and high schools. For instance, in 1928 the paper highlighted a story of a woman who had beaten a man in debate at the Galilee Baptist Church on the topic "Resolved: That woman has done more for humanity than man." The article noted that "it was fairly proven by Miss Shelton that woman had done more for humanity than man. Mr. Bounds made some strong points but came out ten points behind" ("Woman Wins Debate", 1928). The *Sun's* coverage of community forensic activities was commensurate with coverage from other newspapers throughout the country. In the early 1920s, the *Chicago Defender* also covered college and community debate activities. In 1923, the Grace Lyceum in Chicago had a debate on the topic "Slavery has been more of a help than a hindrance to the American Negro" ("Young Women Win Debate", 1928). An event sponsored by the "Older Girls and Young Woman's Conferences" and the young men's council, the teams were split on the basis of gender. The young men argued the affirmative position and the girls argued the negative position. The young women won. In 1924, another Chicago paper, the *Broad Ax*, covered the annual Elbridge L. Adams Prize Debates held at Hampton Institute ("Douglass Society Wins Adams Debate", 1924). That year the Douglass Literary Society beat the Dunbar Literary Society debating the topic, "Resolved: That compulsory military training should be abolished in secondary schools." The Douglass Society team argued the negative.

In 1932, the *Sun* reported that there had been "a revival of intercollegiate debating activities among the schools of the South Central Association of Colleges for Negro Youth." Among those schools were Southern University, Straight College, Alcorn State University, Leland College, and the University of New Orleans. The subject under consideration during the spring 1932 debating season was "Resolved: That Great Britain should give India complete and immediate independence" ("Southern Debaters Win", 1932). These young Black students were engaged in debates over British imperialism and the ethics and value of anti-colonialism in the 1930s. The broad national coverage of community and college debate activities in the Black Press suggests that locally and nationally Black communities valued vigorous debate and discussion and also that they took great pride in seeing young African Americans engage in these activities. The topics also suggest that conversations in Black public culture attended to more general questions of history and social relationships between the sexes as well as debates about contemporary political issues like mandatory military training and the ethics of colonialism. The debates themselves, audience participation, and coverage in the Black Press all participated in raising community literacies and consciousness around these important political issues that certainly had implications for Black communities living in the thick of Southern Jim Crow regimes.

Interracial debates constituted another major aspect of the Black Press's coverage of Black participation in debate. In May 1923, Lewis Burrell, a debater and team captain at Pleasantville High School in Pleasantville, New Jersey, led his white teammates to victory debating Haddonfield High School on the question "Resolved: That the Merchant Marine of the United States should be subsidized by the federal government" ("Leads White Team Mates", 1923). In the 1930s, these interracial exchanges became even more common, particularly among college debaters. In 1932 the Wiley College debaters embarked on a 10,000-mile Goodwill Tour, doing exhibition debates throughout the country. The *Sun* reported that "As a means of promoting better understanding between the races, Wiley has sought to make contacts with some of the white colleges thru [sic] their debating teams." The paper reported that their interactions with teams in Oklahoma, Michigan and Chicago were gratifying, pleasant and profitable.

In 1933, teams from Wiley and the University of Kansas debated the topic "Resolved: That Socialism would be preferable to Capitalism in the United States." Wiley argued the affirmative while Kansas argued the negative. The *Sun* ran this as the lead story in their March 4th issue, with the headline "Interracial Debate Gets Big Ovation." Above the masthead, another headline proclaimed, "Inauguration of a New United States President Today" ("Interracial Debate Gets Big Ovation", 1933). Franklin D. Roosevelt began his first term in office this same day. That an interracial gathering of student competitors from the Midwest and South came together in the early 1930s in the wake of the Great Depression and on the verge of Roosevelt's New Deal to debate the merits of socialism versus capitalism suggests that debates were ideal spaces for capturing the political zeitgeist. Moreover they created opportunities for students from different racial, geographical and cultural backgrounds to come together in a meeting of minds over big ideas. In 1939, the University of Chicago Debate Union traveled to historically Black Lincoln University in Missouri to debate the topic, "Why go to college: To learn how to live or to learn how to make a living" ("Hold Round-Table Discussions", 1939). A picture of the interracial group of debaters sitting and dialoguing ran with the article in the *Shreveport Sun* providing a powerful visual demonstration to the Black readership of the *Sun* about the importance of debate to the work of racial advancement.

The broad swath of issues covered in these debates and the fact that local audiences flocked to see them suggests that local communities were politically engaged and that this engagement was intergenerational, encompassing the political ideas of both the young people who primarily participated in these debates and those adults and elders who served as judges and audience members for such debates. The editorial board of the *Sun* believed that space for discussion and debate was critical to the public life of the city. A 1938 editorial argued that "a city with a colored population as large as ours should have" among other things "a Forum where current questions could be discussed and debated" and "a debating society which might engage in forensic contests with neighboring colleges on important questions of the day" ("More Cultural Organizations Needed", 1938). The clear attention to debate in the press coverage of cities as disparate as Shreveport, Louisiana, and Chicago, Illinois in the 1920s and 1930s suggests that forensic activity was a critical building block not only of African American educational settings but also of African American public culture in the two decades before the formal inauguration of the modern Civil Rights Movement.

As the Civil Rights Movement came to full articulation, beginning with desegregation in 1954 and the Montgomery Bus Boycott of 1955, the importance of formal debate and discussion took on a different meaning. Now Black communities needed to think both ideologically and tactically about what the goals of this latest iteration of the Black freedom struggle were and how to go about achieving them. Many of these debates played out formally among Black male leaders who advocated a liberal integrationist view of the Civil Rights Struggle and those who advocated a radical Black nationalist view. Chief among the Black nationalists was Malcolm X, leader of the Nation of Islam, and a staunch opponent of the philosophy of non-violence that under-girded the public face of the Civil Rights Movement.

As is well documented, Malcolm X honed his oratorical skill as part of the Norfolk Penal Colony Debating Program, during his stint as a prisoner there in the late 1940s and early 1950s. Robert James Branham writes that "Malcolm X was a brilliant debater, adept at dismantling the positions of his opponents, converting their arguments to his own advantage, and most importantly casting the issues of dispute in utter and compelling clarity" (Branham, 1995, p. 117). Malcolm X valued debating as a form of political speech, because, as he famously said in his autobiography:

> Standing up there, the faces looking at me, the things in my head coming out of my mouth, while my brain searched for the next best thing to follow what I was saying, and if I could sway them to my side by handling it right, then I had won the debate – once my feet got wet, I was gone on debating.
> (As cited in Branham, 1995, p. 121)

Despite the fact that Malcolm X became a debater and formidable political thinker while in prison, the presence of the prison debate program represented a moment where prisons were viewed as social apparatuses that could appropriately redirect and prepare inmates for productive lives as citizens upon their release (Branham, 1995, p. 118). In an earlier era, even prisons recognized that teaching people to debate was nothing less than preparing them for a critical and engaged form of participation in democracy.

When Malcolm X was released from prison in the 1950s, now a convert to Islam, he moved to Harlem where he refined his thinking as a street preacher and minister of the Nation of Islam. As the Civil Rights Movement matured, Malcolm X emerged as the most formidable intraracial adversary of Martin Luther King and those proponents of a liberal Civil Rights Tradition. He engaged in a number of debates both throughout the United States and famously in England at the Oxford Union a few months before his death (see also Ambar, 2014; Tuck, 2014). Within the U.S. on more than one occasion he debated Civil Rights figures like James Farmer and Bayard Rustin. Martin Luther King refused to debate Malcolm X, and most Civil Rights leaders were afraid to take him on in public as well, because of his history of fiercely routing his opponents (Ogbar, 2004).

In October 1961, Malcolm X debated Bayard Rustin, one of the key tacticians of the non-violent direct action strategy, on the campus of Howard University. The topic was "Integration or Separation." Each man "spoke for about thirty minutes followed by a ten-minute rebuttal for each." E. Franklin Frazier, the famous sociologist and author of *The Black Bourgeoisie*, moderated the event. In the audience on the front row that night sat a young, spellbound Stokely Carmichael. Before this night, Carmichael had been a devotee of Rustin's non-violent teachings. Freshly back on campus after a summer spent in Nashville organizing with the Student Non-Violent Coordinating Committee (SNCC) and participating in the Freedom Rides organized by James Farmer and the Congress of Racial Equality, Stokely was jubilant when he heard that Malcolm X was planning to visit the campus (Joseph, 2014). Carmichael biographer Peniel Joseph argues that Malcolm's lecture "galvanized racial pride at Howard. He planted seeds of political conversion that would turn many in the audience, over time, into ardent Black nationalists, committed Pan-Africanists, and lifelong political radicals." Carmichael, who would go on to be a key architect of the Black Power Movement, was one such figure. Joseph writes that "Malcolm's physical swagger and intellectual bravado made a lasting impression on Carmichael" (Joseph, 2014, p. 42; see also Ogbar, 2004, p. 54).

James Farmer, national director of the Congress of Racial Equality, proved that when it came to formal debates, swagger and bravado weren't everything. From 1934 to 1938 Farmer served as member and eventually captain of the famous Wiley College debate team. Thus, unlike his fellow Civil Rights counterparts, he was unafraid to debate Malcolm. And he proved to be X's most formidable opponent. On March 7, 1962, the two debated each other at Cornell University also on the topic "Integration or Segregation." This debate represented a convergence of the intellectual, rhetorical and political traditions that brought African Americans into the realms of formal debate, Farmer emerging through Black collegiate debate channels and X emerging from the environs of the prison debate and street preaching.

By all accounts, Farmer bested Malcolm in the first showdown in 1962. Tactically, because Farmer had the first speech in the debate, he laid the historical groundwork for the evils of Jim Crow and segregation. Because X was known to recite a litany of these evils in order to make the case against segregation, by covering that ground first, Farmer claimed the prerogative to reframe the terms. The evils of segregation that instilled a sense of inferiority in Black children, distorted the perceptions of white people about their own supposed superiority, and hurt American business through boycotts, were all reasons, in Farmer's estimation, to support a robust program of integration. Where X frequently cast integrationists as passive recipients of white suprema-cist treatment, Farmer argued that it was prior generations of Black people, people in his father's generation, who had thought "that the way things always had to be and they always would be, so we put up with it, took part in it, decided to exist and stay alive" (as cited in Bosmajian, 1969). In recounting this story with his father, James Farmer Sr., who on his deathbed gave the younger James his blessing to participate in the 1961 Freedom Rides, Farmer situates those actively involved in the desegregation struggle as those who are committed to racial progress. He casts X's desire, vis-à-vis the Nation of Islam, for a separate Black nation-state as the politically retrograde position, one that moved Black people from "forced ghettoism" to "voluntary ghettoism" (as cited in Bosmajian, 1969).

Farmer also pre-empted X's attempts to discredit him as a race man because he had married a white woman. He argued simply that he believed enough in the "virtue of Negroes that I do not even think those virtues are so frail that they will be corrupted by contact with other people" (as cited in Bosmajian, 1969). Finally, and most compellingly, Farmer took on Malcolm's claim that the desire for integration was a bourgeois desire. He argued that historically members of the Black middle class were often against integration because it would hurt Black businesses through competition with white business owners. By the time Malcolm attempted to refute this argument by saying that Farmer still only spoke for a minority of Blacks rather than the majority, the rhetorical heft of his claim has been sufficiently mitigated.

In a subsequent debate with James Baldwin in September 1963, he and Malcolm X tangled masterfully over which accounts of identity, and which accounts of history, Black people should accept as a guide for moving for-ward. Baldwin challenged Malcolm's desire to identify solely with the African or Black part of his heritage and not with the American and white parts of his heritage, particularly the histories of violence, rape and enslavement with which such histories would demand we all grapple. Malcolm simply replied that no other group was asked to give up its cultural and racial identifications in service of identifying with American history. Malcolm challenged the con-tinuing investment of Civil Rights leaders in non-violent strategies, saying to Baldwin, "never do you find white people encouraging other whites to be non-violent." In other words, such tactics in Malcolm's estimation followed a set of rules about non-violence to which white Americans themselves did not even subscribe. In this debate, there were no clear winners and losers. But what emerges is a picture of a robust culture of public debate among African

Americans about the proper ends, aims and goals of the Black freedom project. The Civil Rights Movement and the subsequent Black Power Movement were conceived in a culture of rigorous and powerful debates, the most public of which occurred among Black men, about the ways that history, notions of identity, religion and the politics of power should inform the quest for African American freedom.

Whether we are talking about the life of anti-lynching crusader Ida B. Wells in the post-Reconstruction era or Malcolm X during the Civil Rights Movement, it is simply impossible to understand the rich ideological terrain upon which the quest for African American freedom grew without talking about the importance of formal debates and forensic activity. In the nineteenth century, such activities were critical to the formation of a Black public sphere, as Black people were actively involved in imagining and reimagining their relationship to the larger American body politic in the decades leading up to and following Emancipation. After true emancipation, followed by a century of Jim Crow segregation, proved elusive, the necessity of African American oratical skill and rhetorical prowess became even more important to Black communities throughout the country. Parents wanted their children to have debate training, local communities tried to create debating societies, and the Black Press invested in coverage of high school and collegiate debates both to foster pride in African American achievement and to creatively highlight how issues important to Black people were being engaged publicly. The many debates that took place over the course of the Civil Rights Movement then emerge not as tangential but rather as central and fundamental to steering the course of the movement. As the most vocal proponent of a Black nationalist framework, Malcolm X forced the Civil Rights Movement and its leaders to refine its message, even as his status as the more radical foil to King made King's arguments about inclusion seem imminently more reasonable and attractive to liberal white Americans.

Teaching students to debate means teaching students to invest deeply in the power and possibilities of ideas. Teaching students to debate means teaching them to question more fully and more deeply. Teaching them to debate means that we foster dissatisfaction with easy answers. Debate training emerges as a kind of boot camp for those students who really want to know what it means to grapple with and solve problems that do not have easy or absolute answers. Each of the major leaders profiled here used debate training to push America to be a more inclusive democracy. Ida B. Wells, Pauli Murray, Malcolm X, James Baldwin and James Farmer stood on the frontlines of public discourse, challenging our country to tell ugly truths and to change. Debate helped to teach them how to be the courageous leaders that they were. In a moment when a whole new generation of activists, leaders, thinkers and movers are taking to the street as part of the Black Lives Matter movement, the resonances of these earlier movements insinuate themselves. These earlier movements and the debates on which they stood remind us that the quest for freedom demands our best thinking, and that our best thinking is frequently a product of work in community and contestation with others who are as deeply invested as we are. At the same time, these debates remind us of the importance of civility and respect and a mutual appreciation for the importance of ideas. For no great movement for social justice has ever been achieved without debate.

References

Ambar, S. (2014). *Malcolm X at Oxford Union: Black Politics in a Global Era*. New York: Oxford University Press.

Bosmajian, H. A., & Bosmajian, H. (Eds.). (1969). *The Rhetoric of the The Civil-Rights Movement*. New York: Random House.

Branham, R. J. (1995). 'I was gone on debating': Malcolm X's prison debates and public confrontations. *Argumentation and Advocacy*, 31, 117–137.

Douglass society wins Adams debate – Hampton institute students debate on compulsory military training – Winners in essay contest are announced – Elbridge L. Adams awards prizes. (1924, March 29). *The Broad Ax*.

Giddings, P. (2008). *Ida: A Sword Among Lions*. New York: Amistad.

Hold round-table discussions at Lincoln U, (Mo.). (1939, March 11). *The Shreveport Sun*.

Interracial debate gets big ovation. (1933, March 4). *The Shreveport Sun*.

Joseph, P. (2014). *Stokely: A Life*. New York: Basic Civitas.

Leads white team mates to victory in debating. (1923, May 19). *The Chicago Defender*.

More cultural organizations needed. (1938, August 13). *The Shreveport Sun*.

Murray, P. (1987). *Pauli Murray: The Autobiography of a Black Activist, Feminist, Lawyer, Priest, and Poet*. Knoxville: University of Tennessee Press.

Negative win in debate, "Resolved that the south offers better advantages to the negro than other sections of the U.S." (1927, May 21). *The Shreveport Sun*.

Ogbar, J. (2004). *Black Power: Radical Politics and African American Identity*. Baltimore: Johns Hopkins University Press.

Peterson, C. (2011). *Black Gotham*. New Haven and London: Yale University Press.

Southern debaters win from Straigh and Alcorn colleges. (1932, May 7). *The Shreveport Sun*.

Tuck, S. (2014). *The Night Malcolm X Spoke at Oxford Union: A Transatlantic Story of Antiracist Protest*. Oakland: University of California Press.

Wiley College Debating Team Defeats Howard Univ, 3 Points. (1927, May 28). *The Shreveport Sun*.

Woman wins debate at Galilee Bapt. church. (1928, March 10). *The Shreveport Sun*.

Young women win debate before Grace Lyceum. (1923, June 2). *The Chicago Defender*.

2 Resolved: Debate Disrupts the School-to-Prison Pipeline[1]

Catherine Beane

A 52-pound eight-year-old boy with attention deficit hyperactivity disorder and a history of trauma is handcuffed at school by a Kentucky deputy sheriff for behavior related to his disability; video footage shows the young boy crying as the officer handcuffs his arms at the biceps behind his back (Stolberg, 2015). A 13-year-old boy in Pikesville, Maryland, is arrested and charged with second-degree assault as a juvenile for kissing a girl during school hours without her consent after he was dared to by other students ("Boy charged with assault", 2015). In Columbia, South Carolina, a school resource officer flips over a teenage girl's desk and throws the girl across a classroom for violating the school's policy and refusing to hand over her cell phone (Fausett & Southall, 2015). An African American high-school student is suspended for a day for using a cell phone and an iPod in class; in the same school, a white student with a similar disciplinary history gets detention for the similar infraction of using headphones (Khadaroo, 2015). Stories like the ones shared above – of children as young as preschool being excluded from the classroom as a consequence for non-violent, often age- and developmentally appropriate behavior; and of differential application of school discipline rules along lines of race, ethnicity, gender, disability, and socio-economic status – are at the heart of what has come to be called the "school-to-prison pipeline."

This unique phenomenon in American culture reflects a widespread pattern of pushing students out of school and into the justice system, spurred on by zero-tolerance school discipline policies, increased police presence in public schools, implicit bias, high-stakes testing pressures, and the criminalization of otherwise normal adolescent and childhood behavior. The students pushed into the pipeline are disproportionately black, brown, disabled, and poor. They are the very same students who experience achievement gaps in the classrooms in which they learn and opportunity gaps in the communities in which they live. They are also the very same students for whom, in recent years, debate has opened pathways to greater school engagement, academic achievement, and educational and career opportunities.

No teacher enters the profession wanting to teach to a test or intending to put kids out of the classroom for behavior issues. Yet, tremendous pressure to raise test scores or face being labeled a failure, coupled with the systemic use of zero-tolerance policies by school districts has put teachers in the unenviable position of involving school security officers and relying on suspensions and expulsions when behavior issues arise. Fortunately, teachers who have incorporated debate in their classrooms have found that, by putting students at the center of the learning paradigm, debate offers a powerful tool for managing their classrooms and defusing situations before they escalate.

The central thesis of this chapter is that debate shares common goals, processes, skills, and student outcomes with educational theories, pedagogical practices, and intervention strategies that educators are now using as alternatives to the zero-tolerance and exclusionary discipline policies that fuel the school-to-prison pipeline. This chapter first provides an overview of the school-to-prison pipeline phenomenon – what it is, whom it impacts, and how it fails both students and schools. Thereafter, this chapter examines the alternatives that educators are using to enhance student outcomes and conditions for learning within schools, and it posits that debate provides a structured pedagogical practice and sound strategy for engaging students, enhancing conditions for learning within schools, and disrupting the school-to-prison pipeline.

We are at a moment of profound opportunity for change. Leaders at the highest levels of U.S. government are paying attention to the trends and disparities in our nation's schools and jails, and tremendous strides are being made every day to address the serious crisis that lies at the unnecessary intersection between our education and justice systems. Both former Attorney General Eric Holder and Secretary of Education Arne Duncan are on record emphasizing the importance of this work, with Holder noting, "Every data point represents a life impacted and a future potentially diverted or derailed" (Nicks, 2014), and "ensuring that our educational system is a doorway to opportunity – and not a point of entry to our criminal justice system – is a critical, and achievable, goal" (U.S. Dept. of Education, 2011).

Perhaps most telling about this shifting paradigm are President Barack Obama's remarks when he became the first sitting president to visit a federal prison facility. After touring the facility in Oklahoma and speaking with a group of inmates, President Obama remarked:

> We have a tendency sometimes to almost take for granted or think it's normal that so many young people have been locked up. It's not normal. It's not what happens in other countries. What is normal is teenagers doing stupid things. What is normal is young people making mistakes.
>
> (Baker, 2015)

Debate provides an opportunity for young people to learn, grow, and even recover from mistakes with the support and encouragement of educators and their peers. Debate provides the kind of opportunity that's needed to disrupt the school-to-prison pipeline.

The School-to-Prison Pipeline: What It Is, Who It Impacts, and How It Fails Students and Schools

Discipline in school settings has changed profoundly over the past 25 years, shifting from principals and administrators handling misconduct on a case-by-case basis that takes into account circumstances such as the specific students involved and the impact on overall school safety, to utilizing zero-tolerance policies that limit discretion, often involve law enforcement officers, and that require exclusion from school for even minor misconduct (Kang-Brown, Trone, Fratello, & Daftary-Kapur, 2013). A generation later, the flaws in this approach have become abundantly clear, with experts now concluding that neither schools nor students benefit (Kang-Brown et al., 2013). This section explores multiple dimensions of the zero-tolerance policies, which set students up for the school-to-prison pipeline phenomenon, examining its history and context, and the critique that researchers have put forward based on its very negative, and often unintended, consequences for students and schools.

Zero-tolerance policies are generally understood to be those school- or district-wide policies that mandate predetermined consequences for student misbehavior, regardless of the gravity of the behavior, mitigating circumstances, or the situational context (American Psychological Association, 2008). Most often, these predetermined consequences are severe and punitive in nature, requiring out-of-school suspension or expulsion on a first offense (Kang-Brown et al., 2013). Although originally adopted as responses to weapons, drugs, and violent acts in the school setting, they rapidly expanded to apply to a wide variety of rule violations, and over time, suspensions became commonplace in response to such non-violent conduct as disrespect and non-compliance (National Association of School Psychologists, 2011). In this discussion, "zero tolerance" and "exclusionary discipline" (suspensions and expulsions) are related concepts that often occur together, and each plays a role in the school-to-prison pipeline.

Zero-tolerance policies originated in the 1980s and 90s at a time of rising rates of violent crime by juveniles and a growing perception of young people as dangerous (Kang-Brown et al., 2013). Congress extended its tough-on-crime approach to adult justice issues into the school context through passage of the Gun-Free Schools Act in 1994, which linked a school district's qualification for federal funds to adoption of policies that expelled for at least one year any student who brought a weapon into school (Kang-Brown et al., 2013). Even though juvenile crime rates began to decrease after 1994, the perception of the young urban "super predator" persisted, and 79% of schools had zero-tolerance policies beyond the federal mandate by the 1996–97 school year (Kang-Brown et al., 2013). Zero-tolerance policies gained additional traction in the aftermath of the Columbine shooting, at the same time that federal and state governments increased funding for security guards, school-based law enforcement officers, and the installation of metal detectors in school settings (Kang-Brown et al., 2013). Since the 1990s, school districts have expanded the use of zero tolerance from situations involving possession of a weapon or illegal drugs to less serious offenses such as smoking tobacco; school fighting; and cases involving disruption, willful defiance, or disrespect of educators in the classroom and in the school building (Kang-Brown et al., 2013).

As far back as the year 2000, alarm bells were sounded about the ineffectiveness of zero-tolerance policies and the negative impact such policies have on students. Researchers from the Safe & Responsive Schools initiative at Indiana University (funded by a grant from the U.S. Department of Education Office of Special Education Programs) critiqued such policies along four lines of inquiry: first, there was no evidence that exclusionary discipline changed student behavior or improved school safety; second, exclusionary discipline was utilized inconsistently; third, racial and economic bias often accompanied the imposition of exclusionary discipline; and fourth, over the long term, exclusionary discipline was associated with significant negative impacts for students related to academic achievement (Safe & Responsive Schools, 2000). Ultimately, researchers found that while removing a child from school might be necessary in some circumstances, no evidence existed at that time to support the political assumption that "punishment and exclusion can in and of themselves solve problems of school violence, or teach students alternatives to violence" (Safe & Responsive Schools, 2000).

Leading organizations in the fields of children's health, behavior, and adolescent development have added to the critique. Notably, in 2008, the American Psychological Association found that zero-tolerance policies appear to conflict with what is known about adolescent development: many incidents that result in disciplinary infractions at the secondary level are due to poor judgment on the part of the adolescent involved, and zero-tolerance policies may exacerbate the potential mismatch between an adolescent's developmental stage and the structure of secondary schools (American Psychological Association, 2008). Subsequently, the American Academy of Pediatrics called for schools to focus on teaching and recognizing desired behavior, rather than suspending or expelling students for misconduct (American Academy of Pediatrics, 2013; Lamont, 2013).

Justice and education leaders have also joined the call for change. In 2011, the U.S. Departments of Education and Justice partnered together to launch the Supportive School Discipline Initiative, which seeks to provide alternatives to exclusionary discipline and encourages schools to reduce the disproportionate use of exclusionary discipline for students of color and students with disabilities (U.S. Department of Education, Overview, 2014). In January 2014, the departments issued joint guidance to assist public elementary and secondary schools in meeting their obligations under federal law to administer student discipline without discriminating on the basis of race, color, or national origin (U.S. Department of Education, Dear Colleague Letter, 2014). Contemporaneous with these federal initiatives, seminal reports from the Vera Institute of Justice and the Council of State Governments highlighted the negative consequences of exclusionary discipline on a student's academic progress and the increased risk students face of dropping out and becoming entangled in the juvenile justice system (Kang-Brown et al., 2013; Morgan, Salomon, Plotkin, & Cohen, 2014). Repeating a grade is one of the strongest predictors of dropping out of school, and in one study, nearly 10% of students with at least one disciplinary contact dropped out of school, compared to just 2% of students who had no disciplinary actions (Fabelo et al., 2011).

Most agree that students who engage in violent acts or bring weapons to school should face serious consequences and that exclusion from school through suspension or expulsion is among the acceptable consequences for such serious behavior (Morgan et al., 2014). In reality, however, very few of the serious disciplinary actions in schools involve dangerous conduct, and nationally, almost half (43%) of expulsions and suspensions lasting longer than a week were for insubordination (Kang-Brown et al., 2013). These serious consequences are being applied most often as overly severe responses to minor infractions, such as tardiness, disrupting class, and dress code violations, and in other instances, they are criminalizing what should otherwise be viewed as normal child and adolescent behavior. As former Attorney General Eric Holder noted, "Ordinary troublemaking can sometimes provoke responses that are overly severe, including out-of-school suspensions, expulsions and even referral to law enforcement and then you end up with kids that end up in police precincts instead of the principal's office" (Shanny, 2014). Attorney General Holder's conclusions align with what the research and data on school discipline make clear: "millions of students are being removed from their classrooms each year, mostly in middle and high schools, and overwhelmingly for minor misconduct" (Morgan et al., 2014, Executive Summary p. 1).

Rather than producing a safer climate by removing disruptive students, schools with higher rates of exclusionary discipline seem to have less satisfactory ratings of school climate and seem to spend a disproportionate amount of time on disciplinary issues (American Psychological Association, 2008). Research indicates a negative correlation between the use of school suspension and expulsion and school-wide academic achievement; more exclusionary discipline is associated with lower achievement (American Psychological Association, 2008). Instead of reducing the likelihood of future disruption, school suspension in general appears to predict higher future rates of misbehavior and suspension among those students who are suspended (American Psychological Association, 2008).

Underlying all of these findings and concerns are statistics and disparities that highlight the racial bias implicit in the application of zero-tolerance and exclusionary discipline policies. Reams of data released through the U.S. Department of Education's Civil Rights Data Collection document the extent to which students of color, particularly black and brown males, continue to bear the brunt of exclusionary discipline policies. At each level of the K–12 school system – preschool, elementary, middle, and secondary – students of color are suspended and expelled from school at much higher rates than white students. For example, black middle-school students are suspended nearly four times more often than white students, while Latino students are twice as likely to be suspended or expelled as white students (Kang-Brown et al., 2013). And in the most recent data collection, black children were only 18% of the enrolled preschoolers in America's public schools, but they accounted for 42% of preschool students who were suspended once and 48% of preschool students who received more than one out-of-school suspension (Civil Rights Data Collection, 2014). In releasing this data, U.S. Secretary of Education Arne Duncan noted:

> I simply cannot understand how our public preschool programs could suspend nearly 5,000 young children in a single year – and suspend over 2,500 children more than once. The fact that the school-to-prison pipeline appears to start as early as four years old – before kindergarten – should horrify us.
>
> (U.S. Department of Education, "The New Spotlight", 2014)

A generation of research and statistics paints a portrait of school practices and exclusionary discipline policies that fail both our students and our communities, with devastating impacts for the individual lives touched by them. The tide of public and political opinion is turning, however, and across the country, state legislatures, state departments of education, and municipal school districts are beginning to move away from zero-tolerance policies (Kang-Brown et al., 2013). We can, and must, do better, and the political winds are more favorable than ever for implementing the pedagogical practices and educational policies that more effectively engage students, enhance conditions for learning, and improve school climates. In the next section, this chapter explores the ways in which utilizing debate both as an academically aligned co-curricular activity and as a structured instructional practice are particularly well suited to disrupt the school-to-prison pipeline.

Debate as a Strategy for Disrupting the Pipeline

A growing body of evidence indicates that alternatives to exclusionary discipline can keep young people safely in school. Indeed, there is a "growing consensus that the most effective schools reinforce positive behavior and respond to behavioral problems on a case-by-case basis in ways that suit the student's individual circumstances and needs" (Kang-Brown et al., 2013). Key instructional strategies, communication skills, and academic outcomes related to debate align closely with the educational theories and practices that are driving current thinking about the conditions for teaching and learning that will provide safe and supportive learning environments for educators and students. This section first describes debate as a structured activity and pedagogical practice that produces positive behavioral and academic outcomes for students. Thereafter, this section describes debate's alignment with the various frameworks and approaches that have been effective or shown promise in producing better results in the realm of student discipline and academic achievement, namely, student agency, deeper learning, violence prevention, and restorative practices. Ultimately, this section makes the case that debate can be a powerful force in disrupting the school-to-prison pipeline precisely because it creates the positive conditions for learning that are central to addressing the exclusionary discipline crisis in America's schools.

Debate is a highly structured activity that involves reading and interpreting non-fiction text, developing and writing arguments based on these texts, verbally expressing and defending evidence-based claims, listening to and interpreting an opponent's arguments, collaborating with peers, interacting with teachers/coaches/mentors, and managing one's time (Mezuk, Bondarenko, Smith, & Tucker, 2011). Effective communication is at the heart of the debate activity: in order to be successful, students must be able to communicate their arguments clearly and persuasively to others who have differing backgrounds and perspectives, be they teachers, parents, students, or community leaders. Critical thinking, problem-solving, creativity, and innovation are additional elements of debate that have been noted as enabling students in the 21st century to compete effectively in the global economy (NAUDL, n.d.).

Beyond the academic skills that flow from interscholastic debate competition and that are described more fully in other chapters in this volume (see Winkler, Chapter 6), shifts in student behavior and disciplinary referrals have been documented among students involved in competitive debate activities (Winkler, 2011; Winkler, 2009). In one study examining the impact of debate in reducing early signs of aggression and anti-social behaviors among students at risk of dropping out of high school, the majority of students who entered debate with recorded instances of student misconduct (specifically, school conduct violations and suspensions) reduced their annual number of disciplinary referrals and school suspensions (Winkler, 2011).

In explaining the changes in their school conduct, students reported that "debate offers a path to a hopeful future" and strengthens the communication skills needed to negotiate conflict, namely listening, empathy, and persuasiveness (Winkler, 2011, p. 86). Students also noted debate's positive impact on reading as a reason for their own improved conduct, suggesting that debate's "repetitive focus on oral reading activities coupled with a series of competitions against other students from other schools" provides struggling readers with a low-risk means of improving vocabulary, increasing fluency, and enhancing reading comprehension that avoids the potential embarrassment and acting out/disruption of school classrooms that can result from having to read aloud in front of one's peers (Winkler, 2011, p. 87). In other words, debate practice and competition create the kind of safe-to-fail environment that can alleviate disruptive behaviors that could otherwise lead to the imposition of exclusionary discipline.

Male students reported that debate "helps them build a skill set (reading, listening, taking notes, persuasive speaking, etc.) needed for positive interactions with authority figures, such as their teachers within schools," while female students reported that debate "improves their confidence and listening skills, which reduces their potential conflicts with their peers" (Winkler, 2011, p. 87). Each of these skill sets is crucial to navigating the rocky terrain of school discipline and the non-violent conflicts with peers and teachers that account for so much of the exclusionary discipline that is doled out in America's public schools.

The competitive framework for debate has also been adapted for use in the classroom. "Debate Across the Curriculum" (DAC) is a multi-disciplinary instructional strategy that puts students at the forefront of learning. Classroom debate can address many critical causal factors predicting the decision to drop out: disengagement, boredom, and lack of challenge. Imagine a science classroom where students debate about which of Newton's laws of physics could be violated to produce the best superpower. Students do most of the speaking as they debate in teams in front of classmates who are taking notes to form questions for their own opportunities to enter the debate, with a teacher facilitating group cross-examination and fostering group critique of the ideas being debated (Wade & Zorwick, 2009). A recent study of 326 high-school teachers who are members of the National Speech and Debate Association – strongly associated Debate Across Curriculum instructional methods with implementation of Common Core State Standards, which build critical thinking skills (Zorwick & Wade, 2015). Classroom debates allow students to grow and develop a powerful sense of self and voice, as well as a belief that learning matters and that their actions can make a difference.

Researchers and practitioners are focusing considerable attention on creating positive conditions for learning as a means of developing more effective and appropriate disciplinary practices in our schools:

> The extent to which students are safe, connected, engaged, and supported in their classrooms and schools – collectively known as the 'conditions for learning' – is critical to their academic and personal success. Schools that create welcoming and secure learning environments reduce the likelihood that students will misbehave and improve educators' ability to manage student behavior.
>
> (Morgan et al., 2014, Executive Summary p. 3)

Academic achievement and positive behaviors increase when affirming conditions for learning are in place and students and staff feel physically and emotionally safe, connected, fairly treated, and valued (Morgan et al., 2014).

The skills and outcomes fostered by debate are very much aligned with this focus on conditions for learning. Debate actively engages students in the process of using research to support creative argumentation, thereby increasing student connection to school and engagement in academic inquiry. The use of teachers as coaches and mentors fosters positive relationships with caring adults and increases both the ability of teachers and students to understand each other's perspectives, as well as students' sense that they will be heard and treated fairly. Debate's "safe-to-fail" environment for skill development furthers the sense of connection, emotional safety, and value in the school environment.

Student agency is an area of particular interest among educational experts concerned about creating more positive conditions for learning. Student agency refers to a set of mindsets and instructional strategies that increase learning and achievement by enabling students to take charge of their own learning (Rate, 2013). Engaging students by seeking and respecting their opinions, providing opportunities for students to feel connected to school life, and promoting positive and caring relationships in the school building are among the pedagogical approaches that foster student agency (Values-Centered Schools, Student Agency, 2009). Highly structured environments that support sustained and thoughtful engagement promote a student's capacity to define his or her own learning goals, to ask questions, to use metacognitive strategies, and to self-monitor – all critical components of student agency (Alton-Lee, 2003).

Debate fosters student agency in multiple ways. In competitive debate as well as DAC, learning and achievement are valued and expected by students. Goal-setting and intra-personal skills like persistence are required for success in the activity. Respect for others and inter-personal skills like collaboration and communication are inherent in debate. Autonomy is paired with responsibility, as students identify which arguments best support their position, develop the research base to support those arguments, and ultimately persuade teachers and peers of the merits of their position. Each of these elements – high expectations for student learning and achievement, goal-setting, intra- and inter-personal skills, autonomy, and responsibility – are among the behaviors and examples observed in those schools doing exemplary work to develop student agency (Pearson Foundation, n.d.).

Closely related to student agency is the concept of deeper learning, through which students think, question, pursue, and create to take ownership of their own learning (Briceno, 2013). In so doing, students acquire deeper understanding and become more competent learners both in and out of the classroom (Briceno, 2013). Deeper learning instructional practices include student-centered and self-directed learning methods, encouraging collaboration and incorporating real-world projects and explorations. These practices result in prolific learning, and their impact is significantly enhanced when students are supported in developing a growth mindset ("I can change my intelligence and abilities through effort"), self-efficacy ("I can succeed"), a sense of belonging ("I belong in this learning community"), and relevance ("This work has value and purpose for me") (Briceno, 2013). A key component underlying this approach is reframing mistakes and confusion as opportunities to learn, clarify, and grow; thereby making it safe for students and teachers to try and fail and try again, which in turn de-stigmatizes and encourages effort, innovation, and stretching/growing (Briceno, 2013).

Debate is an instructional method and student engagement strategy that flourishes at this intersection between student agency and deep learning. Reading the descriptions of deep learning is like reading a description of debate itself. At its very essence, debate is an instructional practice and activity in which students think, question, pursue, and create as they drive their own learning. Debate fosters a growth mindset and a sense of efficacy among students as it emphasizes trying again in the next debate round or DAC activity, even if a student doesn't "win" the first time around. No two debate rounds ever play out the same, and students are constantly honing and revising their arguments in order to respond to their opponents and to persuade their teachers and peers of the superiority of their own position.

In addition to the educational and pedagogical approaches that create positive conditions for learning, specific violence-prevention initiatives have been utilized in school settings through the years to enhance school climate and decrease the incidence of violence in schools, thereby decreasing the use of exclusionary discipline and closing the spigot to keep young people out of the school-to-prison pipeline. Peer mediation programs utilize student mediators trained in interest-based negotiation procedure, communication skills, and problem-solving strategies to help peers settle disagreements without resorting to confrontation or violence (Creating a Positive School Climate, 2000). Conflict resolution curricula focus on understanding conflict and learning negotiation-based responses to conflict (Creating a Positive School Climate, 2000). Violence-prevention curricula emphasize increasing knowledge about violence and teaching alternatives to fighting (Creating a Positive School Climate, 2000). Social problem-solving curricula focus on deepening understanding of feelings and teaching problem-solving strategies for resolving personal and inter-personal problems (Creating a Positive School Climate, 2000). In addition, the National Association of School Psychologists (NASP) has pointed to systemic school-wide violence-prevention programs, social skills curricula, and positive behavioral supports as leading to improved learning for all students and safer school communities (National Association of School Psychologists, 2001).

Implicit in each of these curricula and programs is a reliance on communication skills, critical thinking, reflection, negotiation, listening, and empathy – skills noted by students themselves as positive outcomes of their involvement in debate activities (Winkler, 2011). Moreover, debate has been cited by the Institute of Law and Justice as a model for violence prevention in schools. In 2009 the Computer Assisted Debate Program targeting secondary students living in Atlanta Housing Authority communities was one of only two school-based intervention programs in the United States recommended for national replication as an anti-gang youth development program (Institute of Law and Justice, 2009). Additionally, studies in Milwaukee, Boston, and Atlanta have demonstrated sharp reductions in disciplinary actions (e.g., in-school suspension, expulsion, parent conferences) after only one year's participation in debate (Winkler, 2009; Winkler, 2011).

Debate closely aligns with restorative practices, a continuum of formal and informal processes that are on the leading edge of efforts to address the exclusionary discipline crisis that fuels the school-to-prison pipeline. Restorative approaches to discipline focus on relationships, engage collaborative problem-solving, give voice to both the person harmed and the person who caused harm, use a dialogue-based decision-making process, and develop agreed-upon actions aimed at repairing any harm done (Gregory, The promise of restorative practices, 2013). The restorative practices continuum includes the use of (Gregory, Guiding principles, 2013):

- affective statements, which describe how others were impacted by behavior;
- affective questions, which ask who was affected, how, etc.;
- small impromptu conferences, which are brief meetings to address and resolve a problem;
- responsive circles, which are more formal and allow all parties to have a say in what should happen as a result of wrongdoing;
- formal conferences, in which offenders, victims, and communities of support come together to repair harm and promote healing.

When studied, restorative approaches have been shown to significantly reduce discipline incidents, and anecdotal evidence suggests that restorative approaches promote a sense of engagement and community, positive interactions among students and staff, attendance, and achievement (Gregory, Guiding principles, 2013).

As with the other frameworks and approaches described in this section, debate fosters the development of the communication, listening, empathy, respect, and collaboration skills and attitudes that are critical for restorative practices to be effective. Moreover, competitive debate regularly engages students around topics of social justice and race, providing a safe space for students and teachers to listen to and learn from one another. The critical listening inherent in both debate and restorative practices generates mutual respect between students, their teachers, and their peers; a sense of shared dialogue and concern; and a framework for looking at all sides of a situation, which in turn generates empathy and understanding. Debate is thus particularly well suited to serve as a complementary strategy for decreasing the use of exclusionary discipline in schools that utilize restorative approaches.

Conclusion

More than a decade of research has made clear that zero tolerance and exclusionary discipline simply don't work. Rather than making schools safer and enhancing conditions for learning, the imposition of zero-tolerance policies and the overuse of exclusionary discipline adversely affect academic achievement and undermine school climate and conditions for learning in schools that serve some of our most socio-economically challenged students. The discriminatory dimensions of this school-to-prison pipeline are nothing short of astounding: starting as early as preschool, the students who are pushed out of the classroom and into the justice system are disproportionately black, brown, disabled, and poor. This is a problem that must be solved, and must be solved now if we are to prepare the increasingly diverse student body that is served by our public school system for the 21st century economy. We all have a stake in this, and the good news is that there are both approaches that work and growing political will to tackle the problem.

Debate is a powerful tool for engaging students and has tremendous potential to disrupt the school-to-prison pipeline by enhancing conditions for learning, improving school climate, and minimizing exclusion of students from school and their entanglement with the juvenile justice system. As an instructional method and student engagement strategy, debate flourishes at the intersection between student agency and deep learning, and shares common features with restorative practices, violence-prevention initiatives, and other alternatives that work to keep students right where they belong: safely in school. Whether one is focused on transforming an entire school culture or simply reaching and supporting that one student who is struggling, debate opens doorways to greater school engagement, academic achievement, and career opportunities, rather than points of entry into the criminal justice system. That's just the kind of strategy we need to disrupt the school-to-prison pipeline.

Note

1 Author's Note: This chapter reflects the author's research and opinions, which are not attributable to YWCA USA, National Education Association, or the Children's Defense Fund.

References

Alton-Lee, A. (2003). Quality teaching for diverse students in schooling: Best evidence synthesis iteration. Retrieved from the New Zealand Ministry of Education website: http://www.educationcounts.govt.nz/publications/curriculum/2515/5959.

American Academy of Pediatrics (2013). Out-of-school suspension and expulsion. *Pediatrics, 131*, e1000-e1007. Retrieved from http://pediatrics.aappublications.org/cgi/doi/10.1542/peds.2012-3932.

American Psychological Association Zero Tolerance Task Force. (2008). Are zero tolerance policies effective in schools? An evidentiary review and recommendations. *American Psychologist, 63*, 852-862.

Australian Government, Department of Education. (2009). Values-centred schools – A guide: Student agency. Retrieved from http://www.valuescentredschools.edu.au/verve/_resources/StudentAgency.pdf.

Baker, P. (2015, July 16). Obama, in Oklahoma, takes reform message to prison cell block. *The New York Times.* Retrieved from http://www.nytimes.com/2015/07/17/us/obama-el-reno-oklahoma-prison.html.

Boy charged with assault after kissing girl says it was a dare. (2015, September 13). *CBS News.* Retrieved from http://www.cbsnews.com/news/boy-charged-with-assault-after-kissing-girl-says-it-was-a-dare/.

Briceno, E. (2013). Mindsets and student agency. *Unboxed: A Journal of Adult Learning in Schools, 10.* Retrieved from http://www.hightechhigh.org/unboxed/issue10/mindsets_and_student_agency_contributors/.

Fabelo, T., Thompson, M. D., Plotkin, M., Carmichael, D., Marchbanks, M. P., & Booth, E. A. (2011). Breaking schools' rules: A statewide study of how school discipline relates to students' success and juvenile justice involvement. Retrieved from The Council of State Governments Justice Center and Public Policy Research Institute website https://csgjusticecenter.org/wp-content/uploads/2012/08/Breaking_Schools_Rules_Report_Final.pdf.

Fausset, R., & Southall, A. (2015, October 26). Video shows officer flipping student in South Carolina, prompting inquiry. *The New York Times*. Retrieved from http://www.nytimes.com/2015/10/27/us/officers-classroom-fight-with-student-is-caught-on-video.html.

Gregory, A. (2013). Guiding principles and efficacy of restorative practices in schools [PowerPoint slides]. Retrieved from www.nycourts.gov/ip/justiceforchildren/PDF/RestorativePracticeConf/P1-Gregory.pdf.

Gregory, A. (2013). The promise of restorative practices to transform teacher-student relationships and reduce racial disparities in exclusionary discipline [PowerPoint slides]. Retrieved from http://gsappweb.rutgers.edu/rts/equityrsch/equitypdfs/Equity%20and%20Restorative%20Practices.pdf.

Indiana University, Safe & Responsive Schools. (2000). An effective model of school violence prevention: Is zero tolerance an effective response? Retrieved from http://www.iub.edu/~safeschl/emodel.html.

Indiana University, Safe & Responsive Schools. (2000). Creating a positive school climate: Violence prevention and conflict resolution curricula. Retrieved from http://www.indiana.edu/~safeschl/climate.html#can.

Institute of Law and Justice. (2009). Engaging youth in gang prevention. Retrieved from http://www.engageyouth-ilj.org/school_based_programs_cad.html.

Kang-Brown, J., Trone, J., Fratello, J., & Daftary-Kapur, T. (2013). *A generation later: What we've learned about zero tolerance in schools*. New York: Vera Institute of Justice.

Khadaroo, S. T. (2013, March 31). School suspensions: Does racial bias feed the school-to-prison pipeline? *The Christian Science Monitor*. Retrieved from http://www.csmonitor.com/USA/Education/2013/0331/School-suspensions-Does-racial-bias-feed-the-school-to-prison-pipeline.

Lamont, J. H. (2013, March 1). AAP: Positive behavior support should replace zero-tolerance policies in schools. *AAP News*. Retrieved from http://aapnews.aappublications.org/content/34/3/29.1.full.

Mezuk, B., Bondarenko, I., Smith, S., & Tucker, E. (2011). Impact of participating in a policy debate program on academic achievement: Evidence from the Chicago Urban Debate League. *Educational Research and Reviews*, 6(9), 622–635.

Morgan, E., Salomon, N., Plotkin, M., & Cohen, R. (2014). The school discipline consensus report: Strategies from the field to keep students engaged in school and out of the juvenile justice system. Retrieved from The Council of State Governments Justice Center website https://csgjusticecenter.org/wp-content/uploads/2014/06/The_School_Discipline_Consensus_Report.pdf.

National Association of School Psychologists. (2001). Zero tolerance and alternative strategies: A fact sheet for educators and policymakers. Retrieved from http://www.naspcenter.org/factsheets/zt_fs.html.

National Association for Urban Debate Leagues [NAUDL]. (n.d.). Urban debate prepares students for 21st century careers [webpage]. Retrieved from http://urbandebate.org/Our-Results/21st-century-skills.

Nicks, D. (2014, March 21). Report: Black preschoolers suspended more than whites. *Time*. Retrieved from http://time.com/33514/report-black-preschoolers-suspended-more-than-whites/.

Pearson Foundation and Partnership for 21st Century Skills. (n.d.). Patterns of innovation: Showcasing the nation's best in 21st century learning. Retrieved from http://www.p21.org/exemplar-program-case-studies/patterns-of-innovation.

Rate, N. (2013, June 4). Student agency [Web log comment]. Retrieved from http://nickrate.com/2013/06/04/student-agency/.

Shanny, M. (2014, January 10). Justice dept weighs in on racial discrimination in school discipline. *Education News*. Retrieved from http://www.educationnews.org/education-policy-and-politics/justice-dept-weighs-in-on-racial-discrimination-in-school-discipline/.

Stolberg, S. G. (2015, August 3). A.C.L.U. sues over handcuffing of boy, 8, and girl, 9, in Kentucky school. *The New York Times*. Retrieved from http://www.nytimes.com/2015/08/04/us/aclu-sues-over-handcuffing-of-boy-8-and-girl-9-in-kentucky-school.html.

U.S. Department of Education. (2011). Secretary Duncan, Attorney General Holder announce effort to respond to school-to-prison pipeline by supporting good discipline practices. Retrieved from http://www.ed.gov/news/press-releases/secretary-duncan-attorney-general-holder-announce-effort-respond-school-prison-pipeline-supporting-good-discipline-practices.

U.S. Department of Education. (2014). Overview of the supportive school discipline initiative. Retrieved from http://www2.ed.gov/policy/gen/guid/school-discipline/fedefforts.html#guidance.

U.S. Department of Education. (2014). The new spotlight on America's opportunity gaps. Retrieved from http://www.ed.gov/news/speeches/new-spotlight-americas-opportunity-gaps.

U.S. Department of Education, Office for Civil Rights. (2014). Civil rights data collection: Data snapshot (school discipline). Retrieved from http://blog.ed.gov/2014/03/four-new-civil-rights-data-collection-snapshots/.

U.S. Department of Education & U.S. Department of Justice. (2014). Dear colleague letter on the nondiscriminatory administration of school discipline. Retrieved from http://www2.ed.gov/policy/gen/guid/school-discipline/fedefforts.html#guidance.

Wade, J., & Zorwick, M. L. W. (2009). Assigned advocacy, argumentation, and debate in high school classrooms. *The Rostrum*, 83, 13–15.

Winkler, C. (2011). To argue or fight: Improving at-risk students' school conduct through urban debate. *Controversia: The Journal of Debate And Democratic Renewal*, 7(2), 76–90.

Winkler, C. (2009). The impact of policy debate on inner-city schools: The Milwaukee experience. In D. Gouran (Ed.), *The Functions of Argument and Social Context* (pp. 565–571). Annandale, VA: National Communication Association.

Zorwick, M. L. W., & Wade, J. (2015). Using forensic activity to develop the skills identified in Common Core State Standards. *The Rostrum*, 90(1), 46–52.

3 Evaluating Contradictory Evidence

Jon Bruschke

This chapter is written from the perspective of a career debate coach. Being a debate coach means many things, but chief among them is that when you first announce your occupation to new acquaintances you can be sure that the first couple of thoughts they have about your vocation are wrong. The first reaction most lay people have to debate is that it involves some eloquence and public speaking. The second thought, and this one is more intellectual, is that being a good debater implies a sort of shiftiness and lack of commitment to a given position or, more damning, a lack of commitment to the truth.

These reactions are not entirely wrong. Debaters do speak, sometimes publicly, and we do switch sides on the topics we discuss. We aren't always fully committed to the words that come out of our mouths and sometimes offer them, quite literally, for the sake of argument. But these are not the best aspects of debate, nor do they capture its value and power. What is the best part of debate, what makes the best debaters the best thinkers, and what in my view has carried this process from the very first educational institutions founded in ancient Greece 26 centuries ago to my first debate tournament in Hurricane, Utah (circa 1981) to the pages of this volume, is this: debaters try to find the truth by comparing all available evidence on a subject and figuring out what that evidence proves.

This simple description belies the power of the process. To debate well – to find all the best evidence on both sides of the topic, to sift through it in your mind, make connections between what you have found, and put it all together into statements you think will withstand the most vigorous scrutiny – requires a level of thinking that develops a power of mind. Aristotle may have overstated the importance of the process when he declared that unexamined lives were not worth living, but the empowerment gained by exploring all the best ideas on a subject and coming to your own conclusion changes the way you interact with the world forever. And in my experience, for the better.

The quality of our democratic form of government, in fact, depends largely on the ability of citizen-voters to think through ideas, to consider all the contrasting opinions out there and pick candidates they feel offer the best answers. The more citizens can think through ideas at a higher level, the more the "Great Experiment" Abraham Lincoln championed proves to the world that self-governed people can make decisions that are not only popular, but that are the right choices to navigate the nation through the challenges it faces. Democracy cannot succeed if the populace is constantly hoodwinked by charlatans; democracy thrives when the marketplace of ideas moves the best ones to the top.

I will attempt to demonstrate what debate can be by pursuing three core questions. First, what is higher-ordered thinking? Second, how does higher-ordered thinking connect to argument and debate? And finally, how do you teach that process to someone else?

What Is Higher-Ordered Thinking?

I will paint with broad strokes here; more precise definitions of critical thinking can be found in many places including the work of Giroux (1978), Garside (1996), and Patrick Wade's chapter in this volume (Chapter 8). The first broad stroke is that arguments generally include both substance and logic. Substance is one element of the argument; Stephen Toulmin (1958) called this component "grounds" and it includes individual pieces of datum, or what we commonly think of as "facts." (Substance also includes values, which are less amenable to evidence. I don't mean to exclude values, they just won't be the focus of this chapter.) Logic is the way that those individual facts connect to broader points. If I were to say "the Lakers will not win the championship because Kobe Bryant is a lousy basketball player," I would have committed an error based on my substance/grounds/facts. Love him or hate him, Kobe Bryant is one of the highest-scoring basketball players of all time. If I were to say "the Lakers will not win the championship because Kobe Bryant is a lousy dresser," I would have committed an error of logic. The lousiness of Bryant's wardrobe might be a matter of taste, but the factual point in dispute (whether Bryant dresses well or not) has no bearing on the ultimate conclusion (whether the Lakers can win the championship).

The second broad stroke is a point I have made elsewhere (Bruschke, 2012), that the substance of an argument is usually where the core of the matter lies. Logic is hardly irrelevant but is rarely at the heart of a dispute. And these two broad strokes lead me to this conclusion: The highest-ordered thinking is that which brings the thinker the closest to the original evidence. A quick story might help to illuminate my point.

As a younger instructor, I would offer my beginning argument class students several options for their final paper. One option was to read an article and identify any fallacies in it. In a traditional argument class, students are presented with a list of fallacies, defined as common errors of logic. They include names like "hasty generalization" or "slippery slope," but some have more lofty-sounding names like "affirming the antecedent," while the most pretentious simply appear in Latin: *Post hoc ergo propter hoc* ("what came before must be the cause of what came after"). Fallacies are one of the most prevalent ways that the topic of "logic" is covered in argument classes. Although other options for their final paper included writing an editorial of their own or analyzing a Supreme Court case, students flocked in droves to the fallacies paper. To me, it seemed enormously boring. To the students, it apparently seemed like the safest haven.

As I matured, it occurred to me that the students were simply novices at argument. They wanted a form of argument that went something like this: "You committed a fallacy, that' s a foul, you lose, I win." This got me to thinking about what the better debaters – my intercollegiate competitors – were doing, and it almost always involved more and more and more research. Logic wasn't unimportant to the best college debaters; it just never came up because as soon as one team won an important substantive point everyone generally understood how that point connected to the overall dispute.

This engagement with substance is outlined in Table 3.1. The table uses the example of pre-trial publicity, and specifically whether media coverage before a trial can bias a jury against a defendant. The top of the table shows the shallowest engagement with the issue, and thus the lowest-ordered thinking, and the bottom of the table shows the deepest engagement and hence the highest-ordered thinking.

At the top of the table, the skills are basic. The ability to articulate a position is better than knowing nothing; the ability to articulate more than one position on a topic (yours and those of an opponent) is better than only knowing your side. As thinking progresses, the ability to offer evidence is better than simply asserting a position, and the ability to grasp that there might be more than one source of evidence and that the evidence might point to contradictory conclusions is a fairly sophisticated accomplishment.

But resolving inconsistent evidence truly begins to engage higher-ordered skills. As students compare source qualifications, date of publication, and consensus among experts, they engage in what I call "surface" comparisons. Although I am calling these "surface" comparisons, they are not to be dismissed. Few high-school students can engage any issue of importance – be it school uniforms, school funding formulas, or marijuana legalization – and get as far as finding contradictory research and making any comparison at all. It is also worth noting that what makes surface comparisons more highly ordered thinking than simply citing evidence is that students are drawn deeper and deeper into the evidence. Moving beyond the mere existence of the evidence students must now ask: Is this the only evidence? How can different evidence point to different conclusions? How can this evidence be compared? What characteristics might a piece of evidence have that makes it better than another piece of evidence?

The final row, which represents the highest level of thinking, is the most sophisticated precisely because it demands that students find the original research that experts used when making their own judgments. It is no longer enough simply to report that a professor did a study and reported a certain conclusion. Students must be able to understand what data the professor collected and how the researcher reached the conclusion that he or she did. At this point, the thinking that the students are doing is not different in kind from the type of thinking that the researchers themselves used.

In the example of pre-trial publicity, students at the highest level don't simply ask what most experts think about publicity's ability to bias jurors or what study has the most recent publication date. They begin to ask questions particular to the topic at hand. Did the study use mock trials or study actual trials? Was the publicity presented in televised or written form? Was the total exposure to publicity in the study comparable to the levels experienced by actual jurors? If not, did the study use more or less media coverage than an actual juror is likely exposed to? Note that students are now doing exactly what the expert researchers themselves would be doing were they to debate the issues at an academic conference. And, to repeat the point once again, what makes the highest-ordered thinking the highest is that it has the tightest connection between the thinker and the evidence.

Table 3.1 Process of Cognitive Engagement

Cognitive Level	Skill	Example
Lower-Ordered Thinking ↑	No understanding of the issue	"I don't understand how publicity relates to a fair trial."
	Ability to understand one side of an issue	"People who have heard about a case in the media will probably be biased during the trial and that's not fair."
	Ability to explain one side of an issue	"If someone has seen something on TV about a trial, they can't avoid bias, because you can't forget what you've seen."
	Ability to understand and explain more than one side of an issue	"People will be influenced by media coverage of a trial, but they will also be influenced by the evidence at a trial, and the real question is whether biases will remain after trial evidence is presented."
	Ability to offer evidence on an issue	"The Rita Simon study in 1966 compared people who had seen publicity and those who hadn't, and found that those who had seen publicity were more likely to convict."
	Ability to recognize contradictory evidence on an issue	"There are 46 studies on publicity; 16 show a publicity bias, 13 show no publicity bias, and the rest have mixed results."
↓	Ability to compare contradictory evidence at a surface level	"Studies showing no publicity bias are more recent that studies showing a bias." or "The book *Free Press and Fair Trials* compares all the studies and concludes there is no publicity bias."
Higher-Ordered Thinking	Ability to compare contradictory evidence at the level of original data	"Lab studies on college students show a publicity bias, but field research on actual trials shows no publicity bias."

What Is the Connection Between Higher-Ordered Thinking and Debate?

The British psychologist Michael Billig (1987) sought to understand what someone meant when they said they were thinking. The book he produced, *Thinking as Arguing*, more or less equated the internal process of thinking with the social practice of arguing. Thinking, holds Billig, is the process of considering a topic, collecting available points of view and evidence, comparing all those points and counter-points, as well as evidence and contrary evidence, turning it all over in your mind, and trying to piece it all together. This is what Isaac Newton did when pondering gravity and what Martin Luther King did when penning his letter from the Birmingham jail.

Debating or arguing between advocates is more or less the same process except that it engages the minds of multiple individuals rather than relying simply on an individual to come up with all the points and counter-points, all the evidence and contrary evidence. In a debate, different advocates bring up their own points of view and find their own evidence. Evidence that one individual might accept in isolation might be challenged by another; more people trying hard to find more evidence will generally come up with more of it than an individual working alone.

The individual process of thinking and the social process of debating complement rather than compete with one another. The more one engages in debate with others, the more one develops the habit of considering multiple viewpoints when thinking alone. Furthermore, engagement with others increases the number of different viewpoints that an individual is aware of. Conversely, the more an individual is aware of different viewpoints, the evidence in support of each viewpoint, and the ways that certain evidence might connect to certain conclusions, the more skilled that person is when arguing with others. The more skilled advocates come together in interactive debates, the more those debates present only the best ideas and refine them with testing, and the more the participants develop the habits of higher-ordered thinking.

Here is a quick example. Several years ago I was judging a debate at Northwestern University between teams from Iowa and Texas. The topic concerned the environment, all the debaters had a great deal of research, and on one major point each team threw perhaps 20 to 25 different quotations from different sources at each other. During a cross-examination, the debater from Iowa asked her opponent for one of the quotations, observed that at the end of the quotation there was a footnote numbered 47, and asked the Texan if she knew what footnote 47 was. The Texan admitted she did not and dismissed the point as minor if not irrelevant.

In the next speech, the Iowan re-read the Texas quotation, produced the original document containing the quotation and footnote 47, correctly pointed out that the justification for the quotation was actually the source in the footnote, and then read additional evidence disproving the information from the source in the footnote. Truly, the Iowa debater had come much closer to the original evidence than her opponent, easily won the dispute about the specific evidence, and eventually carried the larger point and finally the debate. It is that sort of higher-ordered thinking that debate, at its best, can produce, and the habits of mind the Iowa debater had developed that sparked the decision to look up footnote 47 in the first place had come about due to participation in debates with others.

This is probably not a skill we should collectively expect all 12th graders to have developed. In fact, it isn't even a level that most college debaters attain. But boy, is it pretty to watch when it unfolds, and it is an excellent exemplar to aspire to.

To close the circle, this focus on evidence brings us back to the purpose of argument and debate as both an intellectual exercise and a cornerstone of democracy. What educators need debate to be is a tool to help students develop higher-ordered cognition. My contention here is that focusing on evidence comparisons does that. What democracy needs from argument and argument theory is a way for citizens and policymakers to coherently and rationally approach situations where experts do not always agree and good evidence can point to different and often opposing conclusions. Again, it appears that focusing on evidence allows just that.

In fact, the world frequently presents our democracy with situations that demand action but where the available evidence points to different conclusions. Education that trains students to expect such contradictory conditions and carefully maneuver their way through the evidence is truly a next-generation idea that can propel a nation out of its critical thinking doldrums and empower it to address global challenges. Education that gives students a list of fallacies to apply to the real world is less powerful. The end product of vigorous debate is students who can more effectively produce evidence-driven ideas, and perhaps more importantly, students who are better at judging a public debate for themselves. In short, we need students who can encounter a public issue, hear what each side has to say, and use higher-ordered thinking to decide which set of conclusions is more true to the best available evidence.

How Do You Teach Evidence Evaluation?

Generally speaking, I would divide evidence evaluation into two broad tiers. The first tier is general information literacy and is well covered elsewhere in this volume. Essentially, it is the first screen in evaluating the credibility of information. Is the source credible? Has the information been reviewed or edited by others? Is there a way of verifying (via footnote or otherwise) what the author has to say? How does one separate the trappings of credibility from actual, valid information?

The second tier, which I will dwell on for the rest of this chapter, is how to evaluate a specific piece of evidence. Generic tools of logic and proof are, again, not irrelevant here, but they are not as prevalent as the particular questions a given issue poses. The point, especially as an educator, is not to dictate to students when they have arrived at a correct answer, but to constantly encourage them to engage in the practices that are likely to lead them to it. You are teaching students the highest-level thinking when you encourage them to dive into the specific evidentiary questions of a given dispute.

Consider below two quotations; they are taken from an actual argumentation class. After a class discussion, the students voted to debate the National Affordable Health Care Act, commonly called Obamacare. The students were encouraged to underline those portions of the quotations to be read aloud in the debate; the bolded sentence just before the quotations is the main point the students felt the evidence proved. The first quotation is used to demonstrate that Obamacare will not cost jobs, and the second is used to prove that it will.

Before we proceed, let me offer you some words of warning and encouragement. What is about to happen is higher-ordered thinking. At first pass, it might seem confusing or too detailed. The detail, and the extended elements of logic, are what make the ideas higher-ordered. In a nutshell, there isn't an "easy" version of higher-ordered thinking any more than there is an "easy" version of calculus. All I hope to do is present the ideas in a way that doesn't take the complex and make it confusing. If you find yourself getting lost, I encourage you to simply take a few steps down the higher-order thinking ladder to get re-oriented. What is quotation #1 proving again? (That Obamacare won't cost jobs.) What is it the evidence for the argument that Obamacare will not cost jobs? (Two studies, one by the Congressional Budget Office and one by the National Federation of Independent Businesses.) What's that supply side thing? (Quotation #1 is talking about employee motivations, and quotation #2 is talking about employer motivations.) And so on.

Quotation #1: Obamacare will not cost jobs

Source: Farley, R., & Holan A. (2011, January 20). The health care law a "job killer"? The evidence falls short. *St. Petersburg Times*. Retrieved from: http://www.politifact.com/truth-o-meter/statements/2011/jan/20/eric-cantor/health-care-law-job-killer-evidence-falls-short/.

Basically, the CBO is saying that some people right now are working mostly to keep their health insurance. Once they have other options – to enroll in Medicaid, or to qualify for tax breaks to buy insurance from a health exchange – they might choose to work less. The CBO describes this as a "small segment" of the population. And, because the CBO is describing reduced hours rather than lost jobs, it never uses the 650,000 number that the Republican document cites. The Republican extrapolated that number from the CBO's estimate of one-half percent of the labor supply. Finally, we should point out that a person who voluntarily chooses to work less is not having their job "killed" by federal legislation. Now let's turn to the other piece of evidence, the study that claims that the health care law will result in 1.6 million lost jobs. That number comes from a study by the National Federation of Independent Businesses. The problem with this study is that it isn't based on the law that passed. It was published on Jan. 26, 2009, before a finalized House or Senate bill had even been proposed. In the NFIB study, "Small Business Effects of a National Employer Healthcare Mandate," the authors made hypothetical assumptions based on what they thought the law might include. Specifically, the study assumed that all companies would be required to offer private health insurance to their employees, and that the employers would have to pay for at least half of the cost of the insurance premiums. "The results indicate that without major reductions in the cost of healthcare, the employer mandate would cause the economy to lose over 1.6 million jobs within the first five years of program implementation. Small firms would be most adversely affected by the mandate and account for approximately 66 percent of all jobs lost," the report said. But the report's assumptions don't match up with the final version of the health care law. The law actually exempts companies with 50 or fewer workers from any mandate.

Quotation #2: Obamacare will cost 650,000 jobs

Source: Kennedy, K. (2011, January 19). Debate on health care costs rages on. *USA Today*, p. 06a.

Leading up to today's vote, both sides [Republicans and Democrats] attacked the budgetary implications of repealing or keeping the law, and most of their numbers came from the same place: the non-partisan Congressional Budget Office. The office sent a letter to House Speaker John Boehner this month saying a repeal of the Affordable Care Act would increase the budget by $230 billion. While Democrats embraced that number, Boehner said the savings come from increased taxes and fees, and that the Congressional Budget Office could only work with what the Democrats put in front of it. The law "is loaded with gimmicks," Rep. Tim Griffin, R-Ark., said during a floor debate Tuesday. "We find that it adds $700 billion to the deficit." The Democrats say health care costs will continue to rise no matter what happens, but the Affordable Care Law works to stabilize and, in some cases, decrease those costs. Rep. Chris Van Hollen, D-Md., said Boehner "sang CBO's high praises" when the office came out with a report last fall saying the health care law would increase the deficit. "It's an unprecedented step to say we're going to ignore the CBO," he said. "This is a recipe for fiscal chaos, and we should not go down that road." The Republicans released their own report – "A Budget-Busting, Job-Killing Health Care Law" – and cited the Congressional Budget Office's numbers to say the law will cause companies to not hire new employees because they fear their health care costs will be too high. They say this will create a loss of 650,000 jobs, which will damage the economy. They also say the law will lead to lower wages to make up for taxes and fees employers must pay. "It's an incentive to pay your employees less," said Rep. Mick Mulvaney, R-S.C.

Before I go any further, take a moment, read both quotations carefully, and ask yourself which quotation includes better evidence.

Initially, notice that both quotations pass the first-tier screen. Both are written by journalists for edited publications. Both were published in 2011 shortly before Obamacare was passed. Neither publication is inherently more credible than the other; neither publication date is substantially more current than the other.

What would a second-tier analysis suggest? To examine the specifics of what the evidence is suggesting, of course. An advocate for Obamacare might say this in favor of quotation #1: it references two studies, the first of which is the Congressional Budget Office (CBO) report. It points out that the CBO estimate of job loss concerns voluntary reductions in work for those who can now get healthcare from a source other than their employer. It further points out that the job loss asserted in quotation #2 by the Republicans is based on an extrapolation, not a finding, of the CBO report. Meaningfully, the job reductions identified by the CBO are entirely voluntary, and thus to characterize them as having been "killed" by Obamacare is probably misleading.

Furthermore, quotation #1 suggests that any labor effect is on the supply side; if labor supply goes down, it is not because people can't find jobs any more, and it's a problem for employers because they presumably won't be able to find replacements for the workers who voluntarily leave. This, one would imagine, would pressure employers to increase wages, a conclusion directly contrary to quotation #2.

An advocate for the pro-Obamacare side could further use second-tier reasoning to dismiss quotation #2. While it is true that the underlined part of quotation #2 suggests that Obamacare could cost jobs, that is not the overall conclusion of the article. The article, in classic journalistic fashion, is simply reporting that Republicans believe Obamacare will cost jobs; it is not saying that the author agrees with the conclusion. This is not the case with quotation #1, where the author both reports Republican objections to Obamacare and takes the firm position that they are wrong. Nothing in quotation #2 suggests that Kennedy thinks the Republican position is correct.

Additionally, quotation #2 simply repeats the 650,000 figure that quotation #1 has already proven is simply an extrapolation and not an actual finding of the CBO report. Even more damningly, quotation #2 – in the part that is not underlined – includes a statement by Representative Van Hollen demonstrating that the Republican stance to the CBO report is contradictory and perhaps hypocritical; they accept the CBO findings when they are critical of Obamacare, extrapolate freely when the CBO's statements are ambiguous, and dismiss the CBO entirely when it produces answers that they don't like.

Pause for a moment; does this debate now sound like a slam-dunk for the pro-Obamacare side? Or is there more to be said?

Consider now the flip side and what an anti-Obamacare advocate might say. They might first point out that the second half of quotation #1 is addressing the National Federation of Independent Businesses (NFIB) study, which is nowhere referenced in quotation #2. In essence, it is disproving evidence that hasn't been offered and is thus irrelevant. They might also point out that it is true that source #1 is taking a stance, but it is unclear why a *USA Today* journalist is in a better position to evaluate the meaning of the CBO report than Speaker of the United States House of Representatives John Boehner. This is a tier-one source qualification issue, but it stems from a close reading of the quotation.

A careful reading of quotation #1 also reveals that it is only talking about what incentives workers might have; it says exactly nothing about how employers would react. Because the crux of quotation #2 is that employers would have incentives to cut jobs, quotation #1 does not address the central concern in any important way. Finally, both quotations repeatedly say that the governmental cost savings of Obamacare are due to increased taxes and fees (presumably imposed on the private sector), and nothing in either quotation contests that. This provides a bedrock of agreement in all the evidence – everyone agrees that Obamacare will increase taxes and fees on employers, and the only remaining question is how that will affect employment decisions. It is hard to believe that higher taxes and fees will result in more hiring because increased costs almost always result in retaining fewer workers. While a careful reading of quotation #2 shows that there do appear to be two sides to the question of how Obamacare will affect the deficit, nothing in either quotation shows there is another side to the employment concerns.

To defend quotation #2, an anti-Obamacare advocate might respond that while quotation #2 does not make a conclusion, that simply makes quotation #2 more objective than quotation #1. Quotation #2 is trying to present a balanced view while quotation #1 is opposed to Republicans and thus it is not surprising that they only present a single viewpoint. As for Representative Van Hollen's swipes at House Speaker Boehner, they are immaterial because everyone can agree that the CBO says that about a half-percent of employees will cut back hours, and whether that allows one to conclude that exactly 650,000 jobs will be lost or not, the pressure put on employers suggests that the overall impact on jobs will not be good. The fact that Boehner might inconsistently criticize CBO findings does not mean that the half-percent figure is inaccurate. In fact, the figure is not contested by any side.

Put together, an advocate opposed to Obamacare would say that the only evidence that speaks to how Obamacare will impact employers' hiring and retention decisions demonstrates that employers would have incentives to reduce jobs and that taxes and fees would go up. Adding a bit of logic to these factual questions, the anti-Obamacare advocate could point out that while there might be some dispute about how many jobs Obamacare would cost, and whether the job loss would come from employees working less or employers cutting jobs, there is no evidence at all in either quotation to suggest that Obamacare might save jobs. There is only a risk, based on this evidence, of jobs being lost, and while there can be some quibbling about how many jobs, for what reason, and what the CBO report really meant, the only chance with Obamacare is that some jobs will disappear. Maybe not very many (if quotation #1 is correct), maybe an awful lot (if quotation #2 is correct), but why roll the dice and risk losing any jobs at all?

Pause again, and ask yourself if the arguments now sound a bit better for the anti-Obamacare side. What has happened, I believe, is that after the initial evidence is presented, each side had a plausible claim: quotation #1 did indeed support the notion that Republicans had overstated job loss concerns, and there is some evidence in quotation #2 that Republicans had at least some reason to believe jobs would be lost. More careful consideration of the specifics of what each piece of evidence proved exactly pushed the discussion of the issues forward. The circumstances might not have seemed quite as dire as the Republicans were claiming but their concerns weren't as easy to dismiss as quotation #1 made it seem.

What happens now? One perfectly acceptable conclusion is that the debate (given another rebuttal speech or two) is over and the question moves to the judge or judges to decide which side of the debate they find more persuasive. Another option is to point out that these are not the only two quotations possible on the issue (my class of 25 students produced over 30, in fact) and that a wise debater would be cognizant of some of the finer points and read more evidence into the debate that addresses them. A pro-Obamacare advocate, for instance, might do more to address the concern that employers will have incentives to cut jobs, find evidence that Obamacare would actually save jobs, or do more to develop the point that health care costs, and thus incentives for employers to scale back on hiring, would increase without Obamacare. Similar moves are also possible for the anti-Obamacare side.

And as an educator, the important thing is not that the issue comes to a clean conclusion with a conspicuous winner. The outcomes of recent presidential elections suggest that resolution of important issues does not come so easily and that there are a large numbers of people falling on both sides of most significant issues. But there is the opportunity to push the debaters to take their second-tier arguments even farther: Both sides seem to use the CBO report but disagree on what it means – perhaps the students should find the CBO report and make their own conclusion. A somewhat less demanding step would be for students to research what other sources have to say about the Democrat and Republican interpretations of the CBO report. Sliding back slightly to first-tier concerns, a teacher could encourage students to move beyond popular media and journalistic sources in order to see if any academic or policy journals have an interpretation of the CBO report or if there is another study that speaks to the effect Obamacare would have on jobs. The deeper students get into the original source material, remember, the more they are engaging in higher-ordered thinking and the deeper their appreciation for the notion that to resolve important issues, multiple sources, perspectives, evidence, and conclusions must all be put together. It goes without saying that jobs are only one element of Obamacare, and students should be encouraged to research and develop other concerns, such as Obamacare's impact on the deficit, the benefits of expanded healthcare coverage, and the impact of Obamacare on healthcare costs, etc. (Note that many of these issues are referenced in the quotations though few other than the deficit are really developed.)

Concluding Thoughts

The prior section of this chapter has been less theoretical than the other sections and perhaps overly specific; the last 1,300 words have been dedicated to comparing only two possible quotations that address only one issue surrounding Obamacare. The example is offered as the sort of approach that might be taken on any topic and with any form of evidence. The broader point I am seeking to develop here is that by digging into the specifics of the evidence, a number of context-dependent issues will surely arise, and that by drilling down into those issues, the most higher-ordered thinking will occur.

By teaching these key concepts – arguments have both evidence and logic, individual points connect to each other to form larger conclusions, and the development of key issues requires delving deeply into the specific content of evidence – massive student development is possible, and it will be development that encourages thinking on the highest order. Pursuing arguments in this way will demonstrate that instead of lacking a commitment to truth, debate embodies the deepest commitment to truth, and it is this common misunderstanding I hope to have most centrally addressed.

References

Billig, M. (1987). *Arguing and Thinking*. Cambridge: Cambridge University Press.

Bruschke, J. C. (2012). Argument and evidence evaluation: A call for scholars to engage contemporary public debates. *Argumentation and Advocacy, 49*, 59–75.

Farley, R., & Holan A. (2011, January 20). The health care law a "job killer"? The evidence falls short. *St. Petersburg Times*. Retrieved from: http://www.politifact.com/truth-o-meter/statements/2011/jan/20/eric-cantor/health-care-law-job-killer-evidence-falls-short/.

Garside, C. (1996). Look who's talking: A comparison of lecture and group discussion teaching strategies in developing critical thinking skills. *Communication Education, 45*, 212–227.

Giroux, H. A. (1978). Beyond the writing crisis. *Journal of Education, 160*, 40–49.

Kennedy, K. (2011, January 19). Debate on health care costs rages on. *USA Today*, p. 06a.

Toulmin, S. (1958). *The Uses of Argument*. Cambridge: Cambridge University Press.

4 Making Words Matter

Critical Literacy, Debate, and a Pedagogy of Dialogue

Susan Cridland-Hughes

I was never a debater. My initial exposure to debate occurred when the Baltimore Urban Debate League approached me about coaching debate at Southwestern High School, a high school in one of the most dangerous areas of Baltimore, a school where we had high populations of high-needs students. At Southwestern, 99% of students were on free and reduced lunch, and 98% of students were Black and brown youth. I say this to be clear. In the United States, we are not often clear about how we conflate poverty and race. In this case, students were both poor and considered minorities. The school no longer exists, deemed by state officials to be beyond redemption. Southwestern was not serving its students, not because the teachers were uninterested or the students were "bad," but because a collection of societal struggles and policy failures over time manifested in that space. In my mind, one of the only pro-grams working in the school was debate.

Over a decade has passed since my time at Southwestern, but debate has not changed. Students still try out arguments, research topics to find evidence, and practice speaking drills. While students now use laptops, pass evidence on thumb drives, and have embraced paperless debate over storing quotations of evidence in giant tubs, the questions students deliberate remain the same: how do we weigh the disparate needs of communities, how do we de-escalate conflicts between nations, how do we defend our decisions about personal consumption to ourselves (Ed Lee, personal communication, 2008)? Debaters explore lessons in trade-offs, negotiations, and the difference between the lesser evil and the greater good. This is debate: this is the space where students gather to research, evaluate, and advocate; this is the space where students learn that there may not be a perfect solution but there are better ways to engage with and build a socially responsible world.

Gary Fine's (2001) study *Gifted Tongues* offers a comprehensive examina-tion of elite high-school tournament debate, a community in which the worlds of education, adolescence, and talk intersect (pp. 4–7). Fine describes a world in which students from elite backgrounds, predominantly white and affluent, prepare to participate in a game with specific rules and structures. Student participants learn argumentation skills, presentation skills, and "the ability to understand multiple perspectives" (p. 226). Although Fine diligently documents the experiences of elite high-school debaters, he only briefly acknowledges the existence of the urban debate league (UDL) movement as "attempts to establish debate programs in inner city schools" (p. 13). The UDL movement is more than an attempt to establish debate programs, however; the UDL itself began as a means of challenging the very notion of debate as white, elite, and male. More specifically, the UDL movement is a reaction against the exclusive nature of competitive debate, with the community itself a means of advocacy for a more inclusive debate space. It is important to note that although Fine's bounded examination of high-school debaters pre-dates the massive expansion of the UDL movement, Fine still ignores historical evidence of extensive African American participation in debate in segregated schools, in public debating societies, and in communities beyond affluent, predominantly white spaces (Walker, 1996; Cooper, Chapter 1 in this volume). As just one example, the movie *The Great Debaters* tells the story of a collegiate debate team at Wiley College, a Black liberal arts college, that regularly challenged and defeated debaters at white schools in the 1930s (Beil, 2007; Martin, 2008). By focusing on elite debaters and ignoring the historical participation of African Americans in debate, Fine's study limits our understanding of the multiple ways in which youth can identify as debaters and as community members.

Debate is about identity, youth culture, and social justice; debate participation is also about how students learn to interact with text and with ideas. In a debate round, students call up the ideas of many to shape one precisely honed argument. The arguments presented with extensive cross-disciplinary references related to the topic of the year reveal the myriad ways that debate promotes literacy. In debate, students take text (broadly defined), prepare a speech, deliver and perform that speech, and subsequently create a conversation. This is literacy use at its most rigorous, where the interaction between speech, text, and ideas creates new knowledge.

While literacy is about the creation of new knowledge, it is also about the creation of empowered students. As Fine discusses at length when talking about high-school debate, literacy does not exist separate from the complicated conversations about access and denial. The urban debate league movement emerged as a bridge across a historical rupture in debate participation by communities that were not white and affluent. This bridge is important because it is a bridge between a community with a historical focus on social justice and a community focused primarily on competitive success (Cridland-Hughes, 2010). In this interstitial space, students ask questions, research, and engage in dialogue. In my own work, I have explored the question of how debate participation creates a space of both literacy and social justice, looking specifically at the development of the Atlanta Urban Debate League through both historical and contemporary lenses (Cridland-Hughes, 2011; Cridland-Hughes, 2012). My research has focused on expanding the understanding both of debate as a space of engagement and education and of debaters as activist youth. In this chapter, I seek to answer the question of how debate in general and the urban debate league in particular offer new insights into how we teach literacy skills in K–12 settings.

What Is Critical Literacy and What Is the Connection Between Literacy and Debate?

When discussing literacy, and particularly the connection of literacy and debate, the primary question becomes: How is critical literacy as a curricular orientation linked with debate in the urban debate leagues in ways that enhance and build on literacy skills? The term critical literacy refers to Ira Shor's (1992) definition of "habits of thought, reading, writing, and speaking which go beneath surface meaning . . . to understand the deep meaning, root causes, social context, ideology and personal consequences of any action" (p. 129). Critical literacy is not a traditional literacy paradigm, and traditional notions of literacy as the ability to perform at a certain standard on a reading test still dominate political discussions of what constitutes literacy. Current policy and descriptions of literacy reflect a perception that literacy is still distilled down to the five specific components of reading identified in the National Reading Panel in April 2000: phonemic awareness, phonics, fluency, vocabulary, and text comprehension (National Institute of Child Health and Human Development, 2000). While these components are important, they tell us very little about how to reach students who have historically struggled with reading. As those students move past the primary grades into grades where the skill of reading is linked with the need to be able to synthesize text and make text-based arguments, this definition of reading no longer supports continued literacy growth. In effect, the compartmentalization of reading skills is most useful for understanding and supporting new readers. The real challenge after students have learned to decode and move through the mechanics of reading is finding something that motivates the students to want to read (Conradi, Jang, Bryant, Craft, & McKenna, 2013). This shift from skill to motivation is particularly important for connecting debate and literacy. With youth participants in debate, the processes of reading are less important than what literacy as a tool allows youth to accomplish, either in terms of gaining knowledge or membership or in terms of supporting activism.

This definition of literacy, a literacy of engagement, aligns with both sociocultural literacy as identity (Gee, 1996) and critical literacy as action (Pandya & Avila, 2014). Morrell (2008) argues that critical literacy offers a means of not only "[understanding] the role of language and texts in the construction of the self and the social" but also a way to "speak back and act back against these constructions with counter-languages and counter-texts" (p. 5). In this way, the definition of literacy is extended beyond the use and mastery of basic meaning-making related to text and focuses on applying that meaning-making to transform narratives and the world. It is important to note that critical literacy rests on a foundation of basic literacy skills. However, literacy conceptualized through a critical literacy lens acknowledges that literacy is never solely about the demonstration of basic skills but is rather lived and practiced in communities with a social justice orientation.

It is tempting to see debate as an exercise in political analysis where students who are already good at "doing school" get better, as well as an exercise that values those students who are already skilled consumers of text and argumentation. When considering the skills offered by debate participation, research has centered on both specific skills that link with literacy and academic achievement and on individual characteristics that connect with empowerment. However, in conceptualizing literacy for the 21st century, we must also consider skills used to understand text broadly defined, technology used to access text, and sociocultural spaces that support literate engagement (Reinking, McKenna, Labbo, & Kieffer, 1998). Literacy in our 21st-century world needs to focus on advocacy, which leads to perhaps the most important effect of becoming literate: being able to read and analyze texts opens up subtexts and counter-narratives that challenge historically marginalizing spaces and structures.

How Do Urban Debate Leagues Teach Empowering Literacy?

Understanding the intersection between the urban debate league movement and empowering literacy requires some contextualization of debate broadly considered. Gordon Mitchell (1998) argues that the importance of debate as a pedagogical tool centers on the concept of argumentative agency, "the capacity to contextualize and employ the skills and strategies of argumentative discourse in fields of social action . . . [linking] decontextualized argumentation skills such as research, listening, analysis, refutation, and presentation to the broader political *telos* of democratic empowerment" (p. 45). Although Mitchell connects the skills gained through debate preparation and pedagogy with student empowerment, he cautions that one of the dangers of debate is the "undercultivation of student agency" (p. 44). Debate pedagogy, then, contains both the promise of empowerment and the danger of the intellectualization of real-world problems and situations, seeing these problems and situations only as keys to winning an argument. Mitchell's argument reflects the belief that debate pedagogy by itself is neutral and does not inherently create empowered students. Instead, empowerment comes through the responsible cultivation of civic engagement, including an emphasis on primary research conducted by debaters, public debates, and debate outreach to populations not currently represented.

There have been several conceptual articles discussing the potential of debate as outreach in urban public schools. Greg Huber and Jeffrey Smith (1993) recount their interactions with youth learning debate in urban settings, arguing that urban debate carries the potential of individual and community transformation. They describe these debaters as "caring about more than just winning, that they carry questions of 'should' beyond debate rounds, into homes and hearts, and back to people who once believed they could make a difference in the world" (p. 35). Edward Lee (1998) also published a memoir detailing his experiences in an urban debate league, in which he reflected on the importance of debate for developing his voice and a sense of his own power, and Ede Warner and Jon Bruschke (2001) describe debate-related literacy and performance skills as tools to empower students politically, arguing that "students who can face and overcome [the challenges of debate] and those fears are seldom afraid of public dialogue in any other context, be it a political rally, city board meeting, electoral campaign, legal proceeding, or town hall meeting" (p. 17). Warner and Bruschke see the skills and the structure of competitive debate specifically as practice for later political engagement.

In her recent study of the urban debate league in Chicago, the Chicago Debate League, Briana Mezuk (2009) analyzed ten years' data for African American male student participants, examining performance on three markers of educational outcomes: cumulative GPA in 8th and 12th grade, ACT scores, and high-school completion. She argued that students with higher test scores did select into the activity at a higher rate than students with lower test scores, but that those students "had higher 12th grade GPA, were more likely to graduate from high school, less likely to drop out of high school, and were more likely to be college ready in reading and English" even compared with a control group (p. 299). Her findings indicate that participation in debate uniquely supports the development of academic literacy and higher rates of graduation for African American males. Mezuk's work offers compelling evidence that participation in debate particularly improves student skills in argumentation, vocabulary, comprehension of nonfiction texts, and evaluating evidence.

What Mezuk's research does not and cannot explore is the role of community in motivating students to engage with and sustain their interactions in the urban debate league space. In previous research, I have described this as a particularly UDL community phenomenon, focusing specifically on how leaders such as James Roland, Director of the Atlanta Urban Debate League, emphasize community over competitive success (Cridland-Hughes, 2010). If one of the things Mezuk identifies is a "dosing effect" such that more debate exposure actually increases the positive outcomes, some of that dosing effect comes from the ability to create a community where students want to belong and where they feel welcome.

In one of the few studies specifically examining the practices of the urban debate community, Isaac Wolf (2008) analyzed a middle-school urban debate program as a community of practice. Participants came from lower-income backgrounds and the students involved were predominantly African American, although the volunteers reflected demographic diversity. Wolf's research enhances Fine's findings in that it explores the debate participation of African American students, a group largely ignored by Fine. In Wolf's research, he found that students and program volunteers communicated through three languages: the language of popular culture, the language of African American Vernacular English (AAVE), and the language of debate. For participants, many of whom were experiencing debate for the first time, the participation in competitive debate occupied a secondary role to their membership in a unified, supportive community. Wolf describes urban debate as an access point rather than as a means for students to be competitively successful in the larger debate community. This directly contrasts with the competition-oriented debate community described by Fine. Although Wolf expands the idea of who participates in a debate community and how they participate, the question remains as to how this community-oriented debate model translates to high-school urban debate programs.

Publications about debate primarily reflect the experiences of individuals and conceptions of responsible debate pedagogy. Theoretical conceptions about debate such as those espoused by Mitchell emphasize the structural spaces in which debate offers the greatest potential for supporting critical thinking in youth, while personal narratives offer anecdotal evidence as to the transformative nature of debate participation but lack rigorous scientific evidence reinforcing the beliefs of the authors. Empirical exploration emphasizes both academic gains and community building that supports students both inside and beyond the debate round. The broad overview of research into the urban debate league community tells us that students are welcomed and apprenticed into new and different roles, and that they do see what they are doing as key to developing as thoughtful and engaged citizens (although there is a sense that the development of critical literacy skills happens over time as the competitive aspect is phased out and civic responsibility is phased in). This may offer us some insight into what is missing for students in the schooled environment.

What Can We Learn From the Urban Debate League Movement About Building Critical Literacy Capacity?

The conversation in debate, a conversation about students engaging in high-level, thoughtful conversations around current policy issues using research and perspectives from a range of disciplines, mirrors the trend in literacy research in general toward knowledge broadly construed. We are at a space in what the International Literacy Association terms the "Age of Literacy" where definitions of literacies emphasize multiple understandings of what it means to engage in literate activity and literacy participation as situated in space and time (Clark, 2015; Street, 2003). However, this expansive research understanding of literacy does not hold true for policy initiatives and popular reporting about the state of literacy. We regularly see news articles about how students are struggling with literacy, and the definition of literacy used to label youth as struggling is based on a competency model of reading that asks students to read a passage and then answer comprehension questions. This model of reading competency is divorced from the literacy of engagement I discussed previously, and relies on a narrow definition of literacy as measured through testing to sort students into groups that then have a perceived value to society. As one example of how the policy definition of literacy creates struggling readers, the new South Carolina Read to Succeed Act provides provisions for a summer camp for students to help them in their testing and assessment. Additionally, the act makes provisions for students who do not succeed to be held back, even as research tells us that holding children back does not increase their success. The very existence of this act, put in place in 2015, indicates a deficit model of schooling, teaching, and youth. This act sees schools as a place where we fix students who are not meeting benchmarks and expectations on external evaluations. Paul Gorski (2011) defines deficit ideology as "[a way to] manipulate popular consciousness in order to deflect attention from the systemic conditions and sociopolitical context that underlie or exacerbate inequities" (p. 156). In this sense, the summer camp and remediation plans train the gaze of the public on the failure of the students, rather than on the broader conversation of structural inequity in education in the United States.

In the United States, popular constructions of students, particularly of brown and Black students, do not focus on perspectives of success. Rather, our language around schools and students, particularly students in urban schools, hinges on a deficit model. Evidence of this is rampant. In the most recent Race to the Top call for proposals, the U.S. Department of Education specifically asked for proposals that would support high-needs students, defined as:

> Students at risk of educational failure or otherwise in need of special assistance and support, such as students who are living in poverty, who attend high-minority schools (as defined in this notice), who are far below grade level, who have left school before receiving a regular high school diploma, who are at risk of not graduating with a diploma on time, who are homeless, who are in foster care, who have been incarcerated, who have disabilities, or who are English language learners.
>
> (U.S. Department of Education, 2012)

Even in a program that is ostensibly established to provide funds to support student success, the general framing of high needs is connected with race and class and language in ways that reflect a perspective of these students as struggling. This framing undergirds the literacy instruction and support provided to "high-needs students," with students at the lowest levels of literacy instruction as defined by standardized testing more likely to receive the most rigid and scripted interventions (Berry, 1997).

If we acknowledge Gorski's request that we shift the deficit lens, we as a society are responsible for the fact that, historically, students identified as high needs, who have required more support, have not benefited from as many strong teachers, strong leaders, and strong schools. Instead, however, these policy initiatives reflect an assumption that what is needed is simplified literacy instruction, rather than the rich construction of spaces where reading provides the raw material for dialogue and interaction. The desire to bring students up to grade level through scripted curriculum or some sort of summer reading camp limits their potential by leading them step by step through reading skills instead of creating fertile spaces for text-based dialogue and discussion. In some cases, the teacher is virtually nonexistent as high-school students move through scripted reading programs individually (Duncan-Owens, 2009). Additionally, the reading in which students engage, often using computers, rarely takes on a sense of vibrancy and belonging. In this individualized routine, there is no social interaction around literacy; literacy belongs only to the realm of testing, evaluation, and mastery.

In contrast, critical literacy research describes vibrant spaces where students regularly practice literacy skills through social engagement in their communities and by assessing their own school's welcoming and unwelcoming spaces (Kinloch, 2009; Duncan-Andrade, 2008). This is where debate offers the greatest potential to connect with authentic literacy practices, helping students consider their own lived literacy in a way that is meaningful and analytical.

How Can Debate Solve Some of the Current Problems With the Teaching of Literacy Skills?

While I do not see debate as a panacea, I do see it as offering a different type of engagement with text than traditional perceptions of literacy instruction offer. First, debate pushes students to think beyond their own narrow perception and hold opposing perspectives in their minds simultaneously. In my work with policy debate, I specifically examine how asking students to prepare to present two different arguments on the same topic, the affirmative and the negative, helps them to explore both sides of an argument in a way that discourages dogmatism and encourages critical thinking (Cridland-Hughes, 2012). Some of my participants identified this as a tool that helped them learn to think more broadly, while others suggested that the competitive space of debate subsumed important world issues to the goal of winning the competition, where students would make arguments about the topic that they did not believe in order to establish a competitive advantage rather than engage in a real conversation. Still, debate offers a structural framework in which dialogue challenges implicit assumptions and asks hard questions of those engaged with the text. Classroom debates in particular offer the potential to tease out the implications of those discussions and to guide students toward that engaged dialogue that Mitchell advocates.

Additionally, debate forces a pedagogy of listening to peers as they work through ideas. Paolo Freire argues:

> Only the person who listens patiently and critically is able to speak with the other, even if at times it should be necessary to speak to him or her. Even when, of necessity, she/he must speak against ideas and convictions of the other person, it is still possible to speak as if the other were a subject who is being invited to listen critically and not an object submerged by an avalanche of unfeeling, abstract words.
>
> (Freire, 1998, p. 11)

Debate is a social activity. Unlike the computer intervention described above, youth engaged in a debate are engaged in a conversation around ideas. It is impossible to be successful in a debate round or a classroom debate without listening to the arguments offered by the opposing team. Without careful listening, the nuances of an argument are lost, and those nuances are the spaces where rich dialogue occurs. Yet, research indicates that students spend less than 15 seconds a day on discussion in classrooms by 9th grade and that discourse was mainly used to transmit information and report on what was known (Nystrand, Gamoran, & Carbonaro, 2001). Debate offers a structured framework for not only the presentation of information and oral argumentation, but also the reflection and consideration of peer voices. With guidance, debate pedagogy can provide youth with a model of intellectual and personal investment in careful and precise language that counters the polarizing rhetoric so often seen and heard from political actors, and it helps counter the deficit assumption particularly imposed on high-needs students.

Finally, debate pedagogy allows teachers and students to look for the seams in all ideas and notions, even those related to social justice. A good example of this is Shanara Reid-Brinkley's 2012 article, where she simultaneously acknowledges the value of the urban debate league in her history and questions her positioning as a representative example of a "ghetto kid gone good." For Reid-Brinkley, her involvement in debate in Atlanta prior to the institutionalization and expansion of the Atlanta Urban Debate League helped shape her life and her world, and it helped her question the assumptions of what an "urban" student should be. She tells the story of a time when she refused a second interview with a T.V. crew, because she did not want to reify stereotypes of urban youth. She did not want to normalize the media's dominant narrative of youth in her neighborhood by having her story told as an anomaly. Becoming the spokesperson for an important organization such as the urban debate league with its goals of restoration and support still placed her in a space of complicity with external representations of Black and brown youth. Although Reid-Brinkley's article initially appears critical of the UDL movement, I see her nuanced reflection on the program as an example of what debate pedagogy can and should do – we should create spaces where everything is up for discussion and nothing is sacred, where the gray areas of trade-offs and unintended consequences are the basis for conversations about ideology and difference.

What Have I Learned From a Decade of Watching Debaters?

I was hesitant when I first started coaching debate. I asked why students needed to be able to defend both sides of an issue. Why could they not choose the side they believed and argue passionately in defense of those beliefs? Were we not teaching them to argue against their instincts and their own voices? Over time, I realized that my students learned more from having to argue against their initial beliefs than they learned by having to advocate for them. Two of my most active debaters were sisters whose parents would only let them participate if they debated as a team. Over the year, I heard from teachers about how much more the sisters spoke in class, about how they made interesting points, and about how they looked at things from perspectives others had not considered. These sisters, these students, in this school, were looking for a way to engage with ideas, both inside and outside of the school environment, and debate provided them both the opportunity and the motivation.

Although I no longer coach debate at the high-school level, I continue to advocate for debate pedagogy in public schools. Since my time as a teacher and coach at Southwestern, I have shared what I learned as a debate coach in high-needs communities across the country. I ran a debate workshop in the Central Valley of California at a school with a 40% English Language Learner population, and I co-taught with a teacher who applied debate techniques in his traditional English class as students explored the Delano grape strike. I have taught public-speaking courses where students debated whether we should value privacy over security, how best to ensure responsible policing, and how to hold journalists accountable for the words they use in their reporting. Inevitably, what starts as a debate turns into a conversation, and youth ask probing questions that even adults are uncomfortable asking. These questions are powerful. Can we ever really get rid of racism? How do we hold people accountable for their words without limiting their freedom of speech? Is security a primary requirement for freedom? These are the conversations I want to have with my students, and the only space I have found for student engagement and accountability is debate.

While the urban debate leagues were the first response to a homogenous debate community and they continue to expand that community, I am happy to say they have not been the only response. The Migrant Education program in California runs a bilingual speech and debate tournament every year for the children of migrant farm workers, where students gather to question and compete in both Spanish and English and to debate resolutions such as "Granting amnesty perpetuates illegal immigration" (California Migrant Education Program, 2012). The Women's Debate Institute offers a free debate camp committed to expanding access to competitive debate for women, focusing on "closing the gender gap in competitive debate by advocating for and facilitating a more gender-inclusive environment that advances educational and professional opportunities for marginalized gender identities" (Women's Debate Institute, 2015). Debate is less frequently the monolithic space described by Fine—and we are all the better for it. Debate is changing, and as bell hooks would say, the margins are becoming the center (hooks, 2000). When we combine debate with a critical literacy framework, we help students think carefully about the world and their responsibility for using debate, dialogue, and literacy skills to move our communities toward justice.

References

Beil, L. (2007, December 5). For struggling Black college, hopes of a revival. *New York Times*. Retrieved from http://www.nytimes.com/2007/12/05/education/05wiley.html?fta=y.

Berry, A. (1997). High school reading programs revisited. *Journal of Adolescent and Adult Literacy, 40*(7), 524–531.

California Migrant Education Program. (2012). Preparation manual. Second Annual State Speech and Debate Tournament.

Clark, C. (2015). Welcoming a new age. *Literacy Today, 33*(1), 2.

Conradi, J., Jang, B. G., Bryant, C., Craft, A., & McKenna, M. (2013). Measuring adolescents' attitudes toward reading: A classroom survey. *Journal of Adolescent and Adult Literacy, 56*(7), 565–576.

Cridland-Hughes, S. (2010). Valuing voice: Critical literacy practices in an urban debate community (unpublished doctoral dissertation). Emory University, Atlanta, GA.

Cridland-Hughes, S. (2011). African American community literacy and urban debate. *Reflections: A Journal of Writing, Service-Learning and Community Literacy, 11*(1), 109–123.

Cridland-Hughes, S. (2012). Literacy as social action in City Debate. *Journal of Adolescent and Adult Literacy, 56*(3), 194–202.

Duncan-Andrade, J. (2008). *The Art of Critical Pedagogy*. New York: Peter Lang.

Duncan-Owens, D. (2009, January/February). Scripted reading programs: Fishing for success. *Principal*, 26–29. Retrieved from http://www.naesp.org/resources/2/Principal/2009/J-F_p26.pdf.

Fine, G. A. (2001). *Gifted Tongues: High School Debate and Adolescent Culture*. Princeton: Princeton University Press.

Freire, P. (1998). *Pedagogy of Freedom: Ethics, Democracy and Civic Courage*. Lanham, MD: Rowan and Littlefield.

Jean, W., Hill, L., Michel, P., & Kirkland, J. (1996). The Score [Recorded by The Fugees]. *On The Score*. New York: Columbia Records

Gee, J. (1996). *Social Linguistics and Literacies: Ideology in Discourses*. New York: Routledge.

Gorski, P. (2011). Unlearning deficit ideology and the scornful gaze: Thoughts on authenticating the class discourse in education. In R. Ahlquist, P. Gorski, & T. Montaño (Eds.), *Assault on Kids: How Hyper-Accountability, Corporatization, Deficit Ideology, and Ruby Payne Are Destroying Our Schools* (pp. 152–170). New York: Peter Lang.

hooks, b. (2000). *Feminist Theory: From Margin to Center*. Boston, MA: South End Press.

Huber, G., & Smith, J. (1993). Speaking out: Tapping potential in urban public schools. *Cross Streets: Ideas for Cities and Citizens, 1*(1), 29–36.

Kinloch, V. (2009). *Harlem on Our Minds: Place, Race, and the Literacies of Urban Youth*. New York: Teachers College Press.

Lee. E. (1998). Memoir of a former Urban Debate League participant. *Contemporary Argumentation and Debate, 19*, 93–96.

Martin. D. (2008, March 12). Henrietta Bell Wells, a Pioneering Debater, Dies at 96. *New York Times*. Retrieved from http://www.nytimes.com/2008/03/12/us/12wells.html?_r=0.

Mezuk, B. (2009). Urban debate and high school educational outcomes for African American males: The case of the Chicago Debate League. *Journal of Negro Education, 78*(3), 290–304.

Mitchell, G. (1998). Pedagogical possibilities for argumentative agency. *Argumentation and Advocacy, 35*, 41–60.

Morrell, E. (2008). *Critical Literacy and Urban Youth: Pedagogies of Access, Dissent and Liberation*. New York: Routledge.

National Institute of Child Health and Human Development. (2000). Teaching children to read: an evidence-based assessment of the scientific research literature on reading and its implications for reading instruction (National Reading Panel). Retrieved from http://www.nichd.nih.gov/publications/nrp/smallbook.htm.

Nystrand, M., Gamoran, A., & Carbonaro, W. (2001). On the ecology of classroom instruction: The case of writing in high school English and social studies. In P. Tynjälä, L. Mason, & K. Londa (Eds.), *Writing as a Learning Tool* (pp. 57–81). Dordrecht, The Netherlands: Kluwer Academic Publishers.

Pandya, J., & Avila, J. (Eds.) (2014). *Moving Critical Literacies Forward: A New Look at Praxis Across Contexts*. New York: Routledge.

Reid-Brinkley, S. (2012). Ghetto kids gone good: Race, representation, and authority in the scripting of inner city youths in the urban debate league. *Argumentation and Advocacy, 49*(2), 77–99.

Reinking, D., McKenna, M., Labbo, L., & Kieffer, R. (Eds.) (1998). *Handbook of Literacy and Technology: Transformations in a Post-Typographic World*. Mahwah, NJ: Lawrence Erlbaum.

Shor, I. (1992). *Empowering Education: Critical Teaching for Social Change*. Chicago: University of Chicago Press.

Street, B. (2003). What's "new" in New Literacy Studies? Critical approaches to literacy in theory and practice. *Current Issues in Comparative Education, 5*(2), 77–91.

U.S. Department of Education. (2012). Definitions: Race to the top district competitions draft. Retrieved from the U.S. Department of Education website: http://www.ed.gov/race-top/district-competition/definitions.

Walker, V. S. (1996). *Their Highest Potential: An African-American School Community in the Segregated South*. Chapel Hill, NC: University of North Carolina Press.

Warner, E., & Bruschke, J. (2001). "Gone on debating": Competitive academic debate as a tool of empowerment for urban America. *Contemporary Argumentation and Debate, 22,* 37–44.

Wolf, I. (2008). Learning the language of debate: Literacy and community in the Computer Assisted Debate project (unpublished master's thesis). Emory University, Atlanta, GA.

Women's Debate Institute. (2015). Mission. Retrieved from http://womensdebateinstitute.org/.

5 Discerning the Value of Information in the Digital Age

Gordon Stables

Debate as More Than Disagreement

Even among educators, introducing yourself as someone who teaches debate can produce some interesting reactions, including "You must like to argue" or "I should get into an argument with you." These well-meaning reactions stem from a general cultural unease with confrontation. This discomfort is certainly easy to understand. Very few people enjoy having their opinions and beliefs challenged. However, the value of introducing debate as a formal means of argument has less to do with promotion of disagreement for disagreement's sake and much more to do with the need to develop skills for managing difference. Today's students experience a rapidly changing media environment and must develop successful strategies to address the challenges this environment presents. Debate education offers a unique and dynamic way to address these challenges.

Academic debate offers a forum to introduce and engage differing opinions from a wide range of perspectives. Because debate begins with the expectation of disagreement, debate also provides an opportunity to allow students to accept that a range of perspectives routinely accompany a complex subject. Introducing debate to classrooms isn't the same as introducing disagreement; teaching debate should instead be understood as teaching students how to manage conflict, information, and difference. For all of these reasons, in this chapter academic debate will be explored as a means of improving students' ability to manage information.

The Need to Manage Information: The Importance of New Media Skills

Try to recall the first time you encountered a dramatically different opinion. Perhaps you were a child and visiting a friend's home. Maybe you heard them offering an opinion about a holiday, custom, politician, or sports team that was dramatically different from what you had been raised with. Perhaps this experience took place in a classroom when you met someone from a very different background.

In each of these settings, the presence of physical communities played a large role in determining how we are exposed to different opinions, values, and experiences. This pattern has long-standing traditions within communities; indeed it is how values are often passed down from one generation to another. Today's youth certainly have access to these same traditional (and often physically proximate) communities, but they are also citizens of a networked era. They may learn about a different religious or political view from a friend's home, or perhaps an ambiguous comment left on a their Facebook thread leads them to a series of web searches. Perhaps a news story is shared across their social media networks and they come home with difficult questions and perspectives.

Each day there are untold occasions for exactly this kind of dynamic information engagement. Access to so many sources of information means that the sources of information can be as diffuse as the opinions themselves. A classmate might offer a challenging viewpoint, or perhaps it was a player in an online gaming environment who lives across the globe. Today's youth experience their world through their networks. Meeting a new person or experiencing a new event happens, at least in part, through a quick search on our ubiquitous devices. The Pew Research Center (Lenhart, 2015) confirms so many anecdotal observations: "Aided by the convenience and constant access provided by mobile devices, especially smartphones, 92% of teens report going online daily—including 24% who say they go online 'almost constantly'" (p. 2). It may be easy to trivialize the immediate shift toward "googling" something as the first line of research because it is at times difficult to contextualize just how different today's information consumption is from any other era in human history. James E. Short's (2013) research confirms the recent surge as, across all sources, media consumption is growing at 18% per year and Americans now each consume more than fifteen hours of data daily.

Exposure to a volume of content and different perspectives is only one aspect of the powerful social transitions that are influencing today's students. The growth of social media is part of a larger transition that blurs the notion of media production and consumption. Taking pictures and sharing updates is both a means of keeping in touch with one's friends and also a means of citizen journalism and civic engagement. Anyone with a phone is now able to produce content that captures some understanding of his or her world and to share that view with people around the world. Being exposed to differing opinions isn't limited to specific political or cultural topics; contact with differing ideas is a common feature of modern life.

Given the sensitive nature of working with young students, there can be a powerful temptation to focus on limiting access to such information. Indeed, every school district, principal, teacher, and parent will be required to make judgments about what kinds of information and what sources of technology are made available to students. The limitations of such controls and the importance of developing lifelong skills suggest that there is also a need to influence how students learn to navigate this complex sea of information. Henry Jenkins explains:

Participatory culture is emerging as the culture absorbs and responds to the explosion of new media technologies that make it possible for average consumers to archive, annotate, appropriate, and recirculate media content in powerful new ways. A focus on expanding access to new technologies carries us only so far if we do not also foster the skills and cultural knowledge necessary to deploy those tools toward our own ends.

(Jenkins, 2009, p. 8)

The next section explores how debating can foster those skills and cultural knowledge.

Debate as Information Education

A formal academic debate provides structure to arguments. Topics are selected, competitors are given specific amounts of time to prepare and present, and their efforts are evaluated. Although experienced debate educators can point to a virtual alphabet soup of different formats, they all share a common foundation of encouraging students to discuss important issues.

Academic debates are different from political campaign debates in many ways, not the least of which is that each participant is debating to debate, not to seek a specific office. Classroom debates require their own context. A student may debate because they want a specific grade or because they want to defeat their competitors. Either way, competition is an important feature of motivating students to debate. Student competitors will devote their energies toward whatever allows them the greatest opportunity for success. The format of the debate experience will then influence how students prepare. When the format allows the competitors to prepare for the topic by researching the relevant issues, the debate process naturally lends itself to a highly motivated

Table 5.1 Comparison of Academic Debate Styles

	Time with proposition	# Debaters per team	# Teams per round	Length of debate (mins)	Speaking time per debater (mins)
Policy (college)	1 year	2	2	92	18
Policy (high school)	1 year	2	2	84	16
Lincoln Douglas	2 months	1	2	42	13
Public Forum	1 month	2	2	37	7.5
British Parliamentary	25 minutes	2	4	56	7
Congressional Debate	Variable	1	18–20	180	10
American Parliamentary	Proposed in round	2	2	40	8 or 12
World Schools	Mixed prepared & impromptu (30 minutes)	3	2	56	8 or 12

student researcher. The urgency to compete drives the debater to explore the available means of persuasion.

In the 2014–2015 academic year, one national debate topic was "Resolved: For-profit prisons in the United States should be banned" (Past Public Forums Topics). Once students are assigned this topic they will begin the process of brainstorming the possible options for each contest. Because such a topic may have been recently discussed in the national election, a student may begin with some information. They may not know much about what differentiates for-profit and other prisons. The process of investigating a debate argument is an important process. Jeff Parcher (1998) explained the way debate molds a research experience:

> The creation of an argument is one of the most complex cognitive acts that a person can engage in. Creating an argument requires the research of issues, organization of data, analysis of data, synthesization of different kinds of data, and an evaluation of information with respect to which conclusion it may point.

The student understands that debating requires them to draw conclusions, in this case about for-profit prisons. As Parcher notes, the incentive to compete compels a search to identify and synthesize data. Not all data is going to be useful to the debater. They need to anticipate the judgment of their peers and critics. Are concerns about the ethical treatment of prisoners paramount in this setting? Is it an environment where the financial dimensions of such an issue will be most important to their judges? Debate spurs a dynamic process of research, identifying specific arguments, and assessing their relative value.

In settings where students will debate the same topic more than once, this process is ongoing and can evolve after each individual debate. Repetition can be one of the most significant features of academic debating. In many settings, an individual might develop a perspective from a single engagement with an issue. When the debater is asked to research, evaluate, and debate a topic on multiple occasions, their judgment is informed by the sum total of each of these experiences.

This next section explores two specific information benefits to debate education: curation and role playing.

Debate as Curation

The dramatic expansion of information available to each of us profoundly changes what we can consider as research. When Parcher describes the need for organization, analysis, and synthesis, it presumes that the debater has some context for these tasks. A topic such as for-profit prisons may at first be unfamiliar to a student, but it also possesses a specific set of relevant literature (i.e., from its legal status). What happens when the debate subject engages a far broader subject? Consider the topic "Resolved: Schools should adopt a zero-tolerance policy for bullying." There would certainly be specific state and federal laws to reference. There would also be a robust body of literature on the importance of zero-tolerance academic policies (such as in the anti-drug context). But would the student be justified in focusing on examples more relevant in their community? Should they focus on the most recent examples of bullying or the challenges of such policies? Each of these questions has many reasonable answers. Researching and constructing a topic is a challenge for each student and for students in general. Just as Jenkins encourages us to find ways to empower students as active participants in their media environment, debate education can foster a more robust understanding of information literacy.

Curation, the process of finding, organizing, and sharing content, is a powerful approach for debate research. If we acknowledge that debating offers a robust and unique laboratory for students to engage with a wide range of public policy questions, we can begin to see the tremendous power in debate as a model where student-generated research is both the evidence to support claims in a debate and a remarkable by-product that can improve the quality of publicly available information. The use of wikis, or collaboratively built public sources of information, provides an opportunity for debate education to teach the skill of curation and serve a larger public good.

Instead of asking each debate participant to conduct their own privately held research, the debate educator can create an environment that requires each competitor to share their research on a public wiki. Wikis can then provide a common foundation for any participant in the debates and allow any participant to add their own materials. Because wikis allow each competitor to have an expectation of what will happen in their next debate, the competitor is better able to critique the arguments. Competitors may at first hesitate to share their work, but it is not an unheard-of practice. The legal community operates with a similar norm of disclosure for briefs and legal motions, which demonstrates that curation can be managed and preserves a basic sense of equity in each debate. In other words, educators would balance the incentives for students to constantly seek new information and the importance of reviewing current information.

Awards can function as an additional incentive to encourage curation. Historically, debate events provide awards for the best individual speakers. This model of curation-based research could also include awards for the best student research. The public nature of the research product creates a number of pathways to determine who receives these awards. Experts within the public policy field of a debate topic could, remotely, review and recognize the strongest contributions. Web-based analytics could also provide quantitative information about which student research received the most traffic. A student could be recognized as the best debate researcher in their region, state, or nation.

Teaching debate research through wikis would require instruction in how to identify quality material and then how to organize that material on a simple web template. Many educators currently prohibit engagement with wikis in their research projects because they view the information as flawed. However, teaching debate research through wikis would require students to treat the available wiki information as the beginning and not the end of their research; it would require students to improve, correct, and synthesize information – the essence of curation. If public wikis are flawed, academic debate represents a way to improve them, and as a result, to improve the quality of publicly available information on every topic debated.

The public presentation of student research also results in a number of additional benefits. The students themselves begin to wrestle with the inadequacies of publicly available information on a relevant issue. Instead of the debate research existing solely in an information bubble, student research will live in public contexts available to those who might benefit from higher-quality argument and rationales. Returning to the previous anti-bullying example, if school districts encouraged students to conduct open-source models of research as a requirement of involvement in debate participation on this topic, it would allow the schools to generate a specific body of knowledge that would have benefits to the entire community. The debaters' efforts to identify and organize information can be a public good far beyond their individual competitions.

Debate as Role Playing

In the midst of this information surge we might conclude that today's youth are better able to appreciate the views from different perspectives. Returning to the opening questions about encountering difference, it seems logical that if today's youth experience more perspectives, they are also well trained to make the most of that rich diversity. Access to these diverse sources doesn't automatically translate into building diverse information networks. Instead today's information consumers make choices to rely on information sources that reinforce their pre-existing beliefs. The Pew Research Center (Mitchell, 2014) cautioned that Americans cannot live in an information bubble, but they can be part of a series of choices that limit their engagement with other perspectives. Pew's research suggests that liberals and conservatives have developed patterns of information consumption that mirror their political choices. They trust and listen to the news organizations and individuals that reinforce their views. Perhaps more disconcerting, those on both extremes (and consuming the most isolated sources of information) are the most active in all forms of political participation.

This process of relying on media that validates your prior beliefs explains the controversy over the notion of "epistemic closure," which is a phenomenon whereby political factions become so insular that they undermine their own ability to make effective judgments and, in turn, undermine themselves as a viable source of political agency (Cohen, 2010). If our patterns of utilizing both mass media and social media increasingly limit our exposure to those who do not share our beliefs and values, how can we be confident in our judgments?

Teaching students forms of information consumption should anticipate the manner in which these skills will be deployed. To truly embrace the power of research, students should be encouraged to seek out the arguments necessary to frame their position, even if that forces them to move beyond their current ideological boundaries. In this way, debate truly distinguishes itself from other academic inquiries. An academic debate asking students to examine the desirability of greater regulation of behavior understood as bullying is not primarily about bullying. The subject is the means of allowing students to engage in a manner of inquiry.

Recognizing that the topic will drive student research, debate educators can also consider what perspectives students should directly engage. Henry Jenkins (2006) explains that in today's participatory media and cultural landscape, young people need a core set of skills and competencies to be full participants. These skills include the notion of play as "the capacity to experiment with your surroundings as a form of problem-solving" and the notion of performance as "the ability to adopt alternative identities for the purpose of improvisation and discovery" (Jenkins, 2006, p. 56). Taken together, a debate activity could allow students to either engage (play) with issues that directly engage their communities or to take on new perspectives. The improvisation involved in the performance provides a rare opportunity to ask questions and engage in discussions that may not be consistent with their experiences and beliefs.

Debate possesses an advantage for engaging controversial subjects because the framing of a proposition requires the existence of competing perspectives. As compared to a public speaking assignment where students are required to identify and defend a perspective on a public matter, debate requires the student not only to engage their viewpoint, but also to anticipate and prepare for counter-arguments. The decision to have students repeat these debates, on the same or other sides, provides an opportunity for students to revisit the information they have compiled. In Jenkins' terms, they can play with that information.

Role-playing in debate is a way to distinguish the subject of debates from the method of debating. Many economic classes have discussed Thomas Piketty's (2014) significant work, *Capital in the Twenty-First Century*. An academic setting that requires students to debate about the utility of seeking to reduce income inequality requires the students on both sides of the merits of Piketty's work. An economics teacher who chooses to utilize the book as a text makes a decision to endorse, at some level, its rigor and conclusions. By introducing the subject as a debate, a debate educator invites a range of exploration. There are a significant number of ways for the students to begin exploring the topic, especially because the topic contains the clause "greatest economic challenge." The instructor possesses additional latitude to encourage research on a national level or they could frame the topic closer to their home state or local community. The students can operationalize the topic in any number of ways, including focus on education, tax policy, and job training. As the students on each side begin identifying and assessing the possible arguments to present their position, their own information routines are placed alongside those of their teammates, their competitors, and the competitive demands of the debating experience.

In other contexts, educators might be dissuaded from encouraging discussion of such an important, but politically charged subject. In a debate, students are encouraged to consider both the scope of the problem of income inequality, as well as possible solutions. The requirement of students to consider competing perspectives shifts the conversation away from an embrace of any single perspective. Debate can teach students to consider multiple perspectives on complex topics and reach some form of judgment, as opposed to retreating to familiar media that reinforce their pre-existing beliefs.

Debate as a Way to Teach Information Literacy and Meet Common Core State Standards

The development of the Common Core State Standards (CCSS) has provided an opportunity to revisit many of the rationales for specific approaches to curriculum development. Many school districts have long supported speech and debate education as part of public speaking or oral communication curriculum, but the CCSS provides a broader justification for debate education.

The CCSS Initiative, which presented the CCSS for English Language Arts & Literacy in History/Social Studies, Science, and Technical Subjects (2010, p. 4), calls for "Research and media skills blended into the Standards as a whole" and provides a compelling case for research skills to be integrated across the curriculum:

> To be ready for college, workforce training, and life in a technological society, students need the ability to gather, comprehend, evaluate, synthesize, and report on information and ideas, to conduct original research in order to answer questions or solve problems, and to analyze and create a high volume and extensive range of print and nonprint texts in media forms old and new. The need to conduct research and to produce and consume media is embedded into every aspect of today's curriculum. In like fashion, research and media skills and understandings are embedded throughout the Standards rather than treated in a separate section.

The recognition of the need for research and organization of information as a universal competency provides debate educators with the opportunity to demonstrate how debate can support specific curricula across a range of subjects. Debate can support CCSS skills in two broad categories: the collection and organization of information, and the deployment of arguments.

By conducting research, students gain expertise in subjects. The CCSS initiative (p. 4) describes how students build a foundation of knowledge through research and eventually become qualified (proficient) in these subjects. Debate's competitive requirements to prepare the best possible set of arguments implicitly create incentives to identify and work with well-recognized and well-developed texts. Students are challenged to identify works of quality and substance because they need information that can withstand scrutiny from their opposition. A common concern about the problems of research through googling is the selection of the most common research hit (i.e., the top Google search result). The temptation to rely on the first link in a search result exists with any student project, but the built-in expectation that their peers will challenge this work provides students the incentive to further refine their search terms and investigate beyond the most popular results.

This process of investigation carries the additional benefit of providing a routine that encourages the student to conduct much of this investigation and reading outside of their classroom. In the CCSS standards analysis (p. 3), we are reminded that the National Assessment of Educational Progress (NAEP) "makes clear that significant reading of informational texts should take place outside of the English Language Arts Standards classroom in order for students to be ready for college and careers." By starting with the topic and encouraging the students to identify their resources, the act of investigation will take place prior to the competition. Teachers can certainly help students begin this review, but as students become invested in their argument construction, much of their research happens outside of school.

As the students organize and collect information, they do so in order to persuade their judges (i.e., to win their debates). This process of evidence review and selection encourages judgments about the quality of the specific claims and their rationale. In a vast sea of information, a student's primary challenge is not just identifying who advocates a particular policy, but what are their reasons for support. The use of specific information, the power of the reasoning, and the ability to effectively utilize language are all traits of the best evidence. All of these traits are reflected in the CCSS standards analysis, which describe that college-ready students should "value evidence" and "cite specific evidence when offering an oral or written interpretation of a text" (p. 4).

Within these standards, the CCSS recognize that there is no single standard by which evidence can be deployed. When discussing the expectations of college-ready students the standards offer (p.3):

> Students consider their communication in relation to audience, task, purpose, and discipline. They appreciate nuances, such as how the composition of an audience should affect tone when speaking and how the connotations of words affect meaning. They also know that different disciplines call for different types of evidence (e.g., documentary evidence in history, experimental evidence in the sciences).

In this brief statement, CCSS present the dynamic relationship between argument, evidence, and audience. A debate educator understands that this is the ongoing process of argument research, construction, and evaluation. Similarly, the CCSS contend that students need to engage in an ongoing process of identifying and working with specific texts and evidence. Debate encourages research and organization of information in order to make arguments more understandable. The debate student should appreciate that their decisions about the selection of evidence helps to inform the broader narrative that they offer in their speeches. Similarly, a student demonstrating mastery of CCSS standards should be able to draw upon the evidence contained in nonfiction texts in order to comprehend and critique important arguments.

Conclusion

The rising tide of available information and perspectives shows little sign of abating. The Pew (Lenhart, 2015) and Short (2013) research both suggest that our immediate future will include more information and greater exposure to media. Increasingly, the struggle to understand these trends leads to the amorphous concept of "big data." Even Philip Ashlock (as cited in Dutcher, 2014), the chief architect of the White House's open data platform, Data.gov, describes "'big data' to be about analysis for data that's really messy or where you don't know the right questions or queries to make" – analysis that can help you find patterns, anomalies, or new structures amidst otherwise chaotic or complex data points. The messy and chaotic patterns that Ashlock observes are increasingly the world that today's students will be called upon to manage and improve. Rather than treating these giant data sets as answers in and of themselves, many scholars are now recognizing the importance of making judgments based on available evidence. Kenneth Cukier and Viktor Mayer-Schönberger (2013) argue:

> The Internet has reshaped how humanity communicates. Big data is different: it marks a transformation in how society processes information. In time, big data might change our way of thinking about the world. As we tap ever more data to understand events and make decisions, we are likely to discover that many aspects of life are probabilistic, rather than certain.

This volume of information will require trained inquisitors who are familiar with analyzing evidence and deciphering the logical connections between concepts. Students who have spent time exploring complex public policy challenges are themselves familiar with the probabilistic, not certain, nature of policy implementation. Exploring all sides of a question encourages the students to appreciate which nuances are essential to successful implementation and which are likely to produce unintended consequences.

Teaching debate is one method of acquiring these skills. When high-school and college debate began in the US, research involved a great deal of work to secure a relatively modest amount of information. Today, the most casually involved student possesses greater access to research than the most driven of their historical predecessors could have even imagined, which requires a new approach to information literacy. Today's young people live in an information culture that demands a way to nurture careful student engagement, and debate is well positioned to provide such skills. Students who are exposed to debate education are capable of researching and organizing the evidence that is used to build larger positions. Their work can benefit not only themselves, but also any community who can draw upon that information. Debate-educated students are also nurtured in appreciating the multiplicity of viewpoints involved in complex issues. Daily needs dissuade each of us from seeking out the evidence and arguments that contradict our worldview. Debaters are empowered to be contrarian and explore the judgments that we may find inconvenient. The CCSS recognize that students need to be trained in how to think, not just what is the most compelling judgment of the current moment. As part of a larger curricular emphasis on promoting critical engagement, debate education offers a path for a robust greater information literacy.

References

Bleiberg, J. (2014). What does big data actually mean? *The Brookings Institution.* Retrieved from http://www.brookings.edu/blogs/techtank/posts/2014/09/11-big-data-definition.
Cohen, P. (2010). 'Epistemic closure'? Those are fighting words. *The New York Times.* Retrieved from http://www.nytimes.com/2010/04/28/books/28conserv.html?_r=0.
Cukier, K. N., & Mayer-Schönberger, V. (2013, May/June). The rise of big data: How it's changing the way we think about the world. *Foreign Affairs.* Retrieved from https://www.foreignaffairs.com/articles/2013-04-03/rise-big-data.
Dutcher, J. (2014, September 3). What is big data [Web log post]? Retrieved from https://datascience.berkeley.edu/what-is-big-data/.
Jenkins, H. (2009). Confronting the challenges of participatory culture: Media education for the 21st century. Retrieved from https://mitpress.mit.edu/sites/default/files/titles/free_download/9780262513623_Confronting_the_Challenges.pdf.
Jenkins, H. (2006). *Convergence Culture: Where Old and New Media Collide.* New York: New York University Press.
Lenhart, A. (2015). Teens, social media & technology overview 2015. Retrieved from http://www.pewinternet.org/files/2015/04/PI_TeensandTech_Update2015_0409151.pdf.
Mitchell, A., Gottfried, J., Kiley, J., & Matsa, K. E. (2014, October 21). Political polarization & media habits. Retrieved from http://www.journalism.org/2014/10/21/political-polarization-media-habits/.
Parcher, J. (1998). The value of debate: Adapted from the report of the Philodemic Debate Society, Georgetown University. Retrieved from http://www.parklandsd.org/web/smith/files/2012/09/The_Value_of_Debate.pdf.
Past public forum topics. Speech, Debate: National Speech & Debate Association. Retrieved from http://www.speechanddebate.org/aspx/nav.aspx?navid=144.
Piketty, T. (2014). *Capital in the Twenty-first Century.* (Trans. A. Goldhammer). Cambridge, Massachusetts: Belknap of Harvard University Press.
Short, J. E. (2013). How much media? 2013: Report on American consumers. *How Much Media? 2013.* Retrieved from http://classic.marshall.usc.edu/assets/161/25995.pdf.

6 Engendering Academic Success

Debate as a School Engagement Strategy

Carol Winkler

The need for the nation's schools to identify and implement effective pedagogical strategies remains a societal imperative. Of individuals living in the United States between the ages of 16 and 24, 7% have dropped out, not earned their GED degree, and are not currently attending school (National Center for Educational Statistics, 2015). Dropouts are less likely than their peers to find employment and, if they do, they are more likely to receive lower pay and fewer advancement opportunities (Christle, Jolivette, & Nelson, 2007). They are also more likely to have health complications and lower life expectancies, to rely on social services, and to commit crimes and become incarcerated (Dynarski et al., 2008; Martin, Tobin, & Sugai, 2002).

Disengaged students who remain in school exacerbate the problem. Such students tend to minimize their effort when performing school tasks, prefer easy, quick-to-finish assignments, and do not care (or are negative) about their schoolwork (Appleton, Christenson, & Furlong, 2008; Skinner, Kindermann, & Furrer, 2009). Common student outcomes of such work avoidance behaviors include a lack of self-control (Seifert & O'Keefe, 2001) and lower levels of academic achievement (King & McInerney, 2014). As students become more disengaged, they also exhibit more anti-social behaviors, major depression and bipolar disorders, specific phobias, alcohol and cannabis use disorders, and nicotine dependence (Vaughn et al., 2011).

Increasingly, teachers have recognized that debate serves as a much-needed antidote to the school disengagement crisis plaguing our nation's schools. As the empirical studies referenced here demonstrate, debate improves student participation across a wide range of academic fields including history, communication, English, English as a Second Language, philosophy, science, geography, computational sciences, economics, psychology, political science, economics, sociology, dentistry, social work, pharmacology, nursing, rehabilitative counseling, health care, accounting, marketing, and business.

To explain how debate bolsters school engagement, this chapter will present empirical findings about how debate works as a pedagogical approach. The studies discussed here are diverse. They examine various modes of delivering debate instruction that span in-class activities, online courses, extracurricular programs, and interscholastic debate competitions. They evaluate how debate works at the middle-school, high-school, and college levels, and in both urban and suburban schools. Here, the concept of school engagement will encompass the emotional, behavioral, and cognitive aspects of students' active involvement in school. The chapter will describe how emotional, behavioral, and cognitive factors contribute to student disengagement, explain how educational researchers distinguish the three concepts, and explore how debate facilitates heightened engagement across this spectrum. The chapter will then conclude by reviewing robust studies that demonstrate the positive relationship between debate and academic achievement.

Emotional Engagement

Understanding why students disengage emotionally from school defies any single explanation. A recent Gates Foundation survey revealed that 47% of dropouts reported that they left school because their classes were not interesting enough, while 69% of the same group reported that they simply lacked the motivation to work hard in school. Many other students remained in school but failed to engage because they considered their classes boring, insufficiently challenging, or a needless distraction from their other opportunities and life trials (Bridgeland, DiIulio, & Morison, 2006).

Fredricks, Blumenfeld, and Paris's (2004) meta-review of scholarship on emotional engagement distilled the meaning of the concept to "affective reactions in the classroom, including interest, boredom, happiness, sadness, and anxiety" (p. 63). Their study identified four factors that contribute to emotional engagement: how much the student enjoys school activities, the personal importance of task success, the value of the educational experience for the student's future goals, and the student's negative cost of participating in the task.

Debate heightens emotional engagement by improving student interest and enjoyment in the learning process. While some students show initial reticence toward participating in classroom debates, they develop high levels of satisfaction after they experience the activity (Gervey, Drout, & Wahn, 2009). Classroom teachers who participated in focus groups reported that "students often bring up the debates as their favorite aspect of the course, both from a participation and an audience perspective" (Peace, 2011, p. 235). Instructors in online courses likewise indicated that both students and teachers alike found debate innovative and enjoyable (Park, Kier, & Jugdev, 2011).

One reason debate adds to student enjoyment is because it involves active learning. With its interactive, dialogic approach, debate places "the responsibility of comprehension on the shoulders of the students" (Doody & Condon, 2012, p. 236). The activity has a built-in competitive aspect that engages students (Goodwin, 2003; Healey, 2012), which serves as "a useful tool to put students in the driver's seat of their learning experience with faculty members providing a supporting role" (Roucan-Kane, Wolfskill, & Beverly, 2013, p. 22). Even students participating in online debates remain actively engaged as they utilize databases, build pro and con arguments, and develop team-based strategies (Nedeljković, 2014).

Debate also promotes emotional engagement by reducing student anxiety levels about school performance. The approach reduces students' overall communication anxiety, as well as specific fears associated with communicating in group discussions, interpersonal dyads, and public settings (Kennedy, 2007; Roy & Macchiette, 2005; Winkler, 2009). With active tournament debaters identifying improved communication skills as debate's chief benefit (Littlefield, 2001) and alumni naming argumentation, critical thought, reasoning, synthesis, use of evidence, speech writing, research, speech delivery, listening and persuasion as the activity's lasting benefits (Chandler & Hobbs, 1991), students develop the advocacy skills useful for reducing anxiety about their school performance.

Debate even reduces prejudice, which would otherwise undermine the emotional engagement of some students. Because debate provides opportunities for contact between students who might not otherwise engage one another, because it incorporates the necessary time for students to build acquaintances, because it assumes equal status between competitors, and because it values cooperation for the achievement of goals, students who participate in debate develop coping strategies for overcoming negative, prejudicial peer interactions (Zorwick, Wade, & Heilmayr, 2009).

Debate finally strengthens emotional engagement by empowering youth. Alumni of debate programs that serve students who attend the school districts of the nation's largest cities reported that debate improved their interactions with authority figures and peers alike (Winkler, Fortner, & Baugh-Harris, 2013). Multiple reasons explain why. Debate requires students to take responsibility for their own learning through articulation and defense of their own views (Firmin, Vaughn, & Dye, 2007). Debate also teaches students to either better support their own views (Healey, 2012) or to change them in cases where their perspectives become indefensible (Green & King 1990; Omelicheva & Avdeyeva, 2008; Kennedy, 2009). Additionally, debate makes course content more adaptable to the social and cultural values of its participants (Ziegelmueller, 1998). Through involvement in such processes, debaters become "critical consumers of knowledge, social critics, and agents of change" (Warner & Bruschke, 2001, p. 18).

In sum, debate facilitates students' emotional engagement because it is an active and interesting learning tool. It reduces the communication anxiety and prejudice that hold back some students from reaching their academic potential. It empowers advocates by providing students the emotional fortitude and skill sets needed for successful learning. The beneficial aspects of debate, however, extend beyond productive emotional developments. As the next section will explain, the activity's impact on student conduct also helps maximize students' educational experiences.

Behavioral Engagement

Student behavior in school functions as the second predictive indicator of school disengagement. Middle-school students with high numbers of school absences are more disengaged in the classroom (Finn, 1993; Finn & Rock, 1997), with 59–65 percent of surveyed dropouts reporting that they developed patterns of skipping classes or full school days in the year before they left school (Bridgeland, DiIulio, & Morison, 2006). Early onset of student disciplinary problems is predictive of both dropping out of school and future delinquent behavior (Tremblay & LeMarquand, 2001; Wasserman et al., 2003). While many factors contribute to behavioral disengagement, one central cause is weak communication skills. Students with difficulties communicating experience higher levels of peer rejection, depressive symptoms, and increased aggression (Dumas, Blechman, & Prinz, 1994).

The concept of behavioral engagement in educational research is multifaceted. Its three most common meanings include: (1) "participation in school-related activities such as athletics or school governance"; (2) "involvement in learning and academic tasks and includes behaviors such as effort, persistence, concentration, attention, asking questions, and contributing to class discussion"; and (3) "following the rules and adhering to classroom norms, as well as the absence of disruptive behaviors such as skipping school and getting in trouble" (Fredricks, Blumenfeld, & Paris, 2004, p. 62).

Debate improves behavioral engagement by heightening the level of student participation in the classroom. Instructors in college classes have indicated that debate improves students' verbal assertiveness (Colbert, 1993). As one debate alumna explained: "I am not afraid to speak up in class and whenever a student tries to counter what I stated, I am very good at responding fast without being mean" (Winkler et al., 2013). Another insisted that debate made her "a champion hand-raiser" (Winkler et al., 2013).

Debate also improves behavioral engagement by prompting students to be more optimistic about their futures. One study asked students who had improved their conduct after participating in debate to expound on why they changed their behavior. In response, students identified their level of agreement with 35 possible explanations. The students' most frequent response was "Debate made me believe I could succeed in life," followed in rank-order by "Debate taught me to improve my listening," "Debate taught me to read better," "Debate helps me persuasively present my views," and "Debate helps me see two sides of an issue" (Winkler, 2011). In short, when students believed they had the skills necessary to thrive through debate, they focused more on succeeding in school.

Debate finally improves behavioral engagement by enhancing respect for the viewpoints of others. Students taking classes with debate activities were significantly more likely to "consider alternative points of view" than those taking non-debate courses (Gervey et al., 2009, p. 65). In the words of one student, debate allowed her to see "the importance of embracing many views, opinions, and experiences" (Park et al., 2011, p. 10). Others explained that the experience of defending an opposing viewpoint helped them to better understand alternative perspectives (Park et al., 2011).

Examinations of students involved in debate show that participants reduce both the number and severity of their disciplinary incidents. A three-year study comparing the outcomes for participants in the Atlanta Urban Debate League with those in the Milwaukee Debate League document the activity's positive outcome on student conduct. After only one year of debate participation, 83% of the Atlanta students with recorded disciplinary incidents in the year before they debated had fewer incidents during the year they debated, and 81% of students with recorded suspensions the year before had fewer suspensions (Winkler, 2011). Similarly, in Milwaukee, those with recorded disciplinary incidents in the year before they debated, 53% reduced their recorded incidents and 58% had fewer suspensions (Winkler, 2011).

To date, the most rigorous studies documenting the linkage between debate and behavioral engagement compared outcomes of debaters in the Atlanta Urban Debate League with those of a matched group of their non-debate peers. The students selected for the comparison group were matched for similar demographic, family characteristics, and academic risk factors. The results for female students showed that debate participants in 6th–10th grades were "tardy from school only about half as many times" as the non-debaters (Winkler et al., 2013). Moreover, middle-school debaters of both genders "posted one-third fewer annual school absences and 1.4 fewer annual disciplinary incidents than their non-debate peers" (Winkler, 2015, p. 4).

In sum, debate contributes to behavioral engagement by increasing student involvement in learning. Debate lowers barriers to active participation in the classroom, improves student perceptions that they can succeed, and heightens respect for the viewpoints of others. By motivating students to attend class, arrive on time, and follow school rules, debate helps students perform more productively in the classroom. As the next section will reveal, debate compounds the benefits of improved classroom behaviors through its contribution to cognitive engagement.

Cognitive Engagement

Poor academic achievement serves as the final predictive indicator of student disengagement. In an extensive review of more than five hundred articles, dissertations, theses, and convention papers exploring what factors contribute to high-school failure, Storm and Boster (2007) point out that low academic achievement "has consistently been one of the strongest predictors of dropping out of high schools" (p. 435). Further, students who remain in school after they fall behind academically often find themselves held back a grade, tracked away from college preparatory classes, or without sufficient credentials to achieve their goals.

The concept of cognitive engagement in educational research has two related but distinct meanings. First, students display a psychological desire to exceed academic requirements. Second, they demonstrate a willingness to elevate the level of the tasks they attempt and complete, as well show as a heightened investment in gaining a mastery of knowledge associated with those tasks (Fredricks, Blumenfeld, & Paris, 2004).

To a large degree, debate counters cognitive disengagement because it promotes critical thinking (Allen et al., 1999). When preparing for a debate, students build critical thinking skills by selecting and constructing their arguments in anticipation of the competition to come. During the debate, students listen, reflect, defend their own positions, and counter the expressed views of others. After the debate, participants continue the learning process by reflecting on the feedback they received about their performance (Healey, 2012). As Warner and Bruschke (2001) explained, "Rather than simply taking knowledge offered to them at face value, students almost automatically begin thinking through possible objections to any knowledge claim and developing probing questions about it" (p. 6). By strengthening critical thinking skill development, debate helps serve as the foundation for cognitive engagement.

Debate's ability to augment critical thinking development transcends academic subject boundaries. In the subject of reading, for example, question-based engagement with journal articles through debate clarifies the purpose of the reading, directs attention to relevant content, and promotes critical skills useful for analyzing articles (Chamberlain & Burroughs, 1985). Likewise in science courses, repeated exposure to inquiry-based debates builds skills of "identifying an addressable question (the causal role of a specific feature), seeking informative data via controlled comparison, and drawing appropriate conclusions of causality and non-causality" (Kuhn & Pease, 2008, p. 534). By facilitating the mastery of content and critical skills essential for evaluating content, debate prepares students to encounter new information in new settings (Snider & Schnurer, 2006). A survey of Urban Debate League alumni throughout the United States identified the transcendent skill sets that debate teaches from the students' perspective: "critical thinking, reading comprehension, public speaking, essay writing, study habits, annotation, problem solving, research methodologies, organization, time management, and practical sense" (Winkler, Fortner, & Baugh-Harris, 2013). By building foundational proficiencies, debate positions students to improve their academic performance across the academic spectrum.

Debate also promotes cognitive engagement by introducing an element of educational challenge into student learning. Debate fosters in-depth preparation by encouraging students to imagine a broad array of arguments they could encounter as they face off with their peers. Functioning as a stimulating learning activity (Nyatanga & Howard, 2015) that produces higher-level learning (Peace, 2011), the competitive elements of debate appeal to bored students in particular (Belanger & Stein, 2013). In online courses, debate similarly adds challenge due to its "fast-paced exchange of data, facts and arguments" (Nedeljković, 2014, p. 506). Even students who *only observe* debates enhance their levels of cognitive engagement as they compare how they might outper-form the debaters (Peace, 2011).

Debate's positive impact on cognitive engagement extends to student subgroups that pose unique learning challenges. For example, Johnson and Johnson (1985) examined 6th-grade students with disabilities who studied a controversial issue using materials with pro and con viewpoints and then participated in debate in the classroom environment. The special education students who debated were more likely to verbally rehearse the material and to actively search for more information about their study topics.

In short, debate fosters cognitive engagement by teaching critical think-ing to students and providing a challenging learning environment to test those skills in practice. Regardless of academic risk indicators, debate teaches students transferable skill sets useful in the new learning circumstances that students will encounter in their futures. Through its contributions to emo-tional, behavioral, and cognitive engagement, debate produces higher levels of academic achievement, which serves as the focus in the next section.

Debate and Academic Outcomes

The largest and most robust studies of debate's impact on academic achieve-ment examine urban debate leagues (UDL) or UDL participants. Urban debate leagues are after-school, extracurricular debate programs in over 20 cit-ies nationwide that provide public-school students opportunities to compete against their district peers. Each league offers six to eight monthly interscholas-tic tournament competitions throughout the academic year. Each tournament offers students three to four rounds of debate. While the extracurricular expe-rience of the UDL is certainly distinct from traditional classrooms or online courses, it nevertheless provides convincing evidence of the value of repeated, sustained debate exposure for augmenting learning.

One clear, consistent outcome of debate participation is that students improve their reading ability. Over a three-year period, Winkler (2009) exam-ined the progress made by students who were reading below grade level when they entered the Milwaukee Debate League. Using the Gray Oral Reading Test, Winkler compared each league participant's annual progress level on reading rate, accuracy, fluency, and comprehension with the national norms for annual progress on those measures by students at the same grade level. While attending a failing school district under the No Child Left Behind guidelines, the Milwaukee students who debated exceeded national norms for annual progress in reading on all test measures. They surpassed national norms for annual progress in reading rate by nine months, in accuracy by two months, in fluency by eight months, and comprehension by eight months.

The largest UDL studies to date have focused on the experiences of Chicago high-school students. Briana Mezuk and her colleagues compared a data set of more than 9,000 high-school students who participated in the Chicago Debate League from 1997 to 2006 with their peers in the Chicago Public

School System. The first study (Mezuk, 2009) compared African American male debaters in the league with a random sample of school district students matched for age, grade level, race/ethnicity, sex, GPA, SAT test scores, and whether they completed high school. The study concluded:

> Students who participated in debate had higher 12th grade GPA, were more likely to graduate from high school, less likely to drop out of high school, and were more likely to be college ready in reading and English than those who did not debate.
>
> (p. 299)

The same study found that more exposure to debate increased the likelihood of students posting such positive academic outcomes.

The second Chicago study (Mezuk, Bondarenko, Smith, & Tucker, 2011) examined the impact of the policy debate program on all UDL participants. After using statistical methods to correct for missing data and self-selection into the league, the study concluded that "students who participated in the Chicago Debate League were more likely to graduate from high school, performed better on the ACT, and showed greater gains in cumulative GPA relative to similar comparison students" (p. 630). The stronger ACT performance applied across all content areas of the exam, with particularly robust results in reading and English.

The third Chicago study (Anderson & Mezuk, 2012) focused on debate's impact on "at-risk" school students, which the study defined as those with lower scores on 8th-grade standardized tests scores in reading and math, poverty status (i.e. free lunch eligible or neighborhood poverty based on concentration of poverty in census blocks), and enrollment in special education. The analysis compared debaters considered "at-risk" with a comparable matched group to discover the relationships between high-school graduation rates, performance on standardized tests, and debate. At-risk debaters were "3.1 times more likely to graduate from high school," (p. 1229) "nearly one third as likely to drop out of school," (p. 1229) and "scored significantly higher on all sections of the ACT" (p. 1229) than the matched comparison group of non-debaters. Further, both the quantity of participation and the level of competitive success had a significant association with the likelihood of graduation.

Debate research in Atlanta, by contrast, focused on middle-school participants. Winkler (2015) analyzed the impact of debate participation on more than 150 middle-school debaters from eleven metro-area schools. The Atlanta study compared debaters with a matched group of their peers with similar demographic, family, academic risk, and school records who did not attend debate tournaments. The standardized test scores of tournament debaters in math were higher by 4.5 points, in social studies by 10.5 points, in science by 2 points, and in reading by less than 1 point in comparison to the students who did not compete in interscholastic tournaments.

Finally, an unpublished study of middle- and high-school students who participated in the Boston Debate League from 2008 to 2012 (Winkler & Fortner, 2015) also reported that debate participation had a positive impact on academic outcomes. The study revealed that debaters significantly improved their student growth percentile scores in English/Language Arts, their overall academic GPAs, their subject area GPAs in English/Language Arts and Social Science, and their number of AP exams in comparison to a similarly matched group of non-debate peers. Each of those significant findings held for debaters who were black and Hispanic, as well as for those qualifying for special education status.

Concluding Thoughts

On the whole, students who debate tend to increase their level of student engagement in school. Emotionally, they tend to become more interested, more active, and more willing to interact with peers and teachers alike. Behaviorally, they tend to develop more respect for themselves and others, and are more likely to attend school, arrive on time, and be less disruptive. Cognitively, they tend to improve their critical thinking skills in ways that position them to participate in more challenging learning activities. Unsurprisingly, when students become more engaged in school, they often experience improvements in their academic outcomes. Students who do debate improve their reading levels, subject area GPAs, and standardized test-taking more than similar groups of their non-debate peers at the middle- and high-school levels. They also show strengthened graduation outcomes and reduced dropout rates. Participating students, teachers, and academic records of student progress all agree that debate enhances student learning in ways that transcend course subject matter, instructional delivery methods, student subgroups, student grade levels, and school locations. The documented educational promise of debate leaves little doubt that schools should urgently expand the pedagogical approach in both their classrooms and their after-school programs to enhance the quality of the future lives of the nation's children.

References

Allen, M., Berkowitz, S., Hunt, S., & Louden, A. (1999). A meta-analysis of the impact of forensics and communication education on critical thinking. *Communication Education*, 48(1), 18–30.

Anderson, S., & Mezuk, B. (2012). Participating in a policy debate program and academic achievement among at-risk adolescents in an urban public school district: 1997–2007. *Journal of Adolescence*, 35(5), 1225–1235.

Appleton, J. J., Christenson, S. L., & Furlong, M. J. (2008). Student engagement with school: Critical conceptual and methodological issues of the construct. *Psychology in the Schools*, 45, 369–386.

Appleton, J. J., Christenson, S. L., & Reschly, A. L. (2006). Measuring cognitive and psychological engagement: Validation of the Student Engagement Instrument. *Journal of School Psychology*, 44(5), 427–445.

Belanger, A., & Stein, S. (2013). Closing the academic divide through debate. *Communities and Banking, 24*(2), 16–19.

Bridgeland, J. M., DiIulio, J. J., & Morison, K. B. (2006). *The Silent Epidemic: Perspectives of High School Dropouts*. Report for the Bill and Melinda Gates Foundation. Retrieved from http://files.eric.ed.gov/fulltext/ED513444.pdf.

Bureau of Labor Statistics. (2015). Earnings and unemployment rates by educational attainment. Retrieved from http://www.bls.gov/emp/ep_chart_001.htm.

Chamberlain, K., & Burroughs, S. (1985). Techniques for teaching critical reading. *Teaching of Psychology, 12*(4), 213–215.

Chandler, R. C., & Hobbs, J. D. (1991). The benefits of intercollegiate policy debate training to various professions. *Argument in Controversy: NCA/AFA Proceedings of the Alta Argumentation Conference* (pp. 388–390). Annandale, VA: National Communication Association.

Christle, C. A., Jolivette, K., & Nelson, C. M. (2007). School characteristics related to high school dropout rates. *Remedial and Special Education, 28*(56), 325–339.

Colbert, K. (1993). The effects of debate participation on argumentativeness and verbal aggression. *Communication Education, 42,* 206–214.

Doody, O., & Condon, M. (2012). Increasing student involvement and learning through using debate as an assessment. *Nurse Education in Practice, 12*(4), 232–237.

Dumas, J. E., Blechman, E. A., & Prinz, R. J. (1994). Aggressive children and effective communication. *Aggressive Behavior, 20,* 347–358.

Dynarski, M., Clarke, L., Cobb, B., Finn, J., Rumberger, R., & Smink, J. (2008). *Drop Out Prevention* (NCEE 2008–4025). U.S. Department of Education, Institute for Education Sciences: Washington, DC.

Finn, J. D. (1993). *School Engagement and Students at Risk*. Washington, DC: National Center for Education Statistics.

Finn, J. D., & Rock, D. A. (1997). Academic success among students at risk for school failure. *Journal of Applied Psychology, 82,* 221–234.

Firmin, M. W., Vaughn, A., & Dye, A. (2007). Using debate to maximize learning potential: A case study. *Journal of College Teaching and Learning, 4*(1),19–32.

Fredricks, J. A., Blumenfeld, P. C., & Paris, A. H. (2004). School engagement: Potential of the concept, state of the evidence. *Review of Educational Research, 74*(1), 59–109.

Gervey, R., Drout, M. O., & Wahn, C. (2009). Debate in the classroom: An evaluation of a critical thinking teaching technique within a rehabilitation counseling course. *Rehabilitative Education, 23*(1), 61–74.

Goodwin, J. (2003). Students' perspectives on debate exercises in content area classes. *Communication Education, 52*(2), 157–163.

Green, C. S., & King, H. (1990). Teaching critical thinking and writing through debates: An experimental evaluation. *Teaching Sociology, 18*(4), 462–471.

Healey, R. L. (2012). The power of debate: Reflections on the potential of debates for engaging students in critical thinking across controversial geographical topics. *Journal of Geography in Higher Education, 36*(2), 239–257.

Johnson, D. W., & Johnson, R. (1985). Classroom conflict: Controversy versus debate in learning groups. *American Educational Research Journal, 22*(2), 237–256.

Kennedy, R. (2007). In-class debates: Fertile ground for active learning and the cultivation of critical thinking and oral communication skills. *International Journal of Teaching and Learning in Higher Education, 19*(2), 183–190.

Kennedy, R. (2009). The power of in-class debates. *Active Learning in Higher Education*, 10(3), 225–236.

King, R. B., & McInerney, D. M. (2014). The work avoidance goal construct: Examining its structure, antecedents, and consequences. *Contemporary Educational Psychology*, 39, 42–58.

Kuhn, D., & Pease, M. (2008). What needs to develop in the development of inquiry skills. *Cognition and Instruction*, 26(4), 512–559.

Littlefield, R. S. (2001). High school student perceptions of the efficacy of debate participation. *Argumentation and Advocacy*, 38(2), 83–97.

Martin, E., Tobin, T. J., & Sugai, G. M. (2002). Current information on dropout prevention: Ideas from practitioners and the literature. *Preventing School Failure*, 47(1), 10–18.

Mezuk, B. (2009). Urban debate and high school educational outcomes for African American males. *The Journal of Negro Education*, 78(3), 290–304.

Mezuk, B., Bondarenko, I., Smith, S., & Tucker, E. (2011). Impact of participating in a policy debate program on academic achievement: Evidence from the Chicago Urban Debate League. *Educational Research and Reviews*, 6(9), 622–632.

National Center for Educational Statistics (2015). Fast facts. Retrieved from https://nces.ed.gov/fastfacts/display.asp?id=16.

Nedeljković, D. V. (2014). Debates as a distance learning tool. In I. Roclean (Ed.). *Let's Build the Future Through Learning Innovation: The 10th International Scientific Conference: eLearning and Software for Education*, Vol. 1 (pp. 502–508). Bucharest: Editura Universitatii Nationale de Aparare.

Nyatanga, L., & Howard, C. (2015). Using dialectic debates to enhance innovative teaching of conceptual and historical issues in psychology. *History and Philosophy of Psychology*, 16(1), 27–35.

Omelicheva, M. Y. (2007). Resolved: Academic debate should be a part of political science curricula. *Journal of Political Science Education*, 3(2), 161–175.

Omelicheva, M. Y., & Avdeyeva, O. (2008). Teaching with lecture or debate? Testing the effectiveness of traditional versus active learning methods of instruction. *PS Political Science & Politics*, 41(3), 603–607.

Park, C., Kier, C., & Jugdev, K. (2011). Debate as a teaching strategy in online education: A case study. *Canadian Journal of Learning and Technology*, 37(3), 1–17.

Peace, A. G. (2011). Using debates to teach information ethics. *Journal of Information Science Education*, 22(3), 233–237.

Roucan-Kane, M., Wolfskill, L. A., & Beverly, M. M. (2013). Debates as a pedagogical tool in agribusiness and animal science courses: Various perspectives at the undergraduate and graduate levels. *NACTA Journal*, 57(4), 18–23.

Roy, A., & Macchiette, B. (2005). Debating the issues: A tool for augmenting critical thinking skills of marketing students. *Journal of Marketing Education*, 27(3), 264–277.

Seifert, T. L., & O'Keefe, B. A. (2001). The relationship of work avoidance and learning goals to perceived competence, externality, and meaning. *British Journal of Educational Psychology*, 71, 81–92.

Skinner, E. A., Kindermann, T. A., & Furrer, C. J. (2009). A motivational perspective on engagement and disaffection: Conceptualization and assessment of children's behavioral and emotional participation in academic activities in the classroom. *Educational and Psychological Measurement*, 69, 493–525.

Snider, A., & Schnurer, M. (2006). *Many Sides: Debate Across the Curriculum*. New York: International Debate Education Association.

Storm, R. E., & Boster, F. J. (2007). Dropping out of high school: A meta-analysis assessing the effect of messages in the home and in school. *Communication Education*, 54(4), 433–452.

Tremblay, R. E., & LeMarquand, D. (2001). Individual risk and protective factors. In R. Loeber & D. P. Farrington (Eds.), *Child Delinquents: Development, Instrumentation, and Service Means* (pp. 137–164). Thousand Oaks: Sage.

Vaughn, M. G., Wexler, J., Beaver, K. M., Perron, B. E., Roberts, G., & Qiang, F. (2011). Psychiatric Correlates of Behavioral Indicators of School Disengagement in the United States. *Psychiatric Quarterly*, 82(3), 191–206.

Warner, E., & Bruschke, J. (2001). "Gone on debating": Competitive academic debate as a tool of empowerment. *Contemporary Argumentation and Debate*, 22, 1–21.

Wasserman, G. A., Keenan, K., Tremblay, R. E., Coie, J. D., Herrenkohl, T. I., Loeber, R., & Petechuk, D. (2003, April). *Risk and Protective Factors of Child Delinquency*. Washington D. C.: U.S. Department of Justice, Office of Justice Programs, Office of Juvenile Justice and Delinquency Prevention. Retrieved January 24, 2009 from http://ojjdp.ncjrs.org.

Winkler, C. (2009). The impact of policy debate on inner-city schools: The Milwaukee experience. In D. Gouran (Ed.). *The Functions of Argument and Social Context* (pp. 565–571). Annandale, VA: National Communication Association.

Winkler, C. (2011). To argue or fight: Improving at-risk students' school conduct through urban debate. *Controversia: The Journal of Debate And Democratic Renewal*, 7(2), 76–90.

Winkler, C. (2015). Challenging communities: A perspective by, from, and about argumentation. In C. H. Palczewski (Ed.), *Disturbing Argument: Selected Works from the 18th NCA/AFA Alta Conference on Argumentation* (pp. 4–17). New York: Routledge.

Winkler, C., & Fortner, C. K. (2014). Boston Debate League Results: 2008–2012. Unpublished report.

Winkler, C., Fortner, C. K., & Baugh-Harris, S. (2013). Overcoming educational challenges to women living in at-risk communities through urban debate. *Forum on Public Policy*, 2013 (1). Retrieved from http://forumonpublicpolicy.com/vol2013/no1/vol2013archive/winkler.pdf.

Ziegelmueller, G. W. (1998). The Detroit experience. *Contemporary Argumentation and Debate*, 19, 85–88.

Zorwick, M. L. W., Wade, M. M., & Heilmayr, D. P. (2009). Urban debate and prejudice reduction: The contact hypothesis in action. *Contemporary Argumentation and Debate*, 30, 31–51.

7 Using Debate to Improve Scientific Reasoning

Freddi-Jo Eisenberg Bruschke

Scientists are generally suspicious of public science debates – and with good reason. Often, when people without a science background proffer arguments about scientific concepts, ideas that science has discarded, or even found ridiculous, suddenly have the same weight as the most rigorously studied and vetted scientific truths.

Historically, lay debate of basic scientific concepts has resulted in agonizingly frustrating rejections of such basic tenets as the Theory of Evolution, the Big Bang, the age of the universe/Earth, and even Plate Tectonics (Funk & Rainie, 2015). Clarence Darrow and William Jennings Bryan famously argued the merits of evolution in 1925 (State of Tennessee v. John Thomas Scopes, a.k.a. the Scopes Monkey Trial) and science "lost" despite nearly complete support of evolution by scientists. Ninety years later, Bill Nye and Ken Ham publicly debated the same topic (among other things), and there are still enough people who do not accept the overwhelming evidence for the Theory of Evolution that some states do not teach it as an essential paradigm of biology but as one idea among others (Berkman & Plutzer, 2015). Currently, standards in Texas, Louisiana, Tennessee, Florida, Indiana, Ohio, Arizona, Arkansas, Utah, and others allow the teaching of creationism in public schools (Kirk, 2014). Those of us who teach basic science battle a stream of entrenched student misconceptions, many of which are rooted in abysmal lay interpretation of science and the pseudoscience of intelligent design and the Heartland Institute (Blast, 2013). Echoing the thoughts of many scientists, the National Center for Science Education said of the Nye/Ham debate, "Debate is a tool for showing who's a better orator, not necessarily who's right" (Chowdhury, 2014).

Concluding that debate lends legitimacy to bad and false science is understandable. Debate of a topic naturally implies controversy – two sides, each with valid points. Except there aren't two valid sides in basic scientific Theories; any controversy about the topics is usually long past. Those areas in science that are still without a consensus (euphemistically called an area of "active research") generally require a level of scientific understanding far beyond the basic lay levels. Every beginning science class devotes significant time to explaining how scientists go about doing science, "The Scientific

Method," struggling to put a fine point on why a scientific Theory is not just an idea that someone had. As a scientist and science teacher, the idea of introducing my students to the notion that they can debate the validity of scientific knowledge seems as if that boulder I've been pushing up the hill has just rolled back down despite my best efforts.

Given these concerns, why actually invite debate into the science class-room and potentially reinforce or even open the door to new misconceptions? We don't want students coming out of a debate experience thinking intelligent design is valid or that the Sun revolves around the Earth – which, according to the latest General Social Survey from the National Opinion Research Center, 25% of Americans believe (Science and Engineering Indicators, 2014). Won't classroom debate just make our job harder?

In this chapter, I endeavor to convince you that debate can be a very useful tool in teaching science, despite the misgivings already outlined. Concerns about introducing false controversy are valid, but they can be addressed through careful implementation of debate exercises. The creation of false scientific controversy, not the use of debate, is the underlying problem with many lay science debates. By understanding the nature of formal evidence-based debate and how debate complements the study of science, teachers can take advantage of debate as a useful tool for motivating and applying scientific learning while sidestepping the pitfalls of misconceptions.

Anecdotally, people without a debate background imagine that "arguing" involves any assertion, the ability to use any quality of evidence, and style over substance. Witnessing what passes as debate in the political arena and Congress, it is easy to understand this interpretation. Debate as advocated by this book is more structured and critical, involving a rational progression of ideas supported by evidence that is rigorously evaluated. In other words, not all evidence is treated equally and not all assertions are appropriate topics of debate. In this light, it is easy to see a parallel between evidence-based debate and scientific thinking, both grounded in applying critical thinking to answer a question. For a scientist, I imagine that the difference between evidence-based debate and the common expectations of debate is similar to the distinction between the colloquial use of the word "theory" and what scientists mean by the same word. In other words, the two things are extremely different.

Other chapters of this book delve into the details of debate theory and practice; here I will instead address the unique relationship of debate to sci-ence education. I will discuss some reasons behind the generation of false scientific controversy and how to avoid it when structuring a classroom debate. I then describe the relationship between debate and scientific think-ing, specifically between debate and the scientific method. Next, I examine debate as a natural tool to assist implementing science education aligned with the Next Generation Science Standards (NGSS). The NGSS are sci-ence and engineering content and performance standards developed in 2013 by a team of science educators representing 26 states. Although they are not part of the Common Core State Standards and were developed separately, the NGSS do connect to the ELA/literacy and mathematics standards of the Common Core, as each performance standard is mapped to the relevant portions of the Common Core. As the NGSS are performance-based, they describe not only delivery of specific science content, but also development of a set of scientific practices and larger scale cross-cutting concepts. Debate as a classroom activity can be an excellent method of addressing some of these practices. In the final portion of this chapter, I will make suggestions for implementing debate in a science classroom and discuss how debate can both create better citizen scientists and help future scientists become better communicators.

Avoiding False Scientific Controversy in Debate

In and out of the classroom, scientists struggle to communicate degrees of scientific certainty, almost more than we struggle to explain complicated science. This is seen over and over in public surveys; for example the majority of Americans, 60%, believe that the scientific community is divided on the question of whether human activity is increasing global temperatures (Public Religion Research Institute, 2011). In fact, the scientific community is not divided on this question. Nearly all climate scientists recognize that human activity, specifically the burning of fossil fuels, is contributing to rises in global average temperatures. However, political and corporate interests easily perpetuate the myth of scientific controversy over the existence of human-accelerated climate change by misrepresenting data, cherry-picking, or simply inventing evidence. These areas of false scientific controversy are extremely sensitive in terms of potential for creating even more confusion through the presentation of multiple perspectives. In these cases, students enter the classroom already holding beliefs that may be contrary to the scientific evidence, or misconceptions based on what they might have heard in the popular media. It is much more difficult to displace these established incorrect ideas about science than it is to teach a topic entirely new to the students. If any aspect of a classroom debate seems to affirm a student's misconception, there is a high likelihood that the correct information will be overlooked. At the same time, these are the topics most in need of better science education and more understanding of the evidence.

The critical approach to topics of false controversy is to design a debate that introduces scientifically accepted evidence without leading students to poor (scientifically rejected) evidence from poor sources. For example, a student of mine explained in class that he had read an article in his critical thinking course that argued sunspot activity was responsible for global temperature trends. Assuming that the goal of the critical thinking instructor was to have students analyze and reject the bad science sunspot explanation, the lesson was a complete failure, as the student came away remembering the poor evidence as valid. Not only did this student leave his course with a serious scientific misconception, but he also proceeded to introduce his misconception to another classroom of students. Bad science has no role in a basic science classroom and is completely unnecessary for science debates. Imagine if instead the student had been asked to analyze the carbon dioxide generation of different activities or from different countries and to debate which was more justified/which should be reduced. The students would have learned about the science of global warming and debated something that in reality has no single clear answer.

To practitioners of competitive debate, this approach is recognizable as a policy or values debate – debate in which there is real room for controversy or grounds for argument. Debate topics should be carefully selected so that they generate really interesting questions. Certainly you could assign students to recreate a Galilean debate about whether the Sun or the Earth was the center of the universe to teach about the solar system, but why? One side has no real grounds for argument and is forced into using bad science, bad evidence, and poorly constructed arguments. Although they may be using historically accurate arguments, the risk is high that students come away from the experience without an appreciation of what was wrong with the archaic evidence and thinking. As an alternative topic, students could debate the wisdom of developing a program to mine ore from the asteroid belt – a topic that has generated some really interesting conversations in my classroom. Similar science is covered (the planets, orbits, gravitational effects, the structure of the solar system, perhaps even the mass of the Earth and closed versus open systems), but all sides have the benefit of being able to use good scientific evidence and make reasonable claims. This example demonstrates that debate in the classroom can be most successful when the lesson is careful to avoid introducing a false scientific controversy.

Understanding the underlying sources of false scientific controversies can help us as educators avoid exacerbating them in the classroom as well as provide hints on how to address them effectively. I argue that false scientific controversies are fed by poor scientific literacy, poor understanding of the vetting of scientific knowledge, lack of understanding of the nature of scientific knowledge and lack of faith in the way science develops and changes, poor understanding of how science knowledge is important to the lives of non-scientists, and poor communication of current scientific paradigms to the public.

By poor scientific literacy, I mean that the general public level of science education is poor and does not match general knowledge of other topics. Likely this is a result of the scant time spent studying science in K–12 education (as compared to English language skills, for example). Basic science knowledge by non-scientists is so minimal (and there are numerous polls to demonstrate this) as to hamper the public's ability to assess and often understand scientific concepts.

Another result of the general lack of familiarity with the scientific process is poor understanding of the vetting of scientific knowledge. In general, non-scientists are unaware of the rigor with which scientific ideas are assessed prior to publication, even in scientific media. By the time an idea is supported enough to become part of basic science instruction, let alone an actual scientific Theory, it undergoes a long process of peer review and attempted replication. Without an appreciation of this process, it is hard to understand why scientists consider some evidence better than others, and what we even mean by the term "peer review." To compare the quality of scientific evidence, and weed out that information that masquerades as science but isn't, an understanding of this process is necessary.

The general non-scientist population also demonstrates a lack of understanding of the nature of scientific knowledge and corresponding lack of faith in the way science develops and changes. Confidence in the "truth" of scientific ideas can be shaken by changes in scientific consensus when the evolving nature of scientific knowledge is not understood. For example, as scientists revise our understanding of natural carbon sources and sinks in the Earth, our models of global warming rates and processes change. A potential reaction to these changes, if one does not understand how science constantly makes small adjustments to incorporate new evidence, is to reject the science altogether as unreliable.

Another contributing factor to the ease with which false scientific controversies develop is poor understanding of how science knowledge is important to the lives of non-scientists. A lack of interest in learning science is tied to the sense that this is esoteric information and not relevant to the average person's daily life. A challenge of science education is engaging students, motivating them to study basic science. One way of providing this motivation is to tie these concepts to everyday life. For example, if someone is buying a house, it is very useful to understand what it means if the house is on the 20-year versus the 100-year floodplain before signing the mortgage papers.

Finally, poor communication of current scientific paradigms to the public creates opportunities for non-scientists to sow scientific controversy where none exists. The scientific community recognizes a general problem with how poorly scientists communicate our research to non-scientists. With the expectation that some students in the basic science classroom will one day be scientists themselves, classroom debate is training for their future science communication. It is important to note that science, as a general area of study, is more prone to false controversy than other subjects, as most non-scientists lack the tools to evaluate science – a result of minimal science education.

Not only can classroom debates be designed to avoid the trap of debating a false scientific controversy, but debate as a learning activity can address the factors contributing to false controversies in the first place. By critically analyzing the source and content of scientific evidence through debate, students learn about the process of science knowledge creation. For example, students can develop an understanding that results published in the journal *Science* are of higher scientific quality than a blog post – even on a science website. By debating policies or science applications (otherwise known as engineering) students see precise points at which science intersects the average person's daily life. In sum, good topic selection can create a debate with high-quality scientific evidence and arguments available to both sides, which is the key to avoiding perpetuation of false science in classroom debate.

Debate as a Parallel to the Scientific Method

Every science course through the introductory college level begins with a lesson on the scientific method. We spend time on this abstract topic to differentiate how science practice is different from other methods of knowing. The expectation is not that most, or even any, of these students will become scientists, but that they will need to understand how scientific arguments are constructed so they can evaluate scientific information, especially as compared to non-science. We want to convey why the information that is the end result of the scientific process should be viewed as exceptionally reliable. In the classroom, however, this can translate into students who are able to repeat back that a hypothesis is an "educated guess" but who cannot actually form a hypothesis. Inquiry-based and science-as-argument lessons are methods meant to guide students through the scientific thinking process. Inquiry-based science, depending on the level of structure, models the scientific process in more accessible pieces. It also affords students an opportunity to conduct hands-on science, which carries many advantages beyond learning scientific thinking. A structured inquiry lesson walks students through an experiment step by step after providing them with a hypothesis and asks them to record and analyze the results. Guided and open inquiry lessons provide increasing degrees of control to the students in terms of hypothesis selection and experimental design. Scientific argumentation is tied to inquiry and differentiated from "conventional argumentation" as a set of critical thinking practices that follows a set of rules (Llewellyn, 2013). In a way the argumentation-driven lesson follows what scientists do after conducting experiments, writing up results for publication and engaging other scientists in the field in review of their ideas (Sampson, Grooms, & Walker, 2009). The debate format provides a structure, as well as motivation, for constructing scientific arguments.

It is easy to find direct parallels between the scientific method and the development of an evidence-based argument, as would be done in preparation for a classroom debate.

Table 7.1   Scientific Method and Debate Parallels

Scientific Method	Debate/Debate Preparation
Make primary observations	Broadly research the topic
Formulate and evaluate questions based on observations	Identify important questions and sub-topics
Formulate a hypothesis to answer/ explain a question	Develop a claim/primary argument
Conduct experiment to collect evidence in support of hypothesis	Select evidence to support positions
Analyze results of experiment	Evaluate evidence based on content and source

Generally, we model the scientific method in class with structured or guided inquiries in which students conduct experiments to validate hypotheses. Classroom debate provides another methodology for students to address a given topic. Further, the structure of the debate itself mirrors the scientific process we would like them to understand: specifically, the difference between assertions or anecdotal information and rigorously developed and vetted evidence.

At this point, both science practice and the debate continue by bringing the evidence and ideas to a more public arena. We could continue to draw parallels, for example, between the peer-review process in science and developing rebuttal arguments in debate or in the response from the scientific community upon publication and the judging of the debate, but the general idea of the use of evidence and rigorous evaluation remains the same. Where debate and science practice diverge significantly is in how the results are evaluated, or in case of a debate, judged.

Ideally, although this does not always play out this way in a classroom where fellow students are judges, the judge of a debate round will determine which arguments are the best supported by the evidence, which arguments are the most compelling, and which evidence is better or worse. The debate by necessity has two sides that must present some opposing ideas and, after it has ended, one of the sides is declared better than the other. In scientific thinking, on the other hand, hypotheses are evaluated using principles of falsifiability (Popper, 1959). Thus a hypothesis is false (actually not true) if any reliable counter-example or contrary piece of evidence can be found. The classic example of falsifiability is the Black Swan problem. In a debate, it is conceivable that one could win the argument that "swans are white" because the evidence supports that it is mostly and for all practical purposes true. The scientific hypothesis "swans are white" would be rejected, however, once someone traveled to Australia and found that there are some swans that are black. A new hypothesis would have to be formulated that explained both all the white swans and the newly discovered black swans in order to make a scientifically valid argument.

Hesitation about combining science with debate could be based on misunderstanding the nature of formal evidence-based debate. Debate is not an avenue for students to make wild assertions or get overly emotional; it does not create a situation where style can triumph over content. Rather, debate in a science classroom offers students good practice in evaluating evidence and determining how evidence can support a hypothesis/claim that complements what we teach about conducting science.

The truth is that the science taught at basic levels has already been debated – and definitive decisions have already been made. True debate within science occurs at the edges of fields where usually only the few select people completely immersed in the topic can compete. There are a lot of dues to be paid before one can competently jump into a scientific argument. As I will discuss later in this chapter, these difficulties can be avoided by thoughtful topic selection. If you ask students to debate whether or not the Earth is the center of the Universe, you should be prepared to hear some poor evidence/bad science with the corresponding risk that some student will remember the false information as true. If you instead invite a debate on whether NASA and the European Space Agency should focus investiga- tions on other solar systems or our own, you avoid the introduction of poor arguments (hopefully) and perpetuation of misconceptions. There are even a few current scientific controversies that are probably accessible to a basic science audience. For example, in October 2015, the United States Geologic Survey (USGS) and NASA's Jet Propulsion Laboratory had a rather public disagreement about earthquake risks in southern California, which prompted news headlines like, "USGS slams study's claim of 99.9% chance of large LA earthquake" (Lin, 2015) and "USGS Refutes NASA Earthquake Prediction" (Orwig, 2015). This would be a challenging topic for a classroom debate, but it could explore some of the differences in the USGS versus the NASA earthquake probability models and most definitely allow for exploration of the mechanisms of earthquakes and what tools we have to make predictions. The public nature of the disagreement and the uncertainty in the science itself could make this a motivating and exciting topic for classroom debate.

Debate as a Tool to Teach Scientific Practice

In addition to mirroring much of the scientific process, debate can be used to introduce specific scientific practices and cross-cutting concepts that are part of recent changes in science education. The National Research Council's (NRC) Framework for K–12 Science Education/Next Generation Science Standards identifies seven science and engineering practices to be taught in the science classroom (NRC, 2011):

1   Asking questions (for science) and defining problems (for engineering);
2   Developing and using models;
3   Planning and carrying out investigations;
4   Analyzing and interpreting data;
5   Using mathematics and computational thinking;
6   Constructing explanations (for science) and designing solutions (for engineering);
7   Engaging in argument from evidence;
8   Obtaining, evaluating, and communicating information.

Of these, the newest to appear in a science classroom are likely the last three; for each of these debate makes an excellent vehicle for addressing the prac- tices. By definition debate is "engaging in argument from evidence" (practice 7 above) and also is fulfilling the directive to communicate scientific information. Construction of arguments in preparation for a classroom debate addresses the practices about asking questions, constructing explanations, and analyzing data. The specific goals identified by the NRC to be reached by the end of 12th grade for constructing explanations include: using primary and secondary scientific evidence to support or refute an explanation, identifying gaps in explanatory accounts, constructing explanations using knowledge of scientific theory, and being able to offer informal explanations of the science. For practice 7, engaging in argument from evidence, the specific goals are even more relevant to debate: showing how data support a claim, identifying weaknesses in scientific arguments, identifying flaws in their own arguments, recognizing the parts of an argument, and reading media accounts critically. The counter-argument and rebuttal structure of formal debate uniquely provide an opportunity to both analyze flaws in others' arguments as well as one's own. In order to meet the requirements of these practices, science learning must move beyond experiments and lab reports. Although there are other options for teaching the communication and application practices identified above (e.g., traditional research papers, presentations, role playing), debate provides students with additional motivation; competition and the public nature of the debate can often result in a more serious student effort and more excitement about the class assignment.

Perhaps the biggest advantage of using debate as a science classroom activity is the ability to meet the requirements for engineering applications. Debate is an excellent method of introducing engineering options that are related to science content by a proposed public policy. For example, the Bay Delta Project in northern California is being designed to move water from the Sacramento River under the delta area to help protect the waterways and the water supply, some of which are one or two very large tunnels (California Natural Resources Agency, 2015). The various iterations of the project design, or a new student design, could be used at the topic of a classroom debate about how to address the environmental risks and current problems in the area. In the course of this debate, the students would not only need to include science from a wide variety of disciplines (there are fish population problems, river sediment transport problems, salinization of the water supply, flooding issues, etc.), but would also evaluate engineering applications to solve the problems. Engineering and Technology represents one of the four main content areas of the Next Generation Science Standards (the others are Life Science, Physical Science, and Earth Science), and in most science classrooms, engineering content has not previously been included in the curriculum. Fortunately, debate provides an avenue to approach the engineering issues related to classroom science topics.

These sorts of engineering or policy-related debates effectively simulate the ways in which citizens need to evaluate political proposals and even need to make personal decisions like whether to buy foods that contain genetically modified organisms – essentially what the NGSS Framework proposes a "critical consumer" should know. As the standards place an emphasis on practice, even over additional content, activities like debate that hone students skills in areas of scientific practice are more and more valuable.

Implementing Science Debate

The key to a successful science classroom debate is in good topic selection. Guidance on the format, structure, and general implementation of classroom debate including evidence evaluation and construction of arguments is readily available from other sources (St. John, 2013). These general discussions are certainly applicable to a science debate with the exception of what sort of evidence is introduced in the classroom. In order to ensure that bad science, pseudoscience, and not-at-all science remain outside the classroom, debate topics must be chosen to ensure that each side has a scientifically supportable position. Debate on any topic must have common ground on which the two sides can meet. In the science classroom, the choice of ground is even more important and will determine the success of the exercise from a science education perspective. A defensible position and valid scientific evidence must be available to both sides. This is why a debate on whether global temperatures are increasing may not be appropriate in a classroom and may in fact be educationally dangerous. As educators and scientists, we do not want to put students in the position of using bad evidence, and only bad evidence, to construct an argument, nor do we wish to introduce or reinforce misconceptions.

One way to insure the development of good scientific arguments is to control the sources of information available to the students as evidence. This is often useful pedagogically in any case, as limiting the options for evidence prevents the students from becoming overwhelmed. In all cases, an emphasis on evaluating the evidence in terms of scientific practice (not only source credibility and relevance) will both advance scientific understanding and ensure that debates remain within the arena of science. For example, the previously mentioned disagreement between two extremely reputable scientific research organizations, NASA and the USGS, about the likelihood of a large earthquake occurring in southern California affords a chance to explore why their predictions are different. What makes one model potentially better than the other? How are the assumptions each group made different? What was the intended use of the information for each group? What is the level of scientific certainty/confidence level of each estimate? Assessment of the science practices should be brought into the evidence evaluation part of argument construction along with the more traditional criteria.

Another way to ensure equally defensible sides when selecting a debate topic is to avoid anything that questions established scientific facts or Theories. For similar reasons, re-creations of historic debates should also be avoided. Instead, debate can focus on how we use our understanding of the natural world to better our stewardship and interaction with the world around us. In other words, debate can focus on science policy and engineering solutions to societal problems that involve our natural world. Potential areas that offer nearly limitless topics are allocation of resources as they relate to science policy, science research and engineering solutions to recognized problems like environmental contamination, and human impacts on other species and global climate. Some current controversial issues can also make good topics. The practice of hydraulic fracturing, injecting fluids and sand under extreme pressure into subsurface shale to release hydrocarbons, is politically charged and, scientifically, both sides have plenty of solid ground from which to argue. This is likely because the basic question of whether we as a society should condone "fracking" is a policy question about the value of resources (the classic fossil fuels versus environment debate). Science topics that would be covered in such a debate include at the very least chemistry (dissolution of oil and gasses by the fracking fluid, release of methane), geology (human-induced seismic events from injection of waste fluids), environmental science (fate and transport of contaminants from the waste fluids and effects on the ecosystem), and hydrology (seepage of surface wastewater into aquifers).

As a final note on implementation, it may be worthwhile to draw the distinction between what is required as "proof" in a debate versus in scientific argumentation. As discussed earlier, science is based on falsifiability. Therefore a proven scientific hypothesis must have no counter-examples or unexplained evidence. In a debate, the standard is less strict as students need only argue that their conclusions are more likely. This is another opportunity to clarify the scientific process and identify the nature of scientific knowledge.

Debate as a Powerful Science Teaching Tool

New science standards and parallels with the scientific method aside, the science education received by most citizens in the United States does not provide students with an understanding of basic science concepts that are critical for making informed personal and political decisions. The motivation in reforming and reshaping science standards is to improve the quality of science education in our schools from kindergarten through college. Debate can be an excellent tool to deliver science education. Oral presentations and developing arguments on topics require a deeper understanding than, for example, answering a test question. Further, classroom debate can provide powerful motivation to students to tackle topics, like science, with which they are not entirely comfortable by providing a context more closely related to their experiences. For students in basic and general education science courses, this extra motivation can make an enormous difference in terms of depth of knowledge gained. Debates are a mechanism to relate science concepts to issues that affect everyone, scientists and non-scientist alike, such as what we are willing to do to protect our natural environment or what types of hazards we potentially create in altering the world around us. To use another geology-related example (as I am a geoscientist, these are my go-to), through debate one could relate concepts of slope stability/landslides to construction and development in hilly areas. Debating the trade-offs of such development – housing or new roads versus oversteepening a hillslope – highlights what we consider acceptable costs and risks of how we live in the world. The science content has to do with stable angles of different earth materials, the forces at work on those materials, and the effects of adding or removing stress and/or altering the stresses by adding water. The debate can involve evaluating the acceptable potential risks as well as the costs and effectiveness of the types of things we do to mitigate landslides.

For the future scientists in the classroom, oral presentation skills and the ability to communicate technical information effectively to a general audience are also critical. Attend any general field scientific conference and you will find sessions on effectively communicating research to the public. The key to better science communication is providing instruction and practice in oral presentation to scientists every step of the way in their training. Classroom debate provides this communication experience to future scientists, motivates those not destined for a career in the sciences, and adds the depth of science-based policy to any science classroom.

References

California Natural Resources Agency, State of California. (2015). *Bay Delta Conservation Plan*. Retrieved from http://baydeltaconservationplan.com.

Berkman, M., & Plutzer, E. (2015). Enablers of doubt: How future teachers learn to negotiate the evolution wars in their classrooms. *Annals of the American Academy of Political and Social Science*, 685(1), 253–270. DOI: 10.1177/0002716214557783.

Blast, J. (2013, October 14). IPCC exaggerates risk: an opposing view. *USA Today*. Retrieved from http://www.usatoday.com/story/opinion/2013/10/14/ipcc-climate-change-heartland-institute-editorials-debates/2983941/.

Chowdhury, S. (2014, February 5). Bill Nye versus Ken Ham: Who won? *The Christian Science Monitor*. Retrieved from http://www.csmonitor.com/Science/2014/0205/Bill-Nye-versus-Ken-Ham-Who-won-video.

Funk, C., & Rainie, L. (2015). *Public and scientists' view on science and society*. Retrieved from Pew Research Center website: http://pewinternet.org.

Kirk, C. (2014, January 26). Map: Publicly funded schools that are allowed to teach creationism. *Slate Science*. Retrieved from http://www.slate.com/articles/health_and_science/science/2014/01/creationism_in_public_schools_mapped_where_tax_money_supports_alternatives.html.

Lin, R-G. (2015, October 22). USGS slams study's claim of 99.9% chance of large LA earthquake. *Los Angeles Times*. Retrieved from http://www.latimes.com/local/lanow/la-me-ln-usgs-99-9-percent-chance-20151022-story.html.

Llewellyn, D. (2013). *Teaching High School Science Through Inquiry and Argumentation* (2nd ed.). Thousand Oaks, CA: SAGE Publications.

National Research Council. (2011). *A Framework for K–12 Science Education: Practices, Crosscutting Concepts, and Core Ideas*. Washington, DC: National Academies Press.

NGSS Lead States. (2013). *Next Generation Science Standards: For States, By States*. Washington, DC: The National Academies Press.

National Science Board, Science and Engineering Indicators 2014. (2014). *Science and Technology: Public Attitudes and Understanding*. Retrieved from http://www.nsf.gov/statistics/seind14/.

Orwig, J. (2015, Oct 22). A major scientific organization just refuted NASA's 99.9% prediction that an earthquake will hit LA before 2018. *Business Insider*. Retrieved from http://www.businessinsider.com/usgs-refutes-nasa-earthquake-prediction-2015-10.

Popper, K. (1959). *The Logic of Scientific Discovery*. New York: Basic Books.

Public Religion Research Institute. (2011). *Climate Change and Evolution in the 2012 Elections*. Retrieved from http://publicreligion.org/research/2011/09/climate-change-evolution-2012/#.VlVkKBiG2-c.

Sampson, V., Grooms, J., & Walker, J. (2009). Argument-driven inquiry: A way to promote learning during laboratory activities. *The Science Teacher*, 76(7), 42–47.

St. John, K. (2013). The need to teach about ethics and science, and the credibility of sources. *Journal of Geoscience Education*, 61(1), 1–2.

8 Critical Thinking through Debate
Skills, Dispositions, and Teaching Strategies

W. Patrick Wade

Ironically, much praise for critical thinking is rather uncritical. Critical thinking is often used as a buzzword for politicians or educational administrators to trumpet when describing their goals. Who could disagree, for example, with calls to promote critical problem solving to address the challenges of the 21st century? As teachers, we too are responsible for engaging in uncritical discussions of critical thinking. The phrase enters our teaching philosophy statements and our conversations with our peers, as we try to describe the pinnacle of thinking that we hope our students achieve. But still the concept remains vague and is often assessed intuitively: you know critical thinking when you see it. Too frequently, our discussions of critical thinking are unaccompanied by clear ideas about what critical thinking is, how it should be taught, or how it can be assessed, which makes it very difficult for us to know how our classroom practices can be adapted to encourage critical thought.

This chapter works from a clear, research-based understanding of critical thinking in order to explain how debate can be used in the classroom to promote specific critical thinking skills. A growing body of research already suggests that classroom and co-curricular debate develop such skills (e.g., Colbert, 1987; Garrett, Shoener, & Hood, 1996; Goodwin, 2003; Green & Klug, 1990; Kennedy, 2007; Roy & Macchiette, 2005; Snider & Schnurer, 2006). In a meta-analysis of previous research on the relationship between debate and critical thinking, Allen, Berkowitz, and Louden (1999) found that communication skills training in the form of a course on public speaking, a course on argumentation, or participation in co-curricular competitive debate or speech improved students' critical thinking skills, with the greatest gains for competitive debate or speech relative to the other kinds of communication instruction (see also Allen, Berkowitz, & Louden, 1995). Bellon's review (2000) of the literature examining debate across the curriculum draws insights from educational psychology to provide possible explanations for these critical thinking gains: debate adopts an interactive, student-centered approach to education that gives students ample opportunities to practice verbal and analytical skills.

In spite of this relationship between debate and critical thinking instruction, few studies linking debate and critical thinking have attempted to define critical thinking or engage the controversies in critical thinking research.

Most studies rely on a standardized critical thinking assessment, such as the Watson-Glaser Critical Thinking Appraisal (see the meta-analysis by Allen et al., 1999), and accept the implicit theory of critical thinking adopted by the test maker, without raising basic questions about the nature of critical thinking or the preferability of some measurement approaches over others (Ennis, 1993; Ku, 2009). The problem with not discussing the nature of critical thinking is that, in the absence of an engagement with this literature, it becomes difficult to pinpoint *what* about debate should be understood to produce critical thinking gains.

Knowing more about how debate improves critical thinking can help answer practical questions about how teachers should design debate activities. Should students participate as individuals or work together in teams? How much mentoring should students receive when developing their arguments? What kinds of topics are appropriate for classroom debate? How should students be *positioned* in debates – should they represent their own views, the views of issue stakeholders, or those of policy makers? Who should be responsible for judging debates? By exploring the literature on critical thinking, teachers can find answers to these questions and make better judgments about how to use debate in the classroom.

To demonstrate what teachers can learn from the critical thinking literature, this chapter is divided into two parts: definition and application. First, the chapter reviews the existing critical thinking literature to explain how researchers have defined critical thinking as well as to raise important questions about how critical thinking is best taught. The second part of this chapter applies past critical thinking research in order to explain how teachers can use classroom debate to promote critical thinking. Finally, the chapter suggests that, if education and communication researchers want to popularize debate across the curriculum, they should align their future research with findings in the critical thinking literature.

What Is Critical Thinking and How Should It Be Taught?

Academics, policymakers, business leaders, and civic advocates all recognize the importance of critical thinking. References to critical thinking appear in university vision and mission statements, department curricula, and individual courses across the arts, sciences, and professional programs. As a result of this widespread consensus on its value, critical thinking has become a significant educational goal at the secondary level as well – with Common Core State Standards offering only the most recent in a history of educational reforms aimed at making students better, more critical thinkers (Paul, 1993; Paul, 2005).

Because of critical thinking's significance as a major learning outcome at all levels, researchers have attempted to define critical thinking so that it can be taught, measured, and assessed. In the process, they have made a distinction between critical thinking *skills* and critical thinking *dispositions*. Skills are the mental processes central to critical thinking, such as evaluation, reflection, or synthesis, whereas dispositions are the character traits that encourage the use of the skills, such as inquisitiveness, reasonableness, or fair-mindedness (Ennis, 1996; Facione, Facione, Sanchez, & Gainen, 1995; Facione, 2000). Although the lists of skills and dispositions considered integral to critical thinking vary, a commonly cited definition of critical thinking developed by an interdisciplinary group of 46 scholars, the Delphi panel, provides an approachable definition with authority in a wide variety of disciplines that is often cited in contemporary studies (e.g., Abrami et al., 2008; Abrami et al., 2015; Berkowitz, 2006; Dwyer, Hogan, & Stewart, 2014; Lampert, 2007).

According to the Delphi panelists, critical thinking is "purposeful, self-regulatory judgment which results in interpretation, analysis, evaluation, and inference, as well as explanation of the . . . considerations upon which that judgment is based" (Facione, 1990, p. 6). In other words, critical thinking is the exercise of cognitive skills, such as analysis, inference, and explanation, which are employed in order to come to the best judgment possible given the available evidence. Critical thinking is "purposeful" in that it is applied in context in order to solve problems or support judgments about what we should do or believe (Ennis, 1993). Critical thinking is "self-regulatory" in that it involves reflection on one's own beliefs, such that they can be revised in light of new evidence.

However, critical thinking is not simply a set of thinking skills: it is also a set of character traits or dispositions (Ennis, 1996; Facione, 1990; Facione et al., 1995). According to this view, the ideal critical thinker should value reason and should strive to be well-informed regarding the matters under consideration. He or she should be open-minded and demonstrate a willingness to suspend personal beliefs so that reasons and evidence for opposing or different views can be evaluated without bias. Doing so requires that the critical thinker be capable of thinking from the perspective of another person and understand how his or her own background, social position, and life history have impacted his or her worldview. The ideal critical thinker should be inquisitive and curious – should be interested in finding solutions to practical or conceptual puzzles, and should take pleasure in discovery. Such joy of discovery should not be an end in itself, however, and so the ideal critical thinker should be skeptical by nature and take measure of new ideas presented for his or her consideration.

Although few students (or teachers, for that matter) can easily achieve and maintain such an ideal, the Delphi panelists urged that critical thinking instruction should keep such an ideal critical thinker in sight in order to encourage not just the development of critical thinking skills but the practical willingness for critical thinkers to put those skills into practice when the situation demands it. This early definition advocates for teaching that "combines developing critical thinking skills with nurturing those dispositions which consistently yield useful insights and which are the basis of a rational and democratic society" (Facione, 1990, p. 6).

Moving forward from the Delphi definition, educational researchers have asked a variety of questions about how these skills and dispositions can be taught. Should critical thinking skills be taught in the context of regular disciplinary courses (McPeck, 1981) or should they be treated as a general set of skills to be taught in standalone course (Siegel, 1985)? Although critical thinking skills can be measured through careful test design, how can one measure dispositions such as inquisitiveness or open-mindedness? Even if dispositions could be measured, for example via psychological inventories (Facione et al., 1995), how could such habitual character dispositions be encouraged in the classroom setting?

In the past decade, the critical thinking literature has turned to meta-analysis to begin to provide substantive answers to these questions about course design, instructional methods, and assessment. Such meta-analyses are useful because they synthesize the insights of a large number of studies in order to make judgments in light of the preponderance of evidence presented by scholars working in various fields. The meta-analyses conducted by Abrami et al. (2008; 2015) provide good evidence to suggest which *curricular designs* (following Ennis's categorizations of critical thinking instruction as general, mixed, infusion, or immersion; see Ennis, 1989) are most effective, as well as which specific *instructional strategies* have demonstrated their utility as vehicles for teaching critical thinking.

Abrami et al.'s (2008; 2015) findings are the most rigorous and far-reaching of the various meta-analyses and reviews of critical thinking to date (cf. Bangert-Drowns & Bankert, 1990; Halpern, 1993; Niu, Behar-Horenstein, & Garvan, 2013; Tsui, 2002), as they are the first quantitative assessments focusing exclusively on true experiments and going beyond the question of whether critical thinking can be taught to an investigation of which course designs and specific modes of classroom instruction appear most impactful. In their preliminary analysis, Abrami et al. (2008) found that student critical thinking could be improved as a result of course instruction. They further found that, of course types, *immersion*-based courses, in which critical thinking skills are modeled by the teacher but not explicitly discussed during instruction, were the least effective at producing critical thinking gains, suggesting that explicit instruction in critical thinking produces more robust gains. They also learned that *integrated* or *mixed* courses, which include critical thinking skills training as a component of instruction in a disciplinary course, did a better job of boosting students' critical thinking skills relative to *general* critical thinking courses that exclusively focus on critical thinking instruction.

In their follow-up study, Abrami et al. (2015) proceed from the Delphi panel's consensus definition of critical thinking, which they find to be "suitably broad" to be useful in querying the vast literature on critical thinking, and investigate the findings of various research projects (N = 684) measuring critical thinking gains resulting from classroom interventions. When analyzing this literature, they sought to know if critical thinking could be taught, what kinds of courses (if any) were most effective in producing critical thinking gains, which instructional strategies (if any) were commonly shared in courses that produced critical thinking gains, and which students benefited the most. The researchers identified four different instructional categories. present in varying degrees in various critical thinking interventions: *individual study, dialogue, authentic or anchored instruction*, and *mentoring* (Abrami et al., 2015, p. 15). Individual study refers to aspects of instruction in which students work on their own to develop critical thinking skills, without engagement with peers or teachers; dialogue refers to communication-based aspects of instruction; authentic or anchored instruction refers to teaching that places critical thinking skills in the context of "a well-defined real-world problem" (p.17); and mentoring refers to one-to-one engagement between the instructor and the student.

In examining these instructional techniques, they found that a combination of authentic or anchored instruction, dialogue, and mentorship were particularly productive of critical thinking gains, with opportunities for dialogue about authentic problems being the most impactful when combined. Among teaching techniques associated with dialogue, "teacher poses questions," "whole-class discussion led by the teacher," and "small-group discussion led by the teacher" created the largest effects on critical thinking favoring the experimental over the control group, and among teaching techniques associated with authentic or anchored instruction, "applied problem solving" and "role-playing" produced significant effects on critical thinking favoring the experimental group (p. 25). The recent meta-analysis did not find much support for debate developing critical thinking, but this is because there is not enough research on debate-style teaching practices that qualified for inclusion in Abrami et al.'s (2015) study. Debate advocates should adopt true experimental methods where possible in the future to ensure that debate's benefits can be included in future meta-analyses.

With that said, teachers can and should design debate activities for the classroom in ways that align with conclusions in the critical thinking literature. This can be done when teachers design debate activities in courses adopting *mixed* or *infusion* approaches and by relying on instruction methods where students are called to debate the issues surrounding authentic problems, take on the perspectives of established stakeholders, and are guided not just by their engagement with each other but also in the guiding presence of teachers. Suggestions for how this alignment can be accomplished are the subject of the following section.

Debate as Critical Thinking Pedagogy: Alignments With the Critical Thinking Literature

Through debate students learn critical thinking skills in class regardless of the subject; they can engage with authentic, real-world problems; and they participate in critical dialogues about the issues. By examining each benefit, we will discover not only that debate can be used to improve critical thinking skills but also how it can nurture critical thinking dispositions.

Debate as a Platform for Mixed or Infusion Approaches to Critical Thinking Instruction

Debate can be an effective platform for infusion or mixed approaches to teaching critical thinking because it provides a formal context for explicit instruction in a number of critical thinking skills as a supplement to more topical course content. Definitions of critical thinking shared by the Delphi panelists, philosophers, and psychologists all include argument construction, analysis, and evaluation (Dwyer, Hogan, & Stewart, 2014; Ennis, 1993; Facione, 1990; Halpern, 2014; Morrow & Weston, 2011). Including one or more classroom debates or debate-related activities within the curriculum of a subject course allows for the inclusion of readings, lectures, activities, and class discussion centered around debate theory and argumentation, including discussions of argument structure, argument patterns, argument analysis and evaluation, logical fallacies, and questioning strategies. These more abstract issues can be made specific through topical, course examples.

Take, for example, the "disadvantage," a common argument pattern in competitive policy debate. A disadvantage is an argument pattern that is made up of certain necessary parts: a reasoned claim as well as evidence that a problem is not happening now (termed the "uniqueness" of the disadvantage), a reasoned claim as well as evidence that the proposed course of action would cause the problem (termed the "link" of the disadvantage), and a reasoned claim as well as evidence that the disadvantage would create a large magnitude of harm (termed the "impact" of the disadvantage). A disadvantage of a policy proposal should be unique to that proposal, caused by that proposal, and sufficiently harmful to convince a judge to reject the proposal. As an argument form, the "disadvantage" is a generic pattern of reasoning that can be entertained any time a course of action is considered. But in practice, it can only be understood in relation to a specific policy proposal, such as a tax on carbon emissions or a rise in the minimum wage. And the severity of the disadvantage needs to be weighed against the possible advantages of the course of action, requiring further evaluation and ultimately judgment based on the merits and drawbacks of the course of action.

To engage in such complex forms of reasoning requires detailed knowledge of the issues surrounding the course of action, be they economic, political, ethical, technical, or otherwise specialized. And this is perhaps why mixed approaches or infusion approaches to critical thinking instruction are better than their counterparts (the general critical thinking skills course, on the one hand, and, on the other, the "immersion" of critical thinking into a course that doesn't otherwise discuss it explicitly): they give students an opportunity to present arguments in the context of ongoing debates about particular issues.

Although the above example derives from competitive, co-curricular debate, the infusion of critical thinking via debate can also be applied in the classroom setting. One way of doing so is by selecting course readings that either evaluate debates in the literature or conflict with one another directly. In one of my classes, I asked students to reconstruct the arguments made in a debate between two photography critics about whether a famous photograph, "The Valley of the Shadow of Death," was or was not manipulated by the photographer, Roger Fenton (Morris, 2011). The discussion included an introduction to a simplified version of the Toulmin model of argumentation (Toulmin, 2003; Booth, Colomb, & Williams, 2008), which introduced students to claims, reasons, warrants, and evidence. The class then worked together to map these various elements of argument through small-group and board work, with each group assigned to map a particular critic's view on the issue. In a later assignment in the same unit, students wrote a comparative paper in which they had to evaluate and come to a judgment in a similar debate between two different photography critics, Richard Whelan and Philip Knightley, about a different famous photograph, Robert Capa's "The Falling Soldier," by considering the relative strength and weakness of reasoning and evidence employed by both authors in the debate. Similar topical, argumentative writing courses have been shown to have improved students' argument analysis skills (Wade & See, 2014), as measured by the Halpern Critical Thinking Assessment (Halpern, 2013).

In both cases, presenting course content as conflicting by situating materials in the context of debate allowed students to gain explicit instruction in critical thinking skills and then apply that instruction to deepen their engagement with the readings. This stronger engagement with subject material through debate is supported by Jean Goodwin (2003), whose examination of student self-report data suggests that students believe they gained better knowledge of course content as a result of participation in debate and debate-related activities.

The infusion of critical thinking into subject courses via debate provides students with an opportunity to take on new roles and behaviors in the classroom setting, specifically allowing them to break away from the model of knowledge transmission through authoritative lecture, which encourages students to memorize rather than reflect on and engage with material presented during coursework. Teaching argument analysis and evaluation and asking that students apply these skills to course material (rather than take such material on the authority of the teacher or writer) encourages an appropriately skeptical and critical character disposition that may help students in their approach to materials that they might otherwise take for granted or hold in high esteem. Nurturing students to be reflective and skeptical is particularly important in modern communication environments so that students can practice critical media literacy. With the explosion of political, social, and advertising appeals across traditional mass media and new media, students need to be able to question what they see, hear, and read in order to hold it to ethical and logical standards (Kellner & Share, 2005; Wade, 2014).

Debate as a Platform for Authentic Instruction

A related advantage of debate emerges when one considers the authenticity of the topics that can be addressed. As Abrami et al. (2015) suggest, "whenever there is a well-defined real-world problem that the students are analyzing," authentic instruction is taking place. This suggests that real-world relevance be taken into account when selecting topics for debate. Snider and Schnurer (2006) provide a host of examples of how to incorporate authentic, real-world debates into the classroom in a variety of fields in the sciences, social sciences, and humanities.

One example of a debate activity designed with authenticity in mind is the "simulated public argument" through role-play (Mitchell, 2000). Role-play is one of the specific subcategories of authenticity that Abrami et al. (2015) identify as particularly effective in promoting the development of critical thinking. In role-play debates, students go beyond two-sided arguments and consider a range of possible perspectives toward an issue by adopting the standpoints and perspectives of diverse stakeholders engaging a public issue.

A good example can be taken from an interdisciplinary research-based writing course I taught examining heritage advocacy and public memory in Singapore. A common theme of the course was the conflict between heritage preservation and economic development. In one set of lessons, students were introduced to a number of the organizations involved in heritage-related decisions and advocacy, including the National Heritage Board, the Urban Redevelopment Authority, the Land Transport Authority, the Singapore Heritage Society, and Nature Society Singapore. They were then exposed to newspaper articles and position papers about a recent heritage debate in Singapore: should Bukit Brown cemetery, the largest and oldest Chinese cemetery in Southeast Asia, have a significant number of graves exhumed to make way for the construction of a flyover to ease traffic congestion in the area? Students were divided into groups and each group was asked to take on the perspectives of one of the stakeholder organizations, with a structured presentation and question-and-answer session giving students an opportunity to debate the topic and defend the perspective of their organization.

One benefit of role-play activities as a form of authentic instruction is that they have the potential to reconstruct real-world issues in all of their complexity, and thus encourage students to gather information and take on the perspectives of various participants. Perspective taking is consistently identified as a core critical thinking disposition, for example in Facione's *open-mindedness scale* (1995; 2000). Perspective taking is also identified as one of the major benefits of switch-side or assigned perspective debates in general (Snider & Schnurer, 2006; Goodwin, 2003; Roy & Macchiette, 2005; Yang & Rusli, 2012) and of role-play debates in particular (Mitchell, 2000). Zorwick (Chapter 9 in this volume) provides further evidence from social psychology regarding the value of debate as an avenue for developing students' perspective taking ability. When classroom debate addresses real-world issues and asks students to think about the various stakeholders involved in making decisions about those issues, which can include themselves as regular citizens, it activates the critical thinking skills and dispositions beneficial to healthy democratic decision-making and gives students a sense of their own agency with respect to public decisions (Lundberg, 2010; Mitchell, 2000; Ryan, 2006).

Debate as a Platform for Dialogue and Mentoring

Debate can be a platform for dialogue because debate, fundamentally, is a structured technique for creating meaningful dialogue. Debate always assumes a minimum of two partners involved in a dispute, each with a distinct perspective on the issue to present. This dialogue can include many additional participants, with teams working together to present perspectives – all debates do not have to be "pro/con" or "yes/no" disagreements. There are three elements of dialogue through debate that should be highlighted as potentially beneficial to student critical thinking.

First, debate places dialogue in a context that values rational and critical thought, and in which students are encouraged to back up and defend their perspectives to withstand the critical scrutiny of others. This aspect of classroom debate has been identified in several studies, including research by Goodwin (2003) and Kennedy (2007). By placing conversation in this context, debate asks students to reflect on and justify their beliefs, transforming them from subjective opinions into reasoned arguments that are open to contestation and re-evaluation.

Second, debate creates an active position for the audience by emphasizing the importance of judgment. The goal of a debate is not primarily for the participants to persuade one another of their views (although in certain kinds of debates emphasizing co-operation or collaborative problem solving this may be a significant goal); instead, the goal is for each participant to put their perspective forward strongly so that a third party, either as judge or jury, can weigh the merits of the opposing sides and come to a decision about what to think, feel, believe, or do. Classroom debate practices often use ballot-writing as an activity to encourage audience judgment and to assess student skill at argument evaluation.

Third, debate-based dialogue can be supported and guided by the instructor, who can play the part of a coach, a role model, or co-investigator. Roy and Macchiette (2005) provide a detailed account of the various roles played by the instructor in designing debate activities, laying out expectations for format, and participating in the questioning of debate participants and evaluation or judgment of debate results. Instructors can work with individual debating groups to coach them in the development of their arguments or provide background information in the form of lectures, reading materials, or hand-outs to introduce students to the topic. Debate activities can thus be designed with Abrami et al.'s (2015) identification of the importance of instructor guidance or mentorship in mind, enhancing their potential to develop student critical thinking.

Conclusion

There is much that advocates of debate can learn from the scholarly literature on critical thinking about how to design debate activities. Classroom debates can be scaffolded into content courses across the humanities, sciences, and social sciences, but time should be taken when introducing debate to emphasize aspects of critical thinking that the instructor wants to teach. Goals and learning outcomes related to debate's inclusion should be clear to all participants. Argument creation, evaluation, and reasoning should be explicitly covered by the instructor and then applied back to course content prior to the commencement of debates themselves. Debates should be realistic – drawn either from actual debates in the field or ongoing debates related to course themes in public and private life – and where appropriate they should give students the opportunity to take on perspectives that are different than their own, through group assignment, role-play, or other techniques. Students should not be left alone to develop arguments; teachers should model argument creation during class discussion and provide one-on-one or small-group coaching so that students can receive feedback on the rigor of their arguments.

As teachers design debate activities with critical thinking in mind, they are given a further opportunity to engage in scholarly teaching, studying their own pedagogical interventions and contributing additional research on the impact of debate in the classroom. In doing so, and by adopting true experimental methods when possible, they will contribute back to the literature on debate across the curriculum and critical thinking, and they will provide empirical validation for what many debate alumni already believe: that debate, more than any other educational pursuit, gave them the thinking skills and habits of mind that prepared them for a future of research, teaching, and public engagement.

References

Abrami, P. C., Bernard, R. M., Borokhovski, E., Waddington, D. I., Wade, C. A., & Persson, T. (2015). Strategies for teaching students to think critically: A meta-analysis. *Review of Educational Research, 85*(2), 275–314. doi: 10.3102/0034654314551063.

Abrami, P. C., Bernard, R. M., Borokhovski, E., Wade, A., Surkes, M. A., Tamim, R., & Zhang, D. (2008). Instructional interventions affecting critical thinking skills and dispositions: A stage 1 meta-analysis. *Review of Educational Research, 78*(4), 1102–1134. doi: 10.2307/40071155.

Allen, M., Berkowitz, S., & Louden, A. (1995). A study comparing the impact of communication classes and competitive forensic experience on critical thinking improvement. *The Forensic of Pi Kappa Delta, 81*, 1–8.

Allen, M., Berkowitz, S., Hunt, S., & Louden, A. (1999). A meta-analysis of the impact of forensics and communication education on critical thinking. *Communication Education, 48*(1), 18–30. doi: 10.1080/03634529909379149.

Bangert-Drowns, R. L., & Bankert, E. (1990). Meta-analysis of effects of explicit instruction for critical thinking. Paper presented at the Annual Meeting of the American Educational Research Association, Boston, MA.

Bellon, J. (2000). A research-based justification for debate across the curriculum. *Argumentation and Advocacy, 36*(3), 161.

Berkowitz, S. J. (2006). Developing critical thinking through forensics and communication education: Assessing the impact through meta-analysis. In B. M. Gayle, R. W. Preiss, N. Burrell, and M. Allen (Eds.), *Classroom Communication and Instructional Processes: Advances through Meta-analysis* (pp. 43–59). Mahwah, NJ: Lawrence Erlbaum Associates.

Booth, W. C., Colomb, G. G., & Williams, J. M. (2008). *The Craft of Research* (3rd ed.). Chicago, IL: University of Chicago Press.

Caine, R. N., & Caine, G. (1991). *Teaching and the Human Brain*. Alexandria, VA: Association for Supervision and Curriculum Development.

Colbert, K. (1987). The effects of CEDA and NDT debate training on critical thinking skills. *Journal of the American Forensics Association, 23*, 194–201.

Dwyer, C. P., Hogan, M. J., & Stewart, I. (2014). An integrated critical thinking framework for the 21st century. *Thinking Skills and Creativity, 12*, 43–52. doi: http://dx.doi.org/10.1016/j.tsc.2013.12.004.

Ennis, R. H. (1989). Critical thinking and subject specificity: Clarification and needed research. *Educational Researcher, 18*(3), 4–10. doi: 10.2307/1174885.

Ennis, R. H. (1993). Critical thinking assessment. *Theory into Practice, 32*(3), 179–186.

Ennis, R. H. (1996). Critical thinking dispositions: Their nature and assessability. *Informal Logic, 18*(2), 165–182.

Facione, P. A. (1990). *Critical Thinking: A Statement of Expert Consensus for Purposes of Educational Assessment and Instruction: Research Findings and Recommendations*. Newark, DE: American Philosophical Association.

Facione, P. A. (2000). The disposition toward critical thinking. Its character, measurement, and relationship to critical thinking skill. *Informal Logic, 20*(1), 61–84.

Facione, P. A., Facione, N. C., Sánchez, C. A., & Gainen, J. (1995). The disposition toward critical thinking. *The Journal of General Education, 44*(1), 1–25.

Garrett, M., Schoener, L., & Hood, L. (1996). Debate: A teaching strategy to improve verbal communication and critical-thinking skills. *Nurse Educator, 21*(4), 37–40.

Goodwin, J. (2003). Students' perspectives on debate exercises in content area classes. *Communication Education, 52*(2), 157–163. doi: 10.1080/03634520302466.

Green, C. S. III, & Klug, H. G. (1990). Teaching critical thinking and writing through debates: An experimental evaluation. *Teaching Sociology, 18*(4), 462–471.

Halpern, D. F. (1993). Assessing the effectiveness of critical thinking instruction. *The Journal of General Education, 42*(4), 238–254.

Halpern, D. F. (2013). *The Halpern Critical Thinking Assessment Manual*. Version 22. Moedling, Austria: Schuhfried (Vienna Test System).

Halpern, D. F. (2014). *Thought and Knowledge: An Introduction to Critical Thinking* (5th ed.). New York: Taylor & Francis.

Kellner, D., & Share, J. (2005). Toward critical media literacy: Core concepts, debates, organizations, and policy. *Discourse: Studies in the Cultural Politics of Education, 26*(3), 369–386.

Kennedy, R. (2007). In-class debates: Fertile ground for active learning and the cultivation of critical thinking and oral communication skills. *International Journal of Teaching and Learning in Higher Education, 19*(2), 183–190.

Ku, K. Y. L. (2009). Assessing students' critical thinking performance: Urging for measurements using multi-response format. *Thinking Skills and Creativity, 4*(1), 70–76. doi: 10.1016/j.tsc.2009.02.001.

Lampert, N. (2007). Critical thinking dispositions as an outcome of undergraduate education. *The Journal of General Education, 56*(1), 17–33.

Lundberg, C. O. (2010). The Allred Initiative and debate across the curriculum: Reinventing the tradition of debate at North Carolina. In A. Louden (Ed.), *Navigating Opportunity: Policy Debate in the 21st Century* (pp. 289–321). New York: International Debate Education Association.

McPeck, J. E. (1981). *Critical Thinking and Education*. New York: St. Martin's Press.

Mitchell, G. R. (2000). Simulated public argument as a pedagogical play on worlds. *Argumentation and Advocacy, 36,* 134–150.

Morris, E. (2011). *Believing is Seeing: Observations on the Mysteries of Photography.* New York: Penguin Press.

Morrow, D. R., & Weston, A. (2011). *A Workbook for Arguments: A Complete Course in Critical Thinking.* Indianapolis, IN: Hackett Publishing.

Niu, L., Behar-Horenstein, L. S., & Garvan, C. W. (2013). Do instructional interventions influence college students' critical thinking skills? A meta-analysis. *Educational Research Review, 9,* 114–128. doi: http://dx.doi.org/10.1016/j.edurev.2012.12.002.

Paul, R. W. (1993). *Critical Thinking: What Every Person Needs to Survive in a Rapidly Changing World* (rev. 2nd ed.). Santa Rosa, CA: Foundation for Critical Thinking.

Paul, R. W. (2005). The state of critical thinking today. *New Directions for Community Colleges, 2005*(130), 27–38. doi: 10.1002/cc.193.

Roy, A., & Macchiette, B. (2005). Debating the issues: A tool for augmenting critical thinking skills of marketing students. *Journal of Marketing Education, 27*(3), 264–276.

Ryan, S. (2006). Arguing toward a more active citizenry: Re-envisioning the introductory civics course via debate-centered pedagogy. *Journal of Public Affairs Education, 12*(3), 385–395.

Siegel, H. (1985). Educating reason: Critical thinking, informal logic, and the philosophy of education. *Informal Logic, 7*(2&3), 69–81.

Snider, A., & Schnurer, M. (2006). *Many Sides: Debate Across the Curriculum* (rev. ed.). New York: International Debate Education Association.

Toulmin, S. E. (2003). *The Uses of Argument* (updated ed.). Cambridge: Cambridge University Press.

Tsui, L. (2002). Fostering critical thinking through effective pedagogy: Evidence from four institutional case studies. *The Journal of Higher Education, 73*(6), 740–763.

Wade, W. P. (2014). Bridging critical thinking and media literacy through integrated courses. *CDTL Brief, 7*(2), 2–4.

Wade, W. P., & See, Y. H. M. (2014). Measuring critical thinking as learning outcome: A pilot study from the Ideas and Exposition module. *Asian Journal of the Scholarship of Teaching and Learning, 4*(4), 220–236.

Yang, C., & Rusli, E. (2012). Using debate as a pedagogical tool in enhancing pre-service teachers' learning and critical thinking. *Journal of International Education Research, 8*(2), 135–144.

9 Using Debate to Develop Perspective Taking and Social Skills

M. Leslie Wade Zorwick

I am frequently surprised by the requests my students make. Despite knowing their deadlines months in advance, students request that I write them letters of recommendation with only a few days of notice. After spending hours creating an elaborate review sheet, students tell me that it would be more helpful if I could let them know exactly which questions will appear on the exam. I have even had students request that I have two or three days of evening review sessions, because the time of the scheduled out-of-class review session "doesn't work for them." Over the years, I have come to believe that these requests rarely come from a place of disrespect or entitlement; rather, these requests come from an inability of students to fully consider the perspective of the teacher. When I point out to students that asking a large amount of work from me on short notice is unreasonable – because of the other demands on my time, both at work and at home – students are often apologetic and respond with a phrase I have come to hear a lot: "I hadn't thought about it that way."

It is very easy only to focus on our own needs and wants; in fact, a great deal of research in my field is devoted to the study of humans' profound egocentrism. Moving past a focus on ourselves to consider the needs and feelings of others is a regular struggle in social interactions. We always see the world through our own eyes, so we are fundamentally more aware of our own needs and desires than the needs of almost anyone else. Even in close and intimate relationships, the relationships in which we try to care thoughtfully for other people, we often fall short of this goal because of the inherent limitations in our ability to truly step outside of our own perspective. As a social psychologist, my field offers many theories that might explain both the inherent limitations of our own perspective and the ways in which using our own perspective as a starting point can affect our decisions, perceptions, and interactions. But, for the purposes of this chapter, I am more interested in how people begin to develop and grow the skills that will help them take on the perspective of others more successfully. This chapter will focus on the importance of developing skills in perspective taking and will point to debate as an incredibly effective mechanism for the development of these skills in students. Previous research discussed in this book has identified the many benefits of debate participation for critical thinking and for academic and literacy skills. I will argue that debate also helps to develop meaningful social skills through regular practice in perspective taking.

Empathy

There is no question that, as a society, we value empathy. The idea of considering the thoughts and feelings of others seems to be a topic of interest to parents, educators, and governmental institutions. And, research increasingly suggests that the development of social skills, including empathy, is associated with a host of positive benefits across the lifespan (National Public Radio, 2014). Given the value placed on the development of empathy, it's not surprising that in a commencement speech at Northwestern University, then-senator Barack Obama said:

> There's a lot of talk in this country about the federal deficit. I think it's important for us to talk about that, but I think we should talk more about another deficit, what I call the empathy deficit – the ability to put ourselves in somebody else's shoes; to see the world through those who are different from us.
>
> (Obama, 2006)

Researchers have identified two meaningful components of empathy: affective empathy and perspective taking (Swart, Turner, Hewstone, & Voci, 2011). Affective empathy involves the ability to consider and then take on the feelings of someone else; when people experience affective empathy, they are calling to mind the experience of vicariously experiencing the joy or sorrow of others. The second component, perspective taking, focuses more on the ability to cognitively step into the shoes of another person; perspective taking involves engaging thought processes that allow us to examine and consider the thoughts and experiences of others. In separating out the feeling-based (affective empathy) and thought-based (perspective taking) components of empathy, researchers have been able to separate out situations in which either thoughts or feelings are most impactful in facilitating empathy, as well as identifying the unique benefits when both feelings and thoughts related to empathy are involved. In this chapter, I argue that debate offers a particularly strong opportunity to develop the cognitive skill of perspective taking.

Debate Develops Perspective Taking Skills

Previous research has made the argument that debate can develop perspective taking skills (Budesheim & Lundquist, 1999; Goodwin, 2003; Yang & Rusli, 2012). Budesheim and Lundquist (1999) find that debate is most effective as a way to set the stage for attitude change and to develop more nuanced understanding of issues when it encourages students to argue for positions counter to their own pre-existing beliefs. In fact, the authors argue that:

> Students must learn to question their assumptions, ask new questions, consider novel solutions, and evaluate their possibilities evenhandedly . . . As educators, one tool we can use to promote these mental habits is the in-class debate in which we require students to defend a position with which they disagree.
>
> (Budesheim & Lundquist, 1999, p. 109)

However, I would argue that the opportunity to debate regularly, in extracurricular or in-class settings, would also develop these skills over time. As a debater in both high school and college, I realized very quickly that I would be more likely to win debates if I tried to understand the arguments and logic of my opponents. And, learning to understand the position and background of the authors who were used to provide evidentiary support allowed me to broaden my understanding of the topic. Over time, I found that seeking out evidence that was contrary to my opinion helped my ideas become stronger; even when defending one position, I began to spontaneously research the other position in an attempt to better understand my opponent. Lest you think that this is something unique to my experience, this quote from a middle-school student in New York, who was debating the use of digital enhancement in advertisements, nicely makes this point: "It's really hard, but you have to understand other people's views so that you can prove against their point . . . I need to look at how the companies think, so that I can argue against them" (Schwarz, 2014).

While previous research has argued that debate develops perspective taking, often leaving it at that, I want to clarify and develop the reasons why I think debate has such a unique ability to develop perspective taking skills. I do not necessarily think that debate helps students consider any one person's perspective – in fact, most debate is focused on larger social issues and not the needs or experiences of just one person. Rather, debate develops the skills to understand why different entities (for example, consumers and companies, state and federal government agencies, or even parents and children) could have a different way of thinking about a nuanced issue. And, this broad practice with perspective taking can become a habit that encourages students to consider the context, background, and external and internal forces that shape individuals' positions about complex social issues. I believe that this habit can translate into other areas of study, as students consider the factors that might motivate a politician to support a specific piece of legislation, as well as their own interpersonal relationships, as they try to understand the thoughts and motivations of others.

I believe that debate encourages the development of cognitive perspective taking skills for five reasons. First, many debate opportunities involve debating both sides of an issue. This might manifest in alternating which student or team gets first choice in the side they defend in a classroom debate, or might involve preparing both an affirmative and negative position about the debate topic, the latter of which is more likely in extracurricular debate participation.

For students who will be asked to argue for both a pro and con position, there is a unique competitive incentive for considering the position of the other side. Winning is a powerful motivator, and the desire to present the strongest possible argument in front of peers and teachers can create additional motivation for students to do the thought experiment of considering the other side's position, which offers meaningful practice with perspective taking.

Second, debate requires listening and engaging with the material under consideration. Debate offers a context in which listening skills develop organically; there is a strong incentive to paying attention and an even stronger disincentive to "checking out." The participatory nature of debate means that to win, or to argue effectively, students need to know what has been argued and need to be able to address those arguments. And, the very act of listening and engaging with opposing ideas forces a practice with perspective taking; students are required to logically think through arguments and counter-arguments.

Third, debate forces students to learn more about complicated topics. Debate rewards students who move beyond their knee-jerk responses about policies or issues into a deeper understanding of the topics and constituencies involved. Debate also forces students to learn about topics they may not have experienced directly. And, encountering more information about things that are foreign to the experiences of students, from educational disparities to foreign policy to police use of force, allows them to consider the experiences of a wide range of people.

Fourth, debate often occurs within a social context that invites new perspectives. Whether debate happens on a competitive extracurricular team or within a classroom, there is opportunity for debaters to learn from each other in their preparation. Let's imagine a classroom with 20 students, who are divided into four teams of 5 students. These four teams will be debating gun control with the teacher as a judge. The first two teams will debate the issue at hand and then the next two teams will debate; students who are not debating will listen to the other two teams debate. There are three powerful opportunities for perspective taking in this scenario: a) learning within their group; b) learning while watching the other debate; and c) learning from the teacher/judge. Students can first learn from the other students in their group. In fact, co-operative problem solving within the team can invite new perspectives into the conversation and there is a profound incentive for discussion that allows the strongest arguments to emerge. Students can then learn by watching the debate in which they are not participating. By watching the other debate and witnessing the arguments and counter-arguments, students can strengthen their understanding of the likely position on both sides and practice the cognitive skills of anticipating and taking on the perspective of the opposing team. Finally, students have the opportunity to learn from their teacher and judge. By hearing a critique of the debate, which typically involves a discussion of the most persuasive and least persuasive arguments, students can begin to practice taking on the perspective of someone critically evaluating a debate. This awareness of how an observer is weighing the competing claims and arguments is also incredibly helpful in considering a perspective outside of the debater's personal experience.

Fifth, debate provides opportunities for students to have meaningful interactions with people who are different from them. When working on a team to prepare for a debate, the dimensions along which students differ can more easily fade into the background because of the shared focus on the task at hand; the power of ideas is more important in debate than the differences between people. The power of intergroup, or cross-group, interaction is well documented in social psychology, particularly in the study of the Contact Hypothesis. The Contact Hypothesis argues that prejudice is based on unfamiliarity and that situations that reduce unfamiliarity, and provide an opportunity for two groups to interact co-operatively, will result in less prejudice (Allport, 1954). According to the Contact Hypothesis, four conditions must be met for prejudice reduction to occur: supportive authority figures, equal status between groups, opportunities to develop friendship, and a shared goal that groups must work together to achieve (Brown, 1995). Debate is one scholastic activity that seems to organically create these conditions and, as such, debate is associated with the benefit of social skill development in students, as identified by their teachers (Zorwick, Wade, & Heilmayr, 2009).

My previous research into the ways in which debate can facilitate successful intergroup contact focused on the particular benefits of urban debate league participation. Urban debate leagues were developed with the goal of increasing socio-economic and racial diversity in competitive extracurricular debate by providing coaching and tournament opportunities from local college debate programs, in order to provide access to debate for traditionally underserved student populations (Zorwick, Wade, & Heilmayr, 2009). We found strong evidence that debate participation was associated with feelings of supportive authority figures, meeting on an equal playing field, friendship development, and working on goals so big that students came to see themselves as a "team." One of our focus group participants, a staff member at a summer program for the urban debate league, nicely pointed out the ways in which debate can develop perspective taking, while also combating stereotyping, saying:

> There's an incentive for [students] to understand the lives of other people who are not like them, and there's an incentive for them to understand what policies work, what policies don't, [and] at what level those policies need to be implemented . . . the debate format complexifies the discussion in such a way that causes stereotypes to implode upon themselves and that's the benefit in my mind of debate.
> (Zorwick, Wade, & Heilmayr, 2009, p. 41)

Because students are in a position to focus on their similarities and meet on an equal playing field, friendships can develop; friendships, then, have the opportunity to introduce students to different perspectives and to broaden the social skill development of students. Perspective taking can be aided through intergroup contact and intergroup contact can make perspective taking easier in the future, as students learn about the worldview of people other than themselves; in this way, perspective taking and intergroup contact are mutually reinforcing. Recently published research has found that perspective taking makes people more interested in engaging in intergroup contact, creates more welcoming behaviors which facilitate the success of the contact, and that this interest in contact extends beyond the person in question to the group as a whole (Wang, Tai, Ku, & Galinsky, 2014).

The Benefit of Perspective Taking Skills

It would be nearly impossible to overstate the importance of perspective taking skills. Perspective taking is a foundational skill involved in navigating the social world and it underpins children's development "theory of mind," which is the ability to understand the mental state of others and to realize that their perspective differs from our own (Frith & Frith, 2001). Research has also found that the set of skills that relate to perspective taking are absolutely essential for functioning and navigating the social world on a daily basis, and it is precisely this set of skills that are disrupted for patients with schizophrenia and autism (Sterea, 2015; Frith & Frith, 2001). Perspective taking rapidly grows from the ages of 13 to 18, making the development of these skills during middle and high school of particular importance (Van der Graaff et al., 2014). In addition, stronger perspective taking skills in 13–18 year olds is associated with more trust and more co-operation in social interactions that go positively, which confers clear social benefits (Fett et al., 2014).

Social psychologists also study the benefits of perspective taking as a mechanism to reduce our overreliance on stereotypes, which are cognitive generalizations about groups, in forming impressions of other people. In a foundational study, Galinsky and Moskowitz (2000) showed their research participants a picture of an elderly man and asked their participants to write about a day in the life of this man. Participants were also asked to either try to take on the perspective of the man, try not to use any stereotypes (called stereotype suppression), or gave them no additional instructions. Galinsky and Moskowitz (2000) found that taking on the perspective of a person in the picture reduced the cognitive activation of relevant negative stereotypes, meaning that it was even harder to bring those stereotypes to mind than in the other instruction groups, and resulted in the most positive, and least stereotypical, essays about a subsequent elderly person. Interestingly, perspective taking research has found that stereotypes are reduced for both positively stereotyped (i.e., doctors are intelligent) and negatively stereotyped (i.e., construction workers are not intelligent) individuals, which means perspective taking has the power to get us to see people as individuals and not representations of stereotypic groups, even if those stereotypes are seen as being more positive and socially acceptable to express (Wang, Ku, Tai, & Galinsky, 2014). This line of research finds that when we take on the perspective of someone we don't know when forming an impression about them, we tend to make more positive evaluations, we tend to be less likely to activate and express stereotypes, and we tend to have more positive perceptions of their entire group, even when it's a group we could easily stereotype (Galinsky & Moskowitz, 2000).

Many of the positive benefits of perspective taking seem to come from a process called self–other overlap (Galinsky & Moskowitz, 2000; Galinsky, Ku, & Wang, 2005). Self–other overlap refers to the extent to which our cognitive representations, which can be thought of as a mental file drawer of the things we know and think about a topic, for ourselves and others overlap. In social interactions, when our cognitive representation of our self overlaps with our cognitive representation about other people, we tend to like those people more and see them as being more similar to us (Goldstein, Vezich, & Shapiro, 2014). When we think of close relationships, it makes sense to think that our cognitive representation of our self overlaps with the people who are important to us, because who we are is, in part, defined by the relationships we value. In addition, the groups we belong to also become part of our sense of self and, as a result, our self-esteem is connected to the feelings we have about these groups (Luhtanen & Crocker, 1992). There are many manifestations of the self-esteem we get from groups, but it involves the kind of feelings I have when I hear one of the members of my community won a large award or was awarded a grant, in addition to the pride I feel when my alma mater wins a national championship in athletics. There is a large body of research that shows that once things become connected to our mental representation of ourselves, the more we like them. Interestingly, in the case of individuals who do not feel favorably toward their mental representation of themselves, perspective taking can actually make people feel more positively toward themselves, by getting them to see themselves in terms of groups and other people they value (Peterson, Bellows, & Peterson, 2015).

Recent research has found that just knowing that someone is trying to take on our perspective, called *perceived* perspective taking, is associated with a host of positive benefits, including increased feelings of similarity, liking, desire to help, and self–other overlap (Goldstein, Vezich, & Shapiro, 2014). This research suggests that perspective taking might have a positive cyclical effect in which perspective taking improves our perception of another person, and just knowing that we took their perspective improves their perception of us. It's exciting to consider that perspective taking may beget more perspective taking and better relationships, which will then invite more perspective taking. When conceptualized this way, any work in the classroom that encourages perspective taking may have wider-ranging and longer-lasting positive benefits than research has previously shown.

Research has also found that perspective taking can play an important role in getting people to acknowledge disparate treatment based on group membership, particularly toward groups to which we do not belong (Todd, Bodenhausen, & Galinsky, 2012). When perspective taking, people were more likely to acknowledge that discrimination, as opposed to a lack of motivation, was often responsible for disparities between majority and minority racial groups in housing, employment, and income. In addition, research found that this ability to perceive a larger role played by discrimination made perspective takers more likely to endorse affirmative action and to consider policy solutions to addressing racial disparity. In terms of setting the stage to address structural inequalities, perspective taking allows people to more clearly see the context in which disparity occurs, as opposed to focusing on solely individual responsibility, which has powerful consequences for social change.

In moving through their education, students will be developing skills that will help them as they enter the workforce and become social decision makers. One final benefit of perspective taking speaks to additional benefits of the development of this skill in the long term. Research has found that people who are in positions of power seem less likely to spontaneously take on the perspectives of others (Galinsky, Magee, Inesi, & Gruenfeld, 2006). There are multiple reasons the powerful may engage in less perspective taking, including (a) the feeling that their perspective is most correct because of their status; (b) the demands on their cognitive energy that come from the powerful position; and (c) that power discourages self–other overlap. While power is generally associated with less perspective taking, when power is successfully combined with an explicit focus on perspective taking, the outcome is generally strong and better than either perspective taking or power alone (Galinsky, Magee, Rus, Rothman, & Todd, 2014). Galinsky et al. (2014) argue that power can propel action and ensure things get done, just like the gas pedal in a car, while perspective taking ensures that outcomes and decisions are optimal, just like the steering wheel; so, when power and perspective taking combine, work in groups is more likely to identify the best, or most optimal, solution or decision. This research experimentally induces people to take on the perspective of others either by explicitly instructing them to do so or by creating strong feelings of accountability, which is associated with spontaneous perspective taking. However, it seems possible that people who have made a habit of perspective taking may be more likely to spontaneously consider the perspectives of others, even when they have chronic power or power in a specific situation.

Conclusion

While I struggle to show compassion for the fifth student in any given week who asks for some special consideration on short notice, be it a recommendation or a study guide or just my time, I do realize that encouraging students to take on my perspective is a small way to play a part in helping students develop an incredibly important social skill. I think every time I encourage students to consider the perspective of their teachers, their friends, their roommates, or their fellow students, I am helping their skill at perspective taking to become more automatic and more habitual. And, because we increasingly live in a world where people can surround themselves with media and social interactions that do not require consideration of different perspectives, I think students need more help than ever developing these skills. The ability to spend our social time, and consume media, in an echo chamber of our beliefs prevents us from fully considering the lived experience of others and this is a dangerous thing. Perspective taking is an absolutely essential social and educational skill and it is far too easy for students to avoid learning and developing this skill.

Thankfully, perspective taking can be meaningfully developed through the skills and activities required in structured debate, or argumentation and advocacy assignments, in the classroom. Perspective taking will help students strengthen the skills required for considering multiple sides of an issue, which can lead to more nuanced understanding of issues, other people, and world as a whole. In developing future citizens and leaders, teachers have the unique opportunity to encourage students to develop perspective taking skills. And, lest teachers think they are alone in the fight to instill the value of perspective taking, they need to know that debate is a powerful ally in the struggle to help students consider the world outside their own experiences.

References

Allport, G. W. (1954). *The Nature of Prejudice*. Reading, MA: Addison-Wesley Publishing Company, Inc.

Brown, R. (1995). Reducing Prejudice. *Prejudice: Its Social Psychology* (pp. 235–270). Oxford, UK: Blackwell Publishers Ltd.

Budesheim, T. L., & Lundquist, A. R. (1999). Consider the opposite: Opening minds through in-class debates on course-related controversies. *Teaching of Psychology*, 26(2), 106–110.

Fett, A. J., Shergill, S., Gromann, P., Dumontheil, I., Blakremore, S. J., Yakub, F., & Krabbendam, L. (2014). Trust and social reciprocity in adolescence: A matter of perspective-taking. *Journal of Adolescence*, 37(2), 175–184.

Frith, U., & Frith, C. (2001). The biological basis of social interaction. *Current Directions in Psychological Science*, 10(5), 151–155.

Galinsky, A. D., Ku, G., & Wang, C. S. (2005). Perspective-taking: Increasing social bonds and facilitating social coordination. *Group Processes and Intergroup Relations*, 8(2), 109–124.

Galinsky, A. D., Magee, J. C., Inesi, M. E., & Gruenfeld, D. H. (2006). Power and perspectives not taken. *Psychological Science*, 17(12), 1068–1074.

Galinsky, A. D., Magee, J. C., Rus, D., Rothman, N. B., & Todd, A. R. (2014). Acceleration with steering: The synergistic benefits of combining power and perspective-taking. *Social Psychological and Personality Science*, 5(6), 627–635

Galinsky, A. D., & Moskowitz, G. B. (2000). Perspective-taking: Decreasing stereotype expression, stereotype accessibility, and in-group favoritism. *Journal of Personality and Social Psychology*, 78(4), 708–724.

Goldstein, N. J., Vezich, S., & Shapiro, J. R. (2014). Perceived perspective taking: When others walk in our shoes. *Journal of Personality and Social Psychology*, 106(6), 941–960.

Goodwin, J. (2003). Students' perspectives on debate exercises in content area classes. *Communication Education*, 52(2), 157–163.

Luhtanen, R., & Crocker, J. (1992). A collective self-esteem scale: Self-evaluation of one's social identity. *Personality and Social Psychology Bulletin*, 18(3), 302–318.

National Public Radio (Producer). (2014, December 31). Why emotional learning may be as important as the ABCs (M. Singh, Reporter) [Story transcript]. Retrieved from http://www.npr.org/sections/ed/2014/12/31/356187871/ why-emotional-literacy-may-be-as-important-as-learning-the-a-b-c-s.

Obama, B. (2006, June 19). *2006 Northwestern Commencement*. [Audio File]. Retrieved from http://www.northwestern.edu/newscenter/stories/ 2006/06/barack.html.

Peterson, J. L., Bellows, A., & Peterson, S. (2015). Promoting connection: Perspective-taking improves relationship closeness and perceived regard in participants with low implicit self-esteem. *Journal of Experimental Social Psychology, 56*, 160–164.

Schwarz, A. (2014, November 17). A diverse mix of pupils, learning civilized dissent: New York Debate League involves middle school students of all backgrounds. *The New York Times.* Retrieved from http://www.nytimes.com/2014/11/ 18/nyregion/new-york-debate-league-includes-diverse-mix-of-middle-school-students.html?_r=0.

Sterea, R. (2015). The relationship between social cognition and functional outcomes in schizophrenia. *Procedia: Social and Behavioral Sciences, 187*, 256–260.

Swart, H., Turner, R., Hewstone, M., & Voci, A. (2011). Achieving outgroup forgiveness and outgroup trust: The importance of cross-group friendships, self-disclosure, and empathy. In L. Tropp & R. Mallett (Eds.), *Beyond Prejudice Reduction: Pathways to Positive Intergroup Relations* (pp. 181–200). Washington, DC: American Psychological Association.

Todd, A. R., Bodenhausen, G. V., & Galinsky, A. D. (2012). Perspective taking combats the denial of intergroup discrimination. *Journal of Experimental Social Psychology, 48*, 738–745.

Van der Graaff, J., Branje, S., De Wied, M., Hawk, S., Van Lier, P., & Meeus, W. (2014). Perspective taking and empathic concern in adolescence: Gender differences in developmental changes. *Developmental Psychology, 50*(3), 881–888.

Wang, C. S., Ku, G., Tai, K., & Galinsky, A. D. (2014). Stupid doctors and smart construction workers: Perspective-taking reduces stereotyping of both negative and positive targets. *Social Psychological and Personality Science, 5*(4), 430–436.

Wang, C. S., Tai, K., Ku, G., & Galinsky, A. D. (2014). Perspective-taking increases willingness to engage in intergroup contact. *PLOS ONE.* DOI:10.1371/journal.pone.0085681.

Yang, C., & Rusli, E. (2012). Using debate as a pedagogical tool in enhancing preservice teachers' learning and critical thinking. *Journal of International Education Research, 8*(2), 135–144.

Zorwick, M. L. W., Wade, M. M., & Heilmayr, D. P. (2009). Urban debate and prejudice reduction: The contact hypothesis in action. *Contemporary Argumentation and Debate, 30*, 29–39.

10 Creating Hospitable Communities

Remembering the Emanuel 9 as We Foster a Culture of Humility and Debate

Ed Lee and Ajay Nair

"I have to do it. You rape our women and you're taking over our country. And you have to go."

> Dylan Storm Roof – Charged with killing nine
> people at Emanuel AME Church

"He needs to be praised for the good deed he has done."

> East Texas firefighter Kurtis Cook's
> tweet after Roof's arrest

This chapter is written in honor of the parishioners of the Emanuel African Methodist Episcopal Church who came together on the night of June 17, 2015 in the name of self-reflection and deliberation only to have their hospitality to others result in the brutal massacre of nine members by Dylan Storm Roof. We honor them because, even in light of tragedy, the pursuit of a culturally humble existence that values introspection and open deliberation is inherently good and a necessary antidote to the cultural self-centeredness that encourages Roof and others to rationalize his attack as the appropriate response to our evolution into a more polycultural nation.

Dylan Roof is a child of the internet age. While we cannot and should not attempt to establish a causal relationship between his cyberhate and the shooting spree in Charleston's AME Church, we should not ignore that current uses of social media are fundamentally changing communication norms in ways that discourage critical engagement with those with whom we disagree. Hyper-personalization of social media creates norms and practices that chill self-reflection and debate and that leaves our biases unexposed. We deliberately aggregate our news so that it is "filtered implicitly based on what our friends, contacts, or inner circle" think we should read and "curated to fit our preferences, interests and personality" (Chamorro-Premuzic, 2014, para. 2). Computer technology is so exceptionally effective at weeding out contradictory and confounding information that everyone, regardless of their perspective, leaves their Facebook page justifiably believing that the preponderance of the evidence available supports their views and values. Far too often, social media is used exclusively to confirm who we already are and what we already know instead of challenging us to be introspective and understand others. Meaningful debate over collective values is replaced by 140-character tweets and Facebook activism that only serves to confirm "friendship" via constant agreement and the incessant accumulation of "likes."

These ideologically isolated social spaces where we almost exclusively communicate with people who share our values, perspectives, and beliefs increasingly make us hostile to those who do not. These enclaves of sameness operate under a dangerous illusion of engagement. The ability to vigorously police the membership of our digital social communities and excommunicate those who challenge our vision not only makes negotiated compromise unlikely but reinforces a deadly form of self-centeredness that makes Roof's violent outburst seem rational. His attack was the manifestation of a set of cultural norms that encourage insolence and repulsion of difference and deliberation.

Use of social media is increasingly a concern for teachers. The growing ubiquity of social media among teenagers is undeniable and will challenge how we teach and our ability to produce students who are globally oriented and civically engaged. Teachers are fully aware that social networking has irrevocably altered the communication patterns of the Generations Y and Z. Every student has a smartphone that is rarely used to make phone calls but constantly used to update Facebook pages, snapchat with their friends and retweet the news of the day. Use of social media is part and parcel to adolescence in the United States. A study by Common Sense Media on teen social media consumption reports that nine out of ten teenagers use social media, three-quarters have an active social networking site, and nearly one in three teens visit their social networking site several times a day (Common Sense Media Report, 2012, p. 7). Paula Poindexter's (2012) *Millennials, News, and Social Media: Is News Engagement a Thing of the Past?* concludes that their reliance and dependence on social media for news and information will increase in the future because of their disdain for print and television sources as "garbage," "lies," "propaganda," and "boring."

The time has passed for discussing whether we can or should curtail the social networking of teenagers. Teenage demand coupled with the increasing availability of networking opportunities via numerous technological platforms ranging from smartphones and laptops, to iPads and gaming systems makes it a Sisyphean task. The conversation should shift from whether teenagers should use social media to how teachers can provide students with the skills to use the platform more productively. Our challenge is to equip students with the skills and courage to use social media so that it serves as a source for intercultural exchange instead of fear and disdain.

The stakes cannot be higher. At a minimum, the biases reproduced by current social media consumption patterns legitimized Dylan Roof's attack on one of the most powerful symbols of Black empowerment and progress – South Carolina's Emanuel AME Church. Failure to equip students with the capacity to pursue a culturally humble existence premised on self-reflection and open and honest deliberation will make it increasingly difficult to attenuate hostilities to those deemed as others. Students empowered to respond to difference with empathy and disagreement with curiosity will transform their online social spaces from cultural enclaves of animus and incivility to tools of cultural enlightenment.

W. E. B. DuBois (1903) was correct when he predicted that the problem of the 20th century would be the color line; the problem for us this century will be the demographic shifts along that same line. While US census data predicts that America will become a polycultural majority by 2043, population researchers at Ethnifacts forward that when one accounts for intermarriage and cohabitation of people with different races and ethnicities we have already reached the "tipping point" (Myles, 2014, para. 2). Our communities, workplaces, and schools are increasingly polyracial with profound implications for how we work, live, and learn. As educators, we have reached a crossroads. We can either provide students with the tools to engage, negotiate, and learn from their differences or we can leave them to find refuge in their monocultural online communities that will fail to prepare them for their offline experiences in the new polycultural America.

It is incumbent upon our schools to reimagine the use of social media as having the potential to become radically democratic venues for political, ideological and cultural deliberation. A curriculum that uses debate to facilitate self-reflexive engagement with various and distinct perspectives will transform hyper-personalized MySpace accounts into our space for democratic revival and cultural humility.

Emanuel AME Church: The Freedom House That Hate Attacked

Throughout the 20th century, Charleston's Emanuel African Methodist Episcopal Church has remained a powerful symbol of Black empowerment, cultural renewal, and resistance. For Alton Pollard, dean of the Howard University School of Divinity, the "black church has always been our freedom house," and Emanuel, in particular, is "holy ground" (Foreman, 2015, para. 2). South Carolina historian Robert Greene II argues that Emanuel's creation "was a response to Charleston's importance as one of the largest ports for slave trading in North America" and that its history "is a reflection of the history of African Americans in Charleston and across the state of South Carolina" (Greene, 2015, para. 3).

With Denmark Vesey, planner of one of the largest slave revolts in South Carolina's history, as one its co-founders, resisting discrimination and uplifting the Black community was hardwired into the church's DNA. From its inception in 1816, Emanuel was an iconic symbol of hope and freedom for numerous Black South Carolinians who had no reason to be hopeful and few opportunities to pursue or exercise their freedoms. Throughout the years, the church has remained a potent symbol for the relentless pursuit of Black freedom. Preeminent civil rights leaders from Booker T. Washington to Dr. Martin Luther King Jr. and Roy Wilkins used Emanuel's pulpit to demand voting rights, expand job opportunities, and push for the American dream to be made a reality for all (Kaplan, 2015, para. 16). Given the monumental role the church has played for the past 200 years in the pursuit of justice, liberty, and economic emancipation, it is not shocking that Emanuel was the site of Dylan Roof's heinous killing spree; Roof's attack was and should be understood as an assault on cultural diversity.

Reports indicate that Roof found community on Facebook and other online social mediums. Chat rooms were safe spaces for him to explore Nazism and express his hatred. These zones of ideological homogeneity intensified his affinity for and close alignment with Hitler and white power hate groups. His pictures and texts were littered with symbols of hate including the number "88" – the white supremacist code for "Heil Hitler." He is seen in numerous pictures wearing an "88" T-shirt and writing "88" in the sands of South Carolina's beaches. Roof even restricted his number of Facebook friends to "88" people (Robles, 2015, para. 2). Additionally, his personal website, *The Last Rhodesian*, reveals his disdain for Charleston's cultural diversity:

> I have no choice . . . I am not in the position to, alone, go into the ghetto and fight. I chose Charleston because it is most historic city in my state, and at one time had the highest ratio of blacks to Whites in the country. We have no skinheads, no real KKK, no one doing anything but talking on the internet. Well someone has to have the bravery to take it to the real world, and I guess that has to be me.
>
> (*Last Rhodesian*, n.d., para. 29)

Some may challenge the importance of exploring the role social media played in the death of the Emanuel 9 by asking what is the difference between Roof's hate-filled diatribes via his internet posts and communicating a similar message in a face-to-face conversation? The difference is the opportunity for engagement. The difference is the self-reflexivity that is generated when one has to anticipate disagreement even if it is never delivered. Currently, aggregated and highly curated online communications via social media lack both. We must remain mindful that social media outlets do not function as conveyor belts simply transferring unaltered pictures, texts, and news articles from one iPhone to the next. They create protected communication cocoons that can transform our thoughts and beliefs into universal truisms. With Dylan Roof, the unencumbered message he received from his "88 friends" encouraged him to pursue increasingly more virulent and destructive forms of hate. His excessive filtering of online exchanges to the degree that he was only willing to entertain information from people whom he already knew agreed with his worldview is inherently inhospitable to self-reflexivity and debate – the two things we most need in order to root out animus and discrimination.

Social Media: Can the Medium Truly Be Social If We Ignore the Other?

It is easy to read Roof's *Last Rhodesian* and dismiss it as the work of the mentally ill or a lone wolf assassination so removed from the mainstream that there is nothing we can learn from exploring his use of social media. Unfortunately, his desire to seek shelter in cultural homogeneity is an all too common response for those unable to see difference and argument as communal assets.

While Roof's pursuit of physical violence to resolve his discord with the cultural changes occurring in South Carolina and throughout the United States is very much atypical, our concern is that his use of social media to communicate exclusively with people who will confirm his beliefs is the norm. If we are correct about the ability of social media to facilitate self-centeredness and confirmation bias that can leave hate unchallenged and our personal perspectives uninterrogated, its use should be a major concern for educators interested in producing an ethically stout, collaborative, and democratically engaged citizenry. However, the stakes are even higher. Trend lines point to a continual increase in the share of Americans who get their news from these sites with Facebook becoming a "news powerhouse." (Anderson & Caumont, 2014, para. 2) The trend is even more pronounced among teenagers.

Jose Marichal (2012), political science professor at California Lutheran University, is primarily concerned with what he identifies as social media's architecture of disclosure – the sites' ability to produce a hyper-personalized persona that is widely available but devoid of public engagement and utility (Marichal, 2012, p. 35). The site "encourages more disclosure than listening" and our ability to opt out of engaging when we are uncomfortable "exacerbates the trend toward a more polarized view of the world" (Marichal, 2012, p. 95). Facebook pages are best understood as one-way presentational platforms. They are personal digital billboards built to house our musings about the world, not invitations to negotiate a collective understanding. Contradicting messages are unwanted graffiti. All to often, the offending message is immediately removed and the messenger is summarily barred from posting on the wall. Christopher Sibona's study of unfriending on Facebook concludes that the act of cleansing one's tainted social media spaces is a "widely-used feature of social networking sites" with those most often unfriended being people "discussing polarizing topics too often (politics and religion)" (Sibona, 2014, p. 1683). Sibona continues:

[F]riendships tend to be formed by those who share similar race and ethnicity, followed by age, religion, education, occupation and gender. Strongly held views on polarizing topics such as politics and religion may be difficult to reach agreement on between friends who hold strong opposing views. One way of managing context collapse is to avoid discussing these potentially hazardous topics but not everyone follows the lowest common denominator approach and some may feel quite free to discuss deeply personal matters with their social network.

(Sibona, 2014, p. 1683)

Marichal's overarching concern that an intense focus on presenting an unspoiled caricature of the self leads to an unexplored and intensified polarized world view is supported by Sibona's findings. Additionally, Shannon Rauch and Kimberley Schanz's 2013 study of Facebook posts containing race-related persuasive messages concludes that social networking sites are vectors for the spread of racist messages because the "sites help create a culture where critical thinking is devalued while shallow processing and agreement are promoted" (Rauch & Schanz, 2013, p. 615).

We, as teachers, must be more proactive in using our classrooms to create countervailing forces that offer students opportunities to disagree with conventions, challenge deeply held beliefs, and explore what constitutes credible evidence. We cannot overemphasize the importance of creating an educational environment that encourages and, at times, mandates that our students be curious listeners, apprehensive curators of information, and doubters of the righteousness of their own perspectives. The creation of a culture where social media facilitates critical thinking and deep interrogation of information can not be done without us.

A recent Pew Research Center study suggests that left to their own devices students will quickly abandon a sense of wonder and skepticism for the warm comforts of confirmation, deference, and sameness:

> Facebook and Twitter users were also less likely to share their opinions in many face-to-face settings. This was especially true if they did not feel that their Facebook friends or Twitter followers agreed with their point of view. For instance, the average Facebook user (someone who uses the site a few times per day) was half as likely as other people to say they would be willing to voice their opinion with friends at a restaurant. If they felt that their online Facebook network agreed with their views on this issue, their willingness to speak out in a face-to-face discussion with friends was higher, although they were still only 0.74 times as likely to voice their opinion as other people.
>
> (Hampton et al., 2014, p. 4)

Students are increasingly finding themselves in digital diversity deserts that can only consistently produce vacuous inauthentic self-centered disclosures and trite exploration of otherness used to prove their personal superiority. These barren monocultural wastelands socialize students to forgo ethical deliberation and debate until their cohorts make it "Facebook official" that their thoughts will not stray too far from the norm. We are producing a dangerous form of groupthink that will leave students ethically stunted and unable to negotiate their physical spaces with any degree of sophistication as those physical spaces become more diverse.

One should not read this criticism as an indictment of all uses of social media. In fact, we believe that technology provides an unrivaled opportunity for voices previously silenced by a lack of access to financial resources and print and television mediums. It has the potential to be a powerful force for eliminating communication barriers that prohibit generative disagreements and the spread of innovative ideas. However, the internet's revolutionary potential can only be met if students are prodded and encouraged to explore the worlds that lie beyond their social cocoons. As educators, we can and should be a part of the solution. We can create a curriculum that produces culturally humble students who engage and value vigorous self-reflection, open debate, and the pursuit of justice. We can create a curriculum that encourages them to unlock the revolutionary potential of the numerous social media platforms with which they are engaging.

Cultural Humility: Learning From Others

The classroom is the perfect site for staging a cultural humility revolution. It is one the few places that has not been totally colonized by smartphone technology and ubiquitous access to the internet. Teachers have the authority to use their curricula to encourage meaningful authentic personal encounters with difference that will transform how our students engage others online. With a little creativity, every lesson plan can be modified to manufacture face-to-face exchanges among students that will encourage them to recognize and appreciate the humanity of others. The classroom is where the battle for the production of a culturally humble citizenry can and must be fought. Instilling a sense of cultural humility in our students is the best tribute we can pay to the unfathomable number of people throughout history who lost their lives to hateful violence.

The starting point is making sure cultural humility is infused into the curriculum design. Cultural humility's pursuit of a "lifelong commitment to self-evaluation and critique to redress power imbalances" via "mutually beneficial and nonpaternalistic partnerships" (Tervalon & Murray-García, 1998, p. 123) will enable students to effectively live, work, and learn with people from "any mix of cultural backgrounds" (Juarez et al., 2006, p. 97). Its integration into our curricula will enhance the ability of students to be "both culturally sensitive and culturally competent" (Juarez et al., 2006, p. 101).

Cultural humility's intrapersonal dimension, lifelong self-reflection, encourages us to constantly seek out and eliminate our personal biases. For the culturally humble, there is no discrete end point to their learning. They are forever involved in a process of trying to understand their character, actions, and motives. It is a continual process of thinking about who we are, what we don't know, and how our lack of knowledge informs which relationships we value and which relationships we discard. Educating students to be more culturally humble means insisting that they participate actively in constructing communities of concern and understanding that are attentive to the needs of others and disruptive of social norms that preserve power and resource disparities.

Cultural humility's interpersonal dimension, openness to egalitarian partnerships, is equally important for creating productive relationships and hospitable communities. The culturally humble student tries to maintain an other-orientation that helps to "counteract and regulate the sense of superiority that may occur when cultural differences arise" (Hook, Davis, Owen, Worthington, & Utsey, 2013, p. 354). This openness encourages resistance to the temptation to categorize the world in terms of ingroup and outgroup with the group we belong to being superior and the other deemed disposable.

Racism, sexism, classism and the various other group classifications that are used to justify discrimination and hate are ultimately just derivatives of this self-centered sense of superiority. Dr. Ravi Chandra's (2015) exploration of the role self-centeredness played in Dylan Roof's attack on Emanuel and our collective responsibility to build relationships that will prevent similar events in the future speaks to the importance of incorporating cultural humility into our curricula:

> Evolutionarily speaking, as biologist E. O. Wilson has pointed out, we think in terms of in-group and out-group and are limited by subjective awareness. As long as we are defensive with our group affiliations (racial, religious, national, gender), hatred will be inevitable. Defensiveness occurs on the individual, synaptic level (the amygdala's reactions to threat), but is propagated and reinforced by sociocultural forces that surround us – from movies and pop culture to neighborhoods to, yes, social media. Dylan Roof's Facebook page seems to have been littered with evidence of hatred. He supposedly made racist, hateful statements that were taken as "jokes". By passing up the opportunity to talk to him about his views, society passively reinforced those views.
>
> (Chandra, 2015, para. 10)

In order for us to shoulder our fair share of responsibility for the social climate that produced Dylan Roof, we must actively work to create polycultural communities of humility and care. Academic institutions and teachers must lead the way. Cultivating an other-orientation that challenges hatred and domination requires face-to-face relationships and the willingness to critically engage the ideas of others. Our schools are the perfect locales for harnessing the passions that reside in "the realm of face-to-face relationships" and using them simultaneously to train students to be more introspective and empathetic while laying the groundwork for a radical transformation of our use of social media so that "people are less likely to be treated instrumentally" and the unaccounted for "other" (Greene, 1993, p. 185). This difficult work requires a rethinking not only in what we teach but how we teach. Structures must be created that encourage students to freely explore and disagree without a looming threat of condemnation from their teachers or peers. Coursework needs to provide incentives for our students to create egalitarian partnerships within and across group classifications. We believe debating in a manner that requires introspection and participation in cross-cultural conversations is one of the best instructional methods available for incorporating cultural humility into the curriculum.

Debate and the Power of Play

Creating the conditions where students play together is essential to facilitate impassioned and authentic face-to-face encounters that lay the groundwork for them to become more culturally humble. Greg McKeown argues in *Essentialism: The Disciplined Pursuit of Less* that "we are built to play and built by play" (McKeown, 2014, p. 86). For McKeown, play is the "purest expression of our humanity" and "the truest expression of our individuality" (McKeown, 2014, p. 86). We understand play's importance when we consider that our most memorable experiences and the times we feel most alive usually involve us playing and sharing with others. Scientists studying play are starting to develop a consensus view that it "is a central part of neurological growth and development – one important way that children build complex, skilled, responsive, socially adept and cognitively flexible brains" (Henig, 2008, para. 6). Play's influence on our cognitive development is significant. It has the unique capacity to stimulate the part of the brain that allows both logical reasoning and carefree exploration. Indeed, a life without play is not much of a life at all.

Debate is a type of play that encourages students to interact with new ideas and perspectives. It is an evidence-based game of argument and advocacy that helps students envision a better world, dream big ideas, and see themselves as agents of change. The act of debating creates an educational environment that brings students together to interrogate ideas and pursue a negotiated understanding of their existence that is comprised of information from a multitude of sources and perspectives. Debate as a form of play can fundamentally transform how and what students communicate by encouraging face-to-face encounters on issues of relevance. Debate gamifies the curriculum in ways that will produce students who look forward to learning new ideas and engaging their classmates on ways to improve their communities.

While there are a multitude of ways to incorporate debate into the curriculum, the approaches most suitable for producing more culturally humble students will incorporate the following:

- A competition of ideas – because students will learn that disagreement can be generative and productive and the best solutions usually incorporate the ideas of multiple parties;
- Multiple defensible perspectives – because students will learn the value of openly exploring multiple perspectives and remaining open to new and confounding information;
- An expectation that positions are informed by research – because students will learn that decisions are improved with better and more pertinent evidence;
- Sides that are assigned in some way other than by student preference – because assigning sides depersonalizes the conversation and removes the fear and anxiety from engaging controversial issues; and
- Topics that are socially and culturally relevant – because meaningful topics will increase students' desire to research and engage.

These debates hold the possibility of encouraging students to reach across the cultural divide and play meaningfully together. Students from all races and cultures need the opportunity to practice cross-cultural dialogue on substantive matters that are impacting their lives. Teachers too often avoid exercises that encourage disagreement and exploration of difference because these encounters can be "highly charged," "unpredictable," and "volatile moments of self-discovery" (Murray-García, Harrell, García, Gizzi, & Simms-Mackey, 2014, p. 594). However, debate provides the structure to transform these encounters into valuable, teachable moments that can serve as essential building blocks for constructing an empathetic and humble student. These intellectually and emotionally challenging teaching moments are a necessary component of a student's growth and development. Our evolution into a polyracial society means it is no longer a question of whether teachers should facilitate cross-cultural encounters on difficult issues, but how it should be done. Debate provides the structure and incentives for students to view these exchanges as laboratories to explore who they and how they want to exist instead of harbingers of a cultural onslaught. These inevitable encounters with difference are far more productive when they are within the confines of a debate. Academic debate is the best instructional method available for facilitating the authentic face-to-face encounters necessary for students to begin a lifelong process of self-evaluation while remaining other-oriented.

Debate creates intellectual spaces for students to play around with who they are and what they are willing to defend. It is easy to structure an exercise where students are expected to defend two diametrically opposed propositions in the same setting. Encouraging students to debate from a position they may not agree with challenges their desire to dogmatically defend a particular perspective. Additionally, students are encouraged to critique ideas and not character. Debating can become a model of peer education that encourages students to understand criticism as an opportunity for growth while reassuring them that a challenge to their perspective is not an attempt to prove another's superiority. Debate's emphasis on engaged listening is of paramount importance. Uninterrupted moments of expression are rare. Even more limited are environments where we are expected to listen and entertain the validity of ideas with which we may fundamentally disagree. When the communal norm becomes one that privileges the value of listening over our personal desire to speak, we have reached a point where negotiation and compromise are possible.

Debate as an evidence-based game of advocacy and argument has the potential to create the unique learning environment needed to promote cross-cultural dialogue. Transforming our classroom conversations into games requiring the exploration of well-researched arguments is one way of depersonalizing the exchange and lowering the emotional stakes in the encounter. Laurie Ross's (2010) work on cultural humility offers a similar conclusion. She finds that "a powerful way to develop cultural humility" (Ross, 2010, p. 318) is the use of participatory and interactive learning environments where students share and evaluate each other's ideas. Debate is an example of just that type of learning environment.

If we are truly vested in getting students to participate in productive cross-cultural dialogues on difficult issues, we must find ways to lower the emotional stakes involved in their participation. While a little competition can keep the stakes high enough to encourage students to research and explore ideas that are radically different from the ideas they currently hold, the depersonalization of the encounter will reassure students that their beliefs and culture are not being judged.

Games give students permission to explore. Debating allows students to test ideas and to practice being an advocate. Assigned advocacy provides a safe space for students to defend and challenge policies and worldviews without having to own the conclusion or consequences. It reduces the fear of trying on different beliefs, philosophies, and policy perspectives by removing the fear of openly discussing half-formed ideas in front of their peers. Isn't that what the process of becoming educated is all about – realizing that everyone wakes up every day a different person with substantial room to grow and become a better human being? Humans are social creatures. We cannot grow without others and these face-to-face encounters. We cannot grow without being challenged. Allowing students to play with their words and beliefs provides a safe space for them to practice being lifelong learners on a journey to becoming culturally humble and provides them the tools to transform their online social media experiences.

Conclusion

All indications are that Dylan Roof was a loner. He didn't have many "friends" outside the "88" on Facebook. We would like to think that a sustained commitment to encourage him to play and debate with a wider array of people could have made the night of June 17, 2015 different for him and the Emanuel AME Church. Roof's internet posts on the *Last Rhodesian* are a difficult read for people trying to live culturally humble lives. They also constitute an affront to the pursuit of open and public deliberation as the means to resolve social and political discontent.

More importantly, Roof's cyberhate is a direct challenge to every teacher working to equip their students with the skills to create and sustain more just and hospitable communities. Our commitment to open and honest intercultural deliberation must be central to our effort to build more democratic and welcoming communities and our effort to honor the Emanuel 9 and the many others who have lost their lives in attacks on difference.

While our current use of social media constitutes a challenge, it also has a tremendous amount of potential if we can encourage students to honor the distinct cultural perspectives and intellectual prowess of their classmates by participating in a debate. Students primed to inquire and question will transform our social networks into venues for culturally humble democratic participation and intellectual engagement. That transformation has to start in our classrooms. It starts with encouraging our students to debate everything, all the time.

While we struggle to find much in Roof's *Last Rhodesian* that is socially redeeming, we find it fitting to conclude with the one section of his manifesto we do agree with:

Black people are racially aware almost from birth, but White people on average don't think about race in their daily lives. And this is our problem. We need to and have to.

(*Last Rhodesian*, n.d., para. 6)

References

Anderson, M., & Caumont, A. (2014, September 24). How social media is reshaping news. *Factank*. Retrieved from http://www.pewresearch.org/fact-tank/2014/09/24/how-social-media-is-reshaping-news/.

Chamorro-Premuzic, T. (2014, May 13). How the web distorts reality and impairs our judgement skills. *The Guardian*. Retrieved from http://www.theguardian.com/media-network/media-network-blog/2014/may/13/internet-confirmation-bias.

Chandra, R. (2015, June 19). Forgiving the unforgivable: From hatred to empathy. *Psychology Today*. Retrieved from https://www.psychologytoday.com/blog/the-pacific-heart/201506/forgiving-the-unforgivable-hatred-empathy.

Common Sense Media Report (2012). Social Media, Social Life: How Teens View Their Digital Lives. Retrieved from https://www.commonsensemedia.org/research/social-media-social-life-how-teens-view-their-digital-lives.

DuBois, W. (1903). *The Souls of Black Folks*. New York: Start Publishing LLC.

Foreman, T. (2015, June 20). Church shooting strikes at the heart of black culture. *CNN*. Retrieved from http://www.cnn.com/2015/06/19/living/charleston-ame-church/.

Greene, M. (1993). The passions of pluralism: Multiculturalism and the expanding community. In J. Fraser & T. Perry (Eds.), *Freedom's Plow: Teaching in the Multicultural Classroom* (pp. 185–196). Abingdon: Routledge.

Greene, R. (2015, June 19). Racism can't destroy this Charleston church. *Politico Magazine*. Retrieved from http://www.politico.com/magazine/story/2015/06/charleston-shooting-emanuel-african-methodist-episcopal-church-119205.html#ixzz3dWbg8jYH.

Hampton, K., Rainie, L., Lu, W., Dwyer, M., Shin, I., & Purcell, K. (2014). Social media and the "Spiral of Silence." *Pew Research Center*. Retrieved from http://www.pewinternet.org/2014/08/26/social-media-and-the-spiral-of-silence/.

Henig, R. (2008, February 17). Taking Play Seriously. *New York Times*. Retrieved from http://www.nytimes.com/2008/02/17/magazine/17play.html?pagewanted=all&_r=0.

Hook, J., Davis, D., Owen, J., Worthington, E., & Utsey, S. (2013). Cultural humility: Measuring openness to culturally diverse clients. *Journal of Counseling Psychology*, 60(3), 353–366.

Johnson, B. (2015, June 18). The only comment on Dylan Roof's Facebook photo will bring you to tears. *IJReview*. Retrieved from http://www.ijreview.com/2015/06/347576-the-only-comment-on-dylann-roof-s-facebook-profile-photo-will-bring-you-to-tears/.

Juarez, J., Marvel, K., Brezinski, K., Glazner, C., Towbin, M., & Lawton, S. (2006). Bridging the gap: A curriculum to teach residents cultural humility. *Family Medicine*, 38(2), 97–102.

Kaplan, S. (2015, June 18). For Charleston's Emanuel AME Church, shooting is another painful chapter in rich history. *Washington Post*. Retrieved from http://www.washingtonpost.com/news/morning-mix/wp/2015/06/18/for-charlestons-emanuel-a-m-e-church-one-of-the-oldest-in-america-shooting-is-another-painful-chapter-in-long-history/.

Last Rhodesian. (n.d.). Retrieved from http://lastrhodesian.com/data/documents/rtf88.txt.

Marichal, J. (2012). *Facebook Democracy: The Architecture of Disclosure and the Threat to Public Life.* Burlington, VT: Ashgate Publishing.

McKeown, G. (2014). *Essentialism: The Disciplined Pursuit of Less.* New York: Crown Business.

McLuhan, M. (1964). *Understanding Media: The Extensions of Man.* New York: McGraw Hill.

Murray-García, J., Harrell, S., García, J., Gizzi, E., & Simms-Mackey, P. (2014). Dialogue as skill: Training a health professions workforce that can talk about race and racism. *American Journal of Orthopsychiatry, 84*(5), 590–596.

Myles, R. (2014, August 23). Population experts say America is already a majority multiracial country. *Latin Post.* Retrieved from http://www.latinpost.com/articles/19826/20140823/population-experts-america-already-majority-multiracial-country.htm.

Poindexter, P. (2012). *Millennials, News, and Social Media: Is News Engagement a Thing of the Past?* New York: Peter Lang.

Rauch, S., & Schanz, K. (2013). Advancing racism with Facebook: Frequency and purpose of Facebook use and the acceptance of prejudiced and egalitarian messages. *Computers in Human Behavior, 29,* 610–615.

Robles, F. (2015, June 20). Dylan Roof photos and a manifesto are posted on website. *New York Times.* Retrieved from http://www.nytimes.com/2015/06/21/us/dylann-storm-roof-photos-website-charleston-church-shooting.html?_r=0.

Ross, L. (2010). Notes from the field: Learning cultural humility through critical incidents and central challenges in community-based participatory research. *Journal of Community Practice, 18,* 315–335.

Sibona, C. (2014, January 6–9). Unfriending on Facebook: Context collapse and unfriending behaviors. *47th Hawaii International Conference on System Science,* 1676–1685.

Tervalon, M., & Murray-García, J. (1998). Cultural humility versus cultural competence: A critical distinction in defining physician training outcomes in multicultural education. *Journal of Health Care for the Poor and Underserved, 9*(2), 117–125.

Appendices

James Roland

Appendix A: Common Myths/Concerns About Debate in the Classroom

Myth #1: "I'm not a debate coach – I never debated – this is not for me."

Even if you have never debated, you have likely engaged your students in a similar thinking process. If you are really honest with yourself, you have probably already been providing your students with debate education without labeling it as such. Debate is just a way to teach students how to think in a critical and reflective way. Materials like this book help break down the processes associated with debate. Debate in the classroom is meant to complement, not replace, your current teaching strategies. Remember, debate provides you with a vehicle to better deliver the strong content knowledge you have acquired.

Myth #2: "Debates take too much time!"

While a full debate certainly can take an entire class period, and maybe one or two more classes for students to prepare, many effective debate activities only take 10–30 minutes. Teachers can save full debates for a once-a-unit or once-a-quarter activity. Like any new activity, students will take some time to learn how to prepare for the debate, but once debate becomes a common practice, teachers will be amazed at how little preparation time is necessary. Teachers will be thrilled to find out that almost all of the preparation for debates will consist of students poring over assigned texts to find arguments to attack their opponents – not a bad classroom activity.

Myth #3: "Students will put me on the spot and ask me questions that will hurt my credibility as a teacher."

Teachers naturally understand that debate is a rigorous, interactive, and engaging educational activity. The key is to learn how to use it effectively, and this book provides the educational foundation and justification for this pedagogical approach. For some teachers, debate requires a new way of teaching. No longer can one simply be the "sage on the stage" and preach to the students from Mount Higher Learning; teachers using debate will help facilitate discussion and oftentimes, rather than supply answers, will push for more questions. This type of teaching creates a deeper level of trust and rapport with students because everyone in the class has an incentive to be an integral part of the learning process.

Appendix B: Empowering Students to L.E.A.R.N. – Core Debate Skill Set

What is debate? Debate is about learning and cultivating your voice. Instead of seeing debate as solely an event or extracurricular activity, we encourage you to view it as a core set of skills that equip students and educators to better navigate the learning process. Using these debate skills in and out of the classroom helps teachers to become better teachers and students to learn!

Listening (Critical)

Debate teaches critical listening skills through the frequent need and desire to understand the arguments being made during a debate by others.

Explanation and Evidence

Assigned Advocacy (taking/defending a position)

Reading (Critical) and Research

Debate teaches critical reading skills by encouraging students to search for meaning both in what was written and not written in the text.

Note Taking (Writing)

Note: *These skills should be seen and demonstrated in each debate lesson.*

Source: Roland, J. (2015). *LEARN Manual: Empowering Students to Learn.* Unpublished manuscript (with permission of author).

Appendix C: Designing a Lesson Plan Using Debate in the Classroom

Odds are, if you are a teacher, you are already quite familiar with lesson plans (probably more familiar than you would like). Our goal here is not to tell you something you already have templates and rubrics for, but rather to suggest to you some skill sets and processes you should try to include in your teaching if you seek to use debate as an instructional tool in your classroom. It is VERY

IMPORTANT to use the five guiding principles as a starting point. All you have to remember is that you getting the students to L.E.A.R.N.!

Listening (Critical)
Explanation and Evidence
Assigned Advocacy (taking/defending a position)
Reading (Critical) and Research
Note Taking (Writing)

The best lesson uses all five guiding principles, but the key is to use as many of the LEARN concepts as possible. Here are some additional helpful steps when it comes to designing a debate lesson:

Step One: Choose a Debate Resolution

Choosing a good debate topic (or resolution) can be a difficult task for teachers new to debate. This section has sample debate topics organized by subject. Look at those lists for examples of resolutions for your classes.

When picking a topic, you should generally start with the essential questions and content objectives that you plan to cover in a particular unit and attempt to turn those into debate resolutions. Using course and unit essential questions as debate resolutions also gives students powerful opportunities to debate the most important aspects of the curriculum.

Good debate resolutions will often (but not necessarily) have one of the words in the list below in them.

SHOULD
A person should take a dollar now instead of two dollars next year.
Rome should not have attacked Carthage.

BEST
Which energy source is the best?
Which character in a play is the best intentioned?

WORST
Romeo had the worst motivation for his actions compared to other characters.

WEIRDEST/ COOLEST
Which kingdom of life is the coolest?
Which absolute emperor is the weirdest?

MOST
Which mathematical property is the most important: the associative, commutative, or the distributive properties?

Which character in a play is the most heroic?
Which political philosopher is most followed in America today?
Which organic compound is the most important?

BIGGEST
Gamma radiation has the biggest impact on humanity, when compared with alpha and beta radiation.

INNOCENT
Macbeth should be declared innocent of killing King Duncan due to extenuating circumstances.

GUILTY
Socrates should have been found guilty and sentenced to death.

The topic doesn't need to be phrased exactly like you would phrase a lesson plan. A science teacher is not likely to state in a lesson plan that 'students will know which kingdom of life is the weirdest.' However, a science teacher likely does want students to know the characteristics of each kingdom, and a debate that requires students to read about and understand the different characteristics so that they can argue they are weird accomplishes that goal.

Step Two: Pick Texts

Your goal should be to find text(s) that have information (evidence) that students can use to support the arguments they are going to make. Depending on your course and on how integral specific texts are to your content, you might need to do this in conjunction with step one.

This is easier than it sounds. Imagine a biology class where the content goal is for students to learn the different characteristics of each kingdom of life. The debate structure is to have five different teams argue that their assigned kingdom is the weirdest. The text is simply the pages in the textbook that explain the different characteristics of each kingdom. Students then point to the evidence of a characteristic they found in their textbook and come up with their own argument why that is weird.

The texts that you will use will generally be the texts you would have used if you had students read in class or at home, or maybe worksheets that you were going to pass out.

Step Three: Organize Students

There are two levels to organizing students for a debate: the groups you will put them in, and then what individual roles students will have in that group.

Groups: Make sure you know how you are going to divide the students into groups for the debate.

- If it is a multi-sided debate, make sure you know what the different options are for students.
- If it is a two-sided debate and you have a 20-person classroom, which means 10 people in each group, think carefully about how you are going to sub-divide each group.
- Multi-sided debates tend to be better for large classrooms.

Roles: Within each group, know what roles you are going to have available for students. Some examples of different roles are:

- Opening statement;
- Attacker/Opposition;
- Defender;
- Cross-examiner (the person asking questions of their opponent);
- Cross-examinee (the person answering questions from their opponent);
- Closing statement;
- Trainers;
- Journalists;
- Judges;
- Court of Public Opinion.

Step Four: Choose Your Assessment

Assessing the debate is very important. It is a very effective tool to encourage the academic behaviors that you are hoping the students will adopt. While there are many different activities that can assess many different skills (e.g. ballots, feedback forms, post-debate discussion, etc.), it is recommended that you pick no more than three for each debate. (See Appendix M for more assessment resources.)

(Note: With permission the step-by-step process was developed by Boston Debate League's Evidence Based Argumentation Program, and more info can be found about that program at www.bostondebate.org.)

Appendix D: Introducing Debate in One Week

Day 1: Ask students about how they feel about public speaking. Why is it scary? When is it fun? When is it needed? Explain that students will be talking about a lot of ideas and learning how to debate effectively.

Activity: Hand out a list of topics and pair students to have short debates on a topic they choose. Each pair may choose their topic (even if others choose the same one), and the students must choose sides to support. After a few minutes for students to think and plan what they want to say (they can ask other students what they could argue), begin debates. Each student will have one minute to support their side of the topic. Take volunteers or pick more confident and outgoing students to be in the first debates.

Day 2: Ask students to tell you what an argument is (giving reasons why you believe that something is true). Have them give examples of times when the ability to argue is valuable. Explain the difference between having an argument and making an argument.

Procedures: Explain that a claim is something that you think is true and a reason tells why you think it is true.

A Take a few of the topics used on Day 1 and have the class brainstorm reasons why they might be true.
B Starting at one side of the class, have a student make a claim; the next person explains why it is true (it is true because . . .) (Example: Blue is a good color . . . because a blue sky makes me happy, "because" a blue sky is clear and I can do things outside.) After a student makes a 'because' statement, she then makes a claim for the next student to respond to.
C Divide the class in half and choose one topic from the list. Have one group take each side of the topic, and come up with as many because answers as they can. Then let them read their lists.

Day 3: Talk about proving things. How can you prove that someone is a good basketball player? How do you prove that someone committed a crime? What are different ways to prove something (examples could include the testimony of an expert, statistics, logic, comparisons/analogies)?

Activity: Hand out the articles of the impact of violent video games, and then have the students read the articles. When students have had time to do that, discuss the articles, the arguments that they make, and the evidence that they use, and ask students which ideas are most persuasive and fit with their own experience. Then pair students and have them fill out handout three making an argument explaining or challenging the link between violent video games and youth violence. Share those arguments with the remaining time.

Day 4: Talk to students about the importance of listening when they talk to other people. Then explain that the problem of speaking to others is often really an issue of having things to say. Tell students that talking and listening are natural, and that when we listen to others, we often have questions. And when we are asked questions, answers are natural and comfortable. But sometimes, the best answer is I don't know.

Activity: The topics are listening and questioning. Have each student go to the front of the class and briefly (less than 30 seconds) tell the class something about themselves or something they are especially interested in. After that, have students in the class ask questions for the next two minutes. Each question should have at least one follow-up question that asks about the student's answer to the first question.

Day 5: Divide the class into four groups and assign topics; then give groups time to develop arguments. Two groups will debate the topic: Math is more important to study than Language Arts. The other two groups will debate the topic: Science is more important to study than Social Studies. Explain the format for the debates: the side agreeing with the topic speaks first, for up to two minutes. The other side will have two minutes to respond. Students in the class may add ideas for up to two minutes. After class comments, each team has a different speaker give a two-minute summary speech to explain why their arguments are better than those of their opponents. Non-debating students vote to decide which side made the better arguments. The two winning teams then debate to decide which is the most important subject to study in school. Close the class discussing what makes a good argument, and which arguments in the debate were most persuasive and effective.

Source: Wade. J. (n.d.). *Assigned Argument and Advocacy*. Unpublished curriculum materials (with permission of author).

Appendix E: Potential Debate Activities and Examples

(Note: With permission many of the activities in Appendix E were developed by Boston Debate League's Evidence Based Argumentation Program, and more information can be found about that program at www.bostondebate.org.)

This section provides short and long debate activities you can use in the classroom.

Short Debate Activities

Soapbox

- Create a list of controversial debate topics, and post them in the classroom.
- Tell students about how politicians used to stand on a soapbox and speak to large crowds about their point of view.
- Model this by standing on a chair (the mock soapbox) at the front of the classroom and choose a topic from the list to talk about.
- Ask students to take turns on the soapbox (in pairs, small groups, or whole class instruction). Encourage students to engage their audience by using rhetorical flourish, humor, persuasion, stories, or real-life examples.

Table Debates

- Create a list of debate topics (the first time you do this activity, you will want use controversial topics that are easy for all students to argue), each with two obvious sides.

- Make a stack of "debate cards" for each table (or pair) with the topic and the two sides; put these on each table.
- Ask a student or adult to model a debate with you in front of the class using the debate cards.
- Now the students try it.
- This activity usually works best if the debates are timed for 30–90 seconds. As the teacher, you can call "Next Card" and "Begin" and "End" at the appropriate time to have all students switch to the next topic.

Four Corners

- Create a list of controversial debate topics, and post them in the classroom.
- Label the front of the classroom or four corners of the classroom with large signs: STRONGLY DISAGREE, DISAGREE, AGREE, STRONGLY AGREE.
- Read the first topic, and then ask (ALL!) students to get out of their seats and take a position. No student can be "in the middle"; each person must take a side.
- Ask several students to explain why they chose their spot.
- Read the next topic and continue.
- You can also adapt this activity to build text-based evidence use by asking students to bring their book or notes with them and to be prepared to cite text-based evidence for their position.

Writing Note Cards

- In preparation for a full-length debate, require that all students create note cards (index cards) with information (quotes, facts, etc.) and notes for their speeches or cross-examinations. All students should have speaking roles in the debate and will therefore need to create the cards.
- Pass out 2–3 index cards to each student to complete individually. Encourage students to ask group members for help. Also encourage group members to plan out arguments in each speech that build on each other's work and ideas.
- Require that students write at least X number of quotations from the text(s) used in preparation for the debate.
- Collect note cards after the debate and grade as part of the debate assessment.

Model Note-Taking

- During the debate, use an overhead projector or the board to model note-taking. Students will spend the entire year learning how to take good notes during speeches, while also preparing counter-arguments. As the teacher, you can model how to follow the debate by modeling note-taking in real time.
- Politely interrupt students during their speeches if they forget to number the points.

- Show students when you are confused by the speakers by looking confused and/or writing a "?" when a speaker is unclear.
- Be sure to note when evidence comes from the text.

Adapted Note-Taking

- For students struggling with English or with processing (or at the beginning of the year when debate is new for everyone), provide adapted notes/graphic organizers with more space for writing and more prompts for students.
- Give a copy of your notes to your students after the debate.

Mock Debate

- Before doing the full-length debate, set up the classroom for the debate and ask students to sit in teams.
- Describe the order of speeches and overall structure of the debate to students (*see Appendix M: Online Resources for more information*).
- As you describe the order, ask students to stand up with note cards and move to front of room (or to the podium) for their speech or cross-examination at the appropriate time.
- This activity will help students envision what happens during the debate and how the structures will help to facilitate an orderly debate.
- Also, writing the order of speeches, names of each speaker, and times on the board will help students see the structure of the debate.

Pictionary

- Find a picture or cartoon connected to the lesson for the day. You can make copies for each student, use an overhead, or smartboard as well.
- Tell students to describe the picture – what do they notice?
- Ask them to write three arguments the picture is making.
- Write down one thing that most people would not notice or could "read" into the picture.
- Have students speak and list all the different arguments and ideas the students notice.
- Have groups or individual students debate the reason why they feel they are right about their observations of the picture.
- Have students not speaking take notes during this process and vote on the arguments they think are best.
- Have students discuss what would make arguments better.

Speed Debate

- You need to have 3–5 topic areas prepared in advance with debate resolutions for each topic area. The topics could be related to the content area or topics that are interesting to the students. You may even entertain having your students suggest topic areas.

- Select two student volunteers to come up to the front of the class.
- Remind the debaters and observers about the need to listen, take notes, body language, tone, etc.
- Have one student pick the topic area and the other pick the side.
- Immediately start the debate and have one side give a position speech for one minute.
- Then have the opposition speak for up to one minute.
- Then field questions from the audience. Make sure BOTH sides have to answer questions.
- Then have at least one student (can have more if you like) give support speeches for a particular side.
- Make sure you have students to speak for both sides. These students should help make the case for their particular side.
- Have another round of questions from the audience.
- Give the original two speakers a chance to have a rebuttal or closing speech for up to one minute.
- Afterwards have students vote or just discuss the debate. Regardless, make sure to give both sides some useful and positive feedback. Repeat again with another set of students. Each time remind students of skills they should be demonstrating throughout the debate.

Long Debate Activities

This section will outline four different types of full-length debates. It is important to stress that these are not the only types of full-length debates, but rather a sample of potential options. What makes these debates full-length is that they incorporate all five skills/elements from LEARN, and they will usually take at least one full class period (and sometimes an extra day to prepare). Be creative!

As you get ready for your first full-length debate, consider what type of debate best fits your unit, students, classroom size, and debate resolution. Throughout the year, you may only use one style of full-length debate or you may experiment with multiple styles. Whatever activity or full-length debate style you choose, debate in the classroom should be part of your curriculum, not an add-on to compete with content you already need to cover.

Debate Format #1: The Multiple Perspective Debate

This is a great debate style for a classroom of more than 12 students. There are 3–6 perspectives (or answers to the resolution), and each team defends one of those perspectives. If you have five perspectives, you will have five teams. Teachers assign each group to attack one other group (not at random – teachers should make assignments so all groups will be attacked by one other group). Teams are encouraged to clash with all groups' arguments, but the structure of the debate minimizes the "all against all" that can happen when you bring more than two perspectives to the debate.

The debate typically goes as follows (for the purpose of clarity, we will use the following resolution):

Which foreign policy was best for America in the late 1800s to early 1900s?

- Opening Statements: One person in each group gives a 1–2-minute opening statement explaining why their foreign policy was the best for America in the late 1800s to early 1900s. They should be required to cite at least two pieces of evidence from the text.
- Prep Time: Teams are given a limited prep time to huddle and help the next group member prepare for cross-examination.
- Cross-examination: One member of each group is assigned to cross-examine one member from another group until all the groups are cross-examined, in the order given by teacher.
- Prep Time: Teams are given limited prep time to huddle and help the next group member prepare for the attack.
- Attack: One member of each group is assigned to attack one other group. They should give 2–3 arguments, with evidence from the text, as to why that group's foreign policy was a bad for America.
- Prep Time: Teams are given limited prep time to huddle and help the next group member prepare for the defense.
- Defense: One member of each group is given an opportunity to defend against the attacks made in last round. This person should be required to respond to all arguments made by the attacker in the last group.
- Prep Time: Teams are given limited prep time to huddle and help the next group member prepare for closing statements.
- Closing Statements: One member of each group is given an opportunity to read a closing statement. These statements give the best reasons why their foreign policy is the best, making sure to cite evidence and respond to attacks made against it. It should also explain why the other group's foreign policies are bad. These may not be written before the debate because they must be a summation of what occurred during the debate, including unanticipated arguments made by all groups.

Note: Prep time is given between each round as needed. Prep time is important because it allows students who have already gone to stay engaged by supporting their teammates. Depending on the classroom context, each speech can last for as little as one minute or as long as four minutes.

Debate Format #2: The Socratic Seminar

Socratic Seminars are discussions rather than debates. Students bring multiple perspectives to the discussion and work to understand the ideas, issues, and values reflected in the text being studied. Socratic Seminars are not competitive and require students to build upon the ideas of others in order to come to a deeper understanding of an issue or text. This type of debate works with any class of eight students or more because you do need two separate groups to carry on a discussion with multiple perspectives.

Teachers can assign different perspectives or sources of textual evidence, or encourage students to do perspective taking in a more organic way, requiring that students use multiple perspectives presented in the text.

In the first half of the activity, one group forms an inner circle facing one another and discusses the debate resolution while the other group forms an outer circle taking notes on the discussion. The groups switch seats after 10–15 minutes, with the first outer group now discussing the resolution on the inside circle while the other group listens and take notes. At the end, several students (assigned at beginning by teacher) give closing remarks on the entire discussion.

The debate typically goes as follows:

- Inner Circle Discussion 1: Free-flowing discussion on debate resolution among inner circle/group 1.
- Switch Groups.
- Inner Circle Discussion 2: Free-flowing discussion on debate resolution among inner circle/group 2.
- Closing Statements: Summary of discussion and final reflections given by the student assigned to make closing remarks.
- Wrap-Up: Teacher-led reflection on the seminar.

Debate Format #3: The Committee Meeting Debate

This style is ideal for a large class. There is a committee meeting to determine the best course of action (or answer to the resolution). This can be a Senate Committee deciding policy, a group of mathematicians deciding on the best way to solve a difficult calculus problem, or a historical committee meeting to decide on past issues, such as the abolition of slavery or whether to invade Cuba in the 1960s.

The teacher assigns 3–5 groups, each with a different position to advocate for; the teacher also assigns a team of committee members who run the debate. Teams prepare an initial 3–5-minute presentation for the committee when called to speak at the beginning of the debate, and each team also stands for questioning first by the committee and then by the entire class. At the end, the committee members decide who won the debate and announce the winning team to the class.

The debate typically goes as follows:

- Beginning of Committee Hearing: Committee members call the hearing to order and invite the first group up to speak.
- Opening Statements: Group 1: Each member of the group speaks as part of the opening statements.

- Closed Cross-Examination, Group 1: Committee members cross-examine Group 1.
- Open Cross-Examination: Committee members open the floor to all students to cross-examine Group 1.
- Repeat This Process with Each Team.
- Announce Winners: Committee members discuss decisions privately and then announce decision and reasons to the whole class.

Debate Format #4: Traditional Two-Perspective/Person Debate

Most teachers familiar with policy or parliamentary debate will know this format. There are two teams (of 2–4 people): one argues the affirmative side and one argues the negative side of the topic. This is a debate format that works easily with smaller classes, but is more difficult to implement effectively in larger classes.

To adapt this for use in larger classes, it is helpful to subdivide your two groups. You can break each side into three groups (total of six groups) and assign different groups different texts perspectives, countries, etc. If you have one large group of 10–15 students, you will have difficulty keeping all students engaged.

The debate typically goes as follows*:

- 1st Affirmative Constructive Speech (Opening statements): (4–8 min).
- Cross-examination (Negative questions first Affirmative speaker): (1–3 min).
- 1st Negative Constructive Speech (Opening statements): (4–8 min).
- Cross-examination (Affirmative questions first Negative speaker): (1–3 min).
- 2nd Affirmative Constructive Speech (Attack/Defense): (4–8 min).
- Cross-examination (Negative questions second Affirmative speaker): (1–3 min).
- 2nd Negative Constructive Speech (Attack/Defense): (4–8 min).
- Cross-examination (Affirmative questions second Negative speaker): (1–3 min).
- 1st Affirmative Rebuttal Speech (Attack/Defense): (2–4 min).
- 1st Negative Rebuttal Speech (Attack/Defense): (2–4 min).
- 2nd Negative Rebuttal Speech (Closing Statements): (2–4 min).
- 2nd Affirmative Rebuttal Speech (Closing Statements): (2–4 min).

*Note: You should feel free to adapt the times to fit your class time and learning objectives. The times above are merely suggestions, but each constructive, cross-examination, and rebuttal should be the same allotment of time for each side.

Make sure as the teacher to allow for post-debate discussion. Remind the students that they need to provide constructive comments. One effective strategy is to have every student observer provide one thing the debaters did well and one thing they could improve upon. Finally, you should make some general comments about the debate. Affirm the students for participating in the debate. The more you create a positive climate, the more students will have the courage to participate in future debate activities.

Appendix F: Got a Problem, Got a Solution Handout

The Problem (Describe the nature and scope):

Why is it bad or harmful?

1

2

Plan of action:

_____

_____

_____

_____

_____

Why do you believe it will work?

1 Because _____

_____

_____

Evidence/Proof/Example/Source:

_____

_____

2 Because _____

_____

_____

Evidence/Proof/Example/Source:

_____

_____

3 Because _____

_____

_____

Evidence/Proof/Example/Source:

_____

_____

Source: Roland, J. (2015). *LEARN Manual: Empowering Students to Learn*. Unpublished manuscript (with permission of author).

Appendix G: Speech/Debate Template

Name:

Speech Outline

Topic:_____

In this debate, my position is:

_____

_____

_____

My first argument is:

_____

_____

because _____

_____

_____

My second argument is:

_____

_____

because _____

_____

_____

My third argument is:

_____

_____

because _____

_____

_____

In closing, my arguments in this debate clearly prove:

_____

_____

because _____

_____

_____

Source: Roland, J. (2015). *LEARN Manual: Empowering Students to Learn*. Unpublished manuscript (with permission of author).

Appendix H: Critical Thinking/Reading Comprehension Handout

Name:

Date:

Class:

What is the title of the article?

Who is the author? What are their qualifications?

List two main arguments in the article?

1

2

Do you agree with the author? Why or why not?

What would you add or take away to make the article better?

Would you recommend it to a friend or family member? Why or why not?

Other thoughts:

Source: Roland, J. (2015). *LEARN Manual: Empowering Students to Learn*. Unpublished manuscript (with permission of author).

Appendix I: Developing Your Ideas – Making an Argument

Topics

Honesty is the best policy.
Violence is never necessary to solve disputes.
School uniforms should be required in all public schools.
Homework should be banned.
Students should be able to decide what they learn in school.
More important lessons are learned outside of school than inside it.
Middle-school students should not be allowed to date.
X is a better player than Y. (Students decide the two to be compared.)
X is a better rapper/performer than Y. (Students decide the two to be compared.)
Animals think like humans.
Professional athletes make too much money.

Topic: _____

Side: _____

Argument 1:

_____

_____

Reason:

_____

_____

_____

Argument 2:

_____

_____

Reason:

_____

_____

_____

Argument 3:

_____

_____

Reason:

_____

_____

_____

Source: Wade. J. (n.d.). *Assigned Argument and Advocacy*. Unpublished curriculum materials (with permission of author).

Appendix J: Debate M&Ms (Me and Mind Exercise)

You Can't Have It Your Way!

> *Randy Bailey was on house arrest in St. Paul, Minn., with an ankle monitor that alerts police if he strays more than 150 feet (but also with a little-understood four-minute delay before notification). Hungry on Aug. 12, Bailey thought he could race to the Burger King (nearly a mile away), yet get back in time. However, the drive-through line moved slowly, and an irate, impatient Bailey allegedly kicked in the restaurant's window before he sped away. Employees got his license-plate number and alerted police, but since Bailey had made it back home in just under four minutes, he claimed to be housebound and never to have left. However, police soon figured it out and charged Bailey with felony destruction of property. [Source: St. Paul Pioneer Press, 8–16–06]*

Directions: Answer the questions below.

What are some arguments against Bailey's decision to leave? To kick in the window (try to think of at least two)?

What are some arguments in favor of Bailey's decisions (try to think of at least three)?

What are some alternative decisions that Bailey could have made that would have changed the outcome of the story?

In your opinion, do you agree with the statement "The reward is always worth the risk"? Please explain and give one example related to the story.

Source: Roland, J. (2015). *LEARN Manual: Empowering Students to Learn*. Unpublished manuscript (with permission of author).

Appendix K: Assessment and Evaluation

Establish grading criteria based on teacher goals and course guidelines.

Example 1 – Criteria for Evaluation of a Team

1   Understanding of the topic. A team gets the maximum points if it demonstrates a clear understanding and in-depth knowledge of the issue area of the debate. Debate involves the correct use of concepts and terms.

2   Organization of arguments. A team gets the maximum points if its position has an effective introduction and conclusion, and is well structured, logical, and coherent. The arguments are straightforward, relevant, clearly elaborated, and are not based soley on emotion.
3   Presentation of evidence. A team gets the maximum points if it demonstrates thorough research of the pertinent evidence (facts, statistics, scholarly research, or authorities' statements) in support of its contentions and presents the research effectively.
4   Delivery. A team gets the maximum points if it delivers its position convincingly and effectively, with the right emphasis, variety, and enunciation in argumentation. Debaters should not simply read their notes, but be encouraged to make eye contact with the audience and explain ideas and concepts.
5   Use of effective counter-arguments, questions, and ability to defend arguments. A team gets the maximum points if it demonstrates the ability to use collected evidence and logic to challenge the contentions of its opponents and defend its own contentions.
6   Extending (referring back to initial) arguments. A team gets maximum points when it deals with opposing arguments in rebuttal speeches, comparing issues of both teams and keeping their own team's important arguments as the focus of the debate.

Example 2 – Categories for Evaluation of a Speaker (where 1 is poor and 5 is exceptional)

1   Speaking ability (including tone, clarity, poise, confidence, eye contact);
2   Familiarity with the facts;
3   Recognition of key issues (including ability to stress important points and evidence);
4   Handling of questions (including adaptability, responsiveness, and ability to integrate answers into the general presentation);
5   Organization of argument (including an introduction and a road map);
6   Overall effectiveness.

Source: Wade. J. (n.d.). *Assigned Argument and Advocacy.* Unpublished curriculum materials (with permission of author).

Appendix L

Overview: This research offers insight into how the CCSS can be supported by the expanded use of argumentation and debate-related activities across the curriculum – and how the power of effective pedagogy can improve teacher satisfaction and retention rates.

Survey respondent teachers who think classroom argumentation, advocacy, and debate-related activities have had a *moderate* or *strong* positive impact on these writing and language skills

	Social Studies/ History Teachers (N = 19)	Science or Technical Teachers (N = 35)	English and all other subject Teachers (N = 184)
Write arguments focused on discipline-specific content, with precise claims and counter-claims developed fairly and thoroughly with appropriate evidence and organized clearly (based on CCSS Writing Standard 1)	100%	88.6%	97.8%
Write informative or explanatory texts focused on discipline-specific content, with precise claims and counter-claims developed fairly and thoroughly with appropriate evidence, and organized clearly (based on CCSS Writing Standard 2)	100%	88.6%	97.3%
Conduct short as well as more sustained research projects to answer a question or solve a problem (based on CCSS Writing Standard 7)	94.7%	80%	94.5%
Gather relevant information from multiple authoritative print and digital sources, accessing that information, and integrating it into a text (based on CCSS Writing Standard 8)	94.8%	94.2%	97.8%
Draw evidence from informational tests to support analysis, reflection, and research (based on CCSS Writing Standard 9)	94.7%	94.3%	98.4%
Acquire and use accurately general academic and domain-specific words and phrases (based on CCSS Language Standard 6)	89.5%	85.7%	93.5%

Source: Zorwick, M. L. W., & Wade, J. (2015). Using Forensic Activity to Develop the Skills Identified in Common Core State Standards (CCSS). *Rostrum*, 90(1), 46–52 (with permission).

Survey respondent teachers who think classroom argumentation, advocacy, and debate-related activities have had a *moderate* or *strong* positive impact on these speaking and listening skills

	Social Studies/ History Teachers (N = 19)	Science or Technical Teachers (N = 35)	English and all other subject Teachers (N = 184)
Initiate and participate effectively in a range of collaborative discussions with diverse partners, building on others' ideas and expressing their own clearly and persuasively (based on CCSS Speaking and Listening Standard 1)	**94.7%**	**80.2%**	**94.6%**
Integrate multiple sources of information presented in diverse media or formats, evaluating the credibility and accuracy of each source (based on CCSS Speaking and Listening Standard 2)	**94.8%**	**85.7%**	**97.2%**
Evaluate a speaker's point of view, reasoning, and use of evidence and rhetoric, identifying any fallacious reasoning or exaggerated or distorted evidence (based on CCSS Speaking and Listening Standard 3)	**100%**	**91.5%**	**97.8%**
Present information, findings, and supporting evidence clearly, concisely, and logically such that listeners can follow the line of reasoning and organization (based on CCSS Speaking and Listening Standard 4)	**100%**	**91.4%**	**96.7%**

Source: Zorwick, M. L. W., & Wade, J. (2015). Using Forensic Activity to Develop the Skills Identified in Common Core State Standards (CCSS). *Rostrum*, 90(1), 46–52 (with permission).

Survey respondent teachers who think classroom argumentation, advocacy, and debate-related activities have had a *moderate* or *strong* positive impact on these reading skills

Social Studies/History Teachers (N = 19)

Cite specific textual evidence to support analysis of sources (based on CCSS Reading Standard for Informational Texts 1)	100%
Determine central ideas and provide an accurate summary that makes clear the relationship among key details and ideas (based on CCSS Reading Standard for Informational Texts 2)	100%
Evaluate various explanations for actions or events and determine which explanation best accords with the textual evidence (based on CCSS Reading Standard for Informational Texts 3)	100%
Evaluate authors' differing points of view on the same event or issue by assessing the authors' claims, reasoning, and evidence (based on CCSS Reading Standard for Informational Texts 6)	**94.7%**

Evaluate an author's premises, claims, and evidence by corroborating 100%
or challenging them with other information (based on CCSS
Reading Standard for Informational Texts 8)

Compare and contrast treatments of the same topic in several primary 89.5%
and secondary sources (based on CCSS Reading Standard for
Informational Texts 9)

Science or Technical Teachers (N = 35)

Cite specific textual evidence to support analysis of science and technical 91.4%
texts (based on CCSS Reading Standard for Informational Texts 1)

Determine central ideas or conclusions of a text and summarize complex 85.8%
information by paraphrasing and simplifying accurately (based on
CCSS Reading Standard for Informational Texts 2)

Analyze how the text structures information and demonstrate 82.8%
understanding of the information or ideas (based on CCSS Reading
Standard for Informational Texts 5)

Analyze the author's purpose in providing an explanation in a text, 82.9%
identifying important issues that remain unresolved (based on CCSS
Reading Standard for Informational Texts 6)

Integrate and evaluate multiple sources of information presented in 88.6%
diverse formats and media in order to address a question or solve a
problem (based on CCSS Reading Standard for Informational Texts 7)

Evaluate the hypotheses, data, analysis, and conclusions in a science or 85.7%
technical text, verifying, corroborating, or challenging conclusions
with other sources of information (based on CCSS Reading Standard
for Informational Texts 8)

Source: Zorwick, M. L. W., & Wade, J. (2015). Using Forensic Activity to Develop the Skills
Identified in Common Core State Standards (CCSS). *Rostrum, 90*(1), 46–52 (with permission).

Appendix M: List of Online Resources

http://www.atlantadebate.org
http://urbandebate.org/What-We-Do/For-Coaches
https://www.pinterest.com/pelhamdebate/debate-resources-for-teachers/
http://idebate.org/training/resources/all
http://www.bostondebate.org/eba/
http://www.debatecoaches.org/curriculum/
http://idebate.org/training/resources/all
http://debate-central.ncpa.org
http://debate.uvm.edu
https://www.pinterest.com/pelhamdebate/debate-resources-for-teachers/
http://debatepedia.idebate.org/en/index.php/Welcome_to_Debatepedia!
http://chicagodebateleague.org/debaters/debate-resources/
http://www.educationworld.com/a_lesson/lesson/lesson304b.shtml
http://www.noisyclassroom.com/primary/ideas/preparing-a-debate-with-a-
class.html

http://csdf-fcde.ca/UserFiles/File/resources/teacher_debate_guide.pdf
http://www.brown.edu/about/administration/sheridan-center/teaching-learning/
effective-classroom-practices/debates
http://iteslj.org/Techniques/Krieger-Debate.html
http://www.facdev.niu.edu/facdev/resources/guide/strategies/classroom_
debates.pdf
https://www.speechanddebate.org

Contributors

Catherine Beane, J.D., is Vice President of Public Policy and Advocacy for YWCA USA and an attorney with more than twenty years' experience advocating for equity in our nation's education, justice, and child-serving systems. She was previously a senior policy analyst with the National Education Association, and the policy director for the Children's Defense Fund.

Freddi-Jo Eisenberg Bruschke, Ph.D., is a groundwater hydrologist and computer modeler who teaches geoscience education, general geology and earth science, freshman university skills, hydrology, and environmental engineering at the university level. She has worked with pre-service and in-service K–8 educators in developing projects that integrate geoscience with engineering, and is an Event Writer for the Orange County Regional High School Science Olympiad.

Jon Bruschke, Ph.D., is an Associate Professor in Human Communication Studies at California State University, Fullerton. He received the national debate coach of the year award in 2004, the National Debate Tournament service award in 2009, and the American Forensics Association lifetime service award in 2013. His areas of research are argumentation theory and pre-trial publicity, and he serves as a lead coder on the tabroom.com website.

Brittney Cooper, Ph.D., is an Assistant Professor of Women's and Gender Studies and Africana Studies at Rutgers University. She is author of the forthcoming book *Race Women: Gender and the Making of a Black Public Intellectual Tradition* (University of Illinois Press, 2017). She is also co-founder of the popular feminist blogging group, the Crunk Feminist Collective, and a sought-after public speaker and social commentator for a variety of media outlets.

Susan Cridland-Hughes, Ph.D., is an Assistant Professor of English Education at Clemson University, where she is program coordinator for the undergraduate English Education program. She researches debate as critical literacy and critical pedagogy in out-of-school settings. Additionally, she provides professional development for English and Social Studies teachers geared towards using dialogue and discussion in their classrooms.

Karyl A. Davis, M.A., J.D., directs communications for the Glenn Pelham Foundation for Debate Education and is the owner and principal creative of the consulting firm, kd Alice Communications, which helps small businesses and nonprofits communicate their stories in print, online, and at events. After practicing law for a number of years, Karyl now draws upon her public speaking, acting, directing, writing, publishing, and teaching background in order to empower clients to create stories and build communities.

Ed Lee, M.A., is executive director of forensics in the Barkley Forum Center for Debate Education at Emory University. He has earned every national intercollegiate debate coaching recognition in the field and is a regular national media commentator for U.S. presidential debates. He was formerly Director of Debate at the University of Alabama and won the President's Award from the University of California-Berkeley during his tenure as director of the Bay Area Urban Debate League.

Ajay Nair, Ph.D., is the Senior Vice President and Dean of Campus Life at Emory University, whose scholarly interests include immigration, race, ethnicity, quality assurance in educational systems, service learning and civic engagement, and Asian American identity. He served as Senior Associate Vice Provost for Student Affairs at University of Pennsylvania and held academic and administrative positions at Columbia, Penn State, and Virginia. His co-edited book, *Desi Rap: Hip-Hop in South Asian America* (Lexington Books, 2008), focuses on the complexities of second-generation South Asian American identity. His current book project explores the current state of multiculturalism in higher education.

James Roland is Senior Director of Community Programs and Engaged Scholarship, Barkley Forum Center for Debate Education at Emory University, where he also coached numerous national intercollegiate debate champions. He is executive director of the Atlanta Urban Debate League and has served as a debate consultant to the U.S. State Department, Atlanta Housing Authority, Atlanta Public Schools, and Open Society Institute. He serves on the Board of the National Association of Urban Debate Leagues and advises UDLs in 15 cities.

John Sexton, Ph.D., J.D., is the fifteenth President of New York University, the Benjamin Butler Professor of Law, and NYU Law School's Dean Emeritus, having served as Dean for 14 years. He is a Fellow of the American Academy of Arts and Sciences, a member of the Council on Foreign Relations, and a past member of the Executive Committee of the Association of American Universities.

Gordon Stables, Ph.D., is Assistant Dean for Student Affairs and Director of Debate & Forensics in the Annenberg School for Communication & Journalism at the University of Southern California. Gordon's research focuses on how changing social and technological norms influence the expectations for argumentative and debate education. His work includes direction of a research project to integrate academic debate with mediated technological platforms.

Melissa Maxcy Wade, M.A., M.T.S., Th.M., is President of the Glenn Pelham Foundation for Debate Education, served for 40 years as executive director of forensics in the Barkley Forum Center for Debate Education at Emory University, was a faculty member in the Division of Educational studies, and is a principal founder of the Urban Debate League education movement. She serves on the Academic Board of Directors of the International Debate Education Association, the Board of Directors of the International Public Policy Debate Forum, and is a noted political commentator for U.S. presidential debates for various national media.

W. Patrick Wade, Ph.D., is a Lecturer at the Centre for English Language Communication, National University of Singapore, where he teaches writing-intensive courses on photography and memory studies. His disciplinary research examines the role of public arts like photojournalism in processes of visual culture and rhetorical action, and his classroom-based research examines critical thinking instruction and media literacy.

Carol Winkler, Ph.D., is the Associate Dean of Humanities for the College of Arts and Sciences and a Professor of Communication at Georgia State University. She is a scholar of presidential foreign policy rhetoric, argumentation and debate, and visual communication. Her book, *In the Name of Terrorism* (SUNY Press, 2006), won the outstanding book award in political communication from the National Communication Association. Winkler is past President of the American Forensics Association and currently serves as the Co-Executive Director of the National Debate Project.

M. Leslie Wade Zorwick, Ph.D., is Associate Professor of Psychology at Hendrix College. She conducts research on stereotyping and prejudice, identity, and the use of perspective taking to improve the quality of social interactions. She has also written about debate and argumentation as an instructional tool that can help develop social skills and create an environment conducive to prejudice reduction.

Index